The Spirit of Liberalism

Frank Chesser

Publishing Designs, Inc.
Huntsville, Alabama

Publishing Designs, Inc.
P. O. Box 3241
Huntsville, Alabama 35810

Second Printing: March 2002

Printed in the United States of America

ISBN 0-929540-27-1

To my parents,
W. C. and Elizabeth Chesser,
whose love for God, the truth, and the church
left an indelible mark on my life;

to my wife
Cherry
whose attributes as a wife and mother
are unexcelled among women;

and to my sons,
Jason and Jared,
my daughter-in law Wendy
and my grandchildren, Aiden and Brooke,
who have filled my life with incomparable joy.

CONTENTS

Foreword

Frank Chesser is a Christian gentleman who loves God, Jesus Christ, the church of Christ, and the word of God. He loves them so intensely that he is grieved to the very depths of his soul that liberalism is subverting so many. Frank loves the church—his fellow Christians so much that he desperately wants to warn every brother and sister about the sinister threat posed by liberalism.

With eloquence, clarity, and precision, the author exposes liberalism's inner workings. In mournful tones of sadness, he pleads with brethren to reject the spirit of liberalism. Employing Scripture skilfully, he issues fervent biblical admonitions not to be seduced by liberalism's subversive tactics. His insightful, penetrating logic goes straight to the heart of human motivation. His words are challenging, uplifting, and therapeutic, while generating a healthy sense of urgency.

Frank has pinpointed the essence of liberalism and done the church a great service. He has issued a sober call to return to our senses. His book will enrage the liberal, disgust the apostate, and alarm the lukewarm. But for the honest and sincere individual—the seeker of truth—this book will warm the heart and propel one to embrace the God and Christ of the Bible. It will deepen one's love for the church for which Jesus died.

Dave Miller, Director
Brown Trail School of Preaching
June 2001

Preface

This book commenced with the intention of penning two or three articles for a local publication. However, it soon became apparent that this subject could not be adequately covered in a few articles. This book closes with a yet deficient depiction of the true nature of the spirit of liberalism.

This book is candid. It could not be otherwise. It is based on divine truth, and truth is candid. The prophets were blunt when they addressed the errors and sins of their day. Jesus Christ was love personified, but He confronted all things inconsistent with truth in a most forthright manner. Jesus made many statements that, when repeated by teachers of truth today, are branded by liberalism as unloving, mean-spirited, and bigoted.

This book is intolerant. It has zero tolerance for the spirit of liberalism. Liberalism is the breeding ground for pride, self-will, and human's tampering with things divine. Toleration for liberalism is toleration for sin. Did God tolerate Cain's self-will worship? Nadab and Abihu's strange fire? Saul's sparing Agag? David's oxen and cart? Ananias and Sapphira's lie? Or Elymas's defiance of the truth? Truth has no tolerance for anything incompatible with itself.

This book believes truth can be known. Liberalism loves to ask, "Do you think you know all truth?" Liberalism, which is pride incarnate, thinks only pride would answer affirmatively. Jesus said, "And ye shall know the truth and the truth shall make you free" (John 8:32). All truth essential for spiritual freedom can be known.

This book was composed in sorrow. The harm that liberalism has done to the church for which Jesus died, the truth of the Bible, and the souls of men is incalculable. The insidious evil of liberalism that necessitates this effort and kindred endeavors by faithful brethren to defend the faith is a brotherhood tragedy. The church is full of Jeremiahs, weeping over the gaping wounds in the bride of Christ, the result of liberalism's injurious work.

Much appreciation is expressed to Dave Miller for his review of this work and for his kind and encouraging words. His own book, *Piloting the Strait,* is a classic in confronting the efforts of liberalism to implement Jereboam-like changes in God's pattern for the church. Also to James Andrews, who encouraged this effort and edited and typeset the material, and did his usual professional job in the publishing thereof.

This book is being sent forth in hopes that it will encourage the faithful, serve as a deterrent to those who are considering embarking on the road of liberalism, and snatch yet receptive souls from the devouring jaws of this stupendous evil.

Frank Chesser
May 1, 2001

1

Liberalism
Does Not Tremble

The superlative majesty and transcendence of God are inexpressible. If a man possessed the oratorical skills of the Ciceros of the ages and had at his disposal the riches of all the vocabularies of the earth, he could not commence to clothe man's mind with an adequate portrait of God. If all of the genes of genius could be implanted into one mind, that man could not begin to comprehend God. If a man could live to the age of Methuselah and spend every conscious moment in deep study and reflection on things divine, in contrast to what there is to be known of God, he would close his life in mental poverty. "O the depth of the riches both of the wisdom and knowledge of God! How unsearchable are his judgments, and his ways past finding out" (Rom. 11:33).

With the gentle movement of the mind of God, Heaven was infused with innumerable angels. God spoke and light appeared, water divided, seas formed, the earth was dressed in green, the heavens were filled with luminaries, the deep pulsated with life, the firmament resounded with avian melody, and the earth moved with living things. God dipped His hand in dust and created man, and from a solitary rib, formed woman. God is sovereign over all creation. Arising from the bed of affliction, Nebuchadnezzar gazed heavenward and exclaimed,

> And all the inhabitants of the earth are reputed as nothing; and he doeth according to his will in the army of heaven and

among the inhabitants of the earth; and none can stay his hand, or say unto him, What doest thou? (Dan. 4:35).

God is, and God has spoken. God's Word is an expression of His nature. One can read the character of God by reading the Word of God. God is powerful; thus, His Word is powerful (Heb. 4:12). God is sovereign; hence, His Word is authoritative (1 Pet. 4:11). God is holy; therefore, His Word demands holiness (1 Pet. 1:15-16). God is merciful; consequently, His Word calls for mercy (Matt. 5:7). God is love; thus, love is the supreme commandment (Matt. 22:37-38). Therefore, rejecting the Word of God is tantamount to rejecting God (John 12:48).

As a result, it is not possible to separate God from His Word. Can a man be viewed apart from his words? Not unless he can be divorced from his mind, for his mind gives birth to his words. Jesus said, "For out of the abundance of the heart, the mouth speaketh" (Matt. 12:34). Man's speech constitutes his character on display. Even so, the mind of God that points to the character of God is the source of the Word of God. There are deep things in the mind of God (1 Cor. 2:10). The Holy Spirit entered the mind of the Father, took from that infinite reservoir of truth every verity essential for man's journey from earth to Heaven, and revealed it to man (1 Cor. 2:10-13). Thus, the Bible is God's mind in human language.

Therefore, indifference toward the Word of God is indifference toward God. A lack of reverence for the Word of God is a lack of reverence for God. An assault on the Word of God is an assault on God. It is inconceivable that a mere man, weak, wretched, and helpless at his best, a microscopic dot on the unending walls of eternity, would attack God by assailing the Word of God with a pompous "so what" disposition toward a single aspect of biblical teaching. Who could be so presumptuous, so lacking in reverence for God as to thus posture himself in the presence of divine authority? Only a man compelled by the spirit of liberalism.

A preacher for the liberal movement in the church has described the use of the mechanical instrument in worship as "no big deal." Just three words, yet in contrast to their destructive power, the nuclear bomb is a mere handclap. Only three words, yet their ramifications are as deep and wide as the oceans of the world. Three ordinary words, but the basis for volumes. Three scant words, yet in comparison to the spiritual erosive power inherent therein, acid is as harmless as dew, as it lies gently upon the earth. Just three words, yet consistently applied, undermines the totality of God's revelation to man.

These three words sum up the spirit of liberalism. In spite of its intense denial, liberalism has no respect for the absolute, unmitigated authority of the Word of God. Liberalism is self on the throne. It is self with a propensity for its own way. It is emotions over mind, flesh over spirit, and man over God. Liberalism is man's refusing to "cease from his own doings, nor from his stubborn way" (Judg. 2:19). It is man's doing that which is "right in his own eyes" (Judg. 21:25). It is man's moving in harmony with a pattern that he has "devised in his own heart" (1 Kings 12:33). Liberalism is man's feigning reverence for God and His Word while paying homage at the shrine of self-will.

Liberalism does not tremble. Eli was so full of reverence for that which symbolized the presence of God with Israel that his heart "trembled for the ark of God" (1 Sam. 4:13). "The Lord reigneth; let the people tremble" (Ps. 99:1). Just a glance from God causes the earth to tremble (Ps. 104:32). Judah's blushing cheek had been replaced by the arrogant brow (Jer. 8:12). While admitting that the prophet spoke "in the name of the Lord," they arrogantly averred, "We will not hearken unto thee" (Jer. 44:16). They had adopted the liberal "no big deal" attitude toward God's will and way, and thus had lost the ability to tremble (Jer. 5:22).

Judah was eighty years removed from the cold chains of captivity. Jerusalem had cast off the garments of widowhood (Lam. 1:1). Her streets, once bathed in silence, now echoed with the laughter of children (Zech. 8:5). The temple had been rebuilt and its priests and sacrificial system restored (Ezra

6:16-18). Tragically, however, the inhabitants of Jerusalem were just one step away from embracing the idolatry of the heathen nations about them. Some of the princes declared, "The holy seed have mingled themselves with the people of these lands" (Ezra 9:2). Upon hearing this news, Ezra rent his garment, plucked hair from his head and, prostrate before the temple, bathed in his own tears. The situation appeared hopeless.

Suddenly, one by one, family by family, the people began assembling before the temple, joining Ezra in deep penitence, confession, and bitter weeping (Ezra 10:1). They affirmed, "We have trespassed against our God, and have taken strange wives of the people of the land" (Ezra 10:2). With a determined resolve, they declared, "Now therefore let us make a covenant with our God to put away all the wives, and such as are born of them" (Ezra 10:3). What contriteness of heart! What penitence of spirit! What confession of sin! What determination to do right at great cost! What was their motivation? Twice, the inspired record states, they trembled at the Word of God (Ezra 9:4; 10:3). If Judah had espoused the liberal "no big deal" attitude toward the Word of God, such penitence would never have been forthcoming, and Shechaniah would not have been able to say, "Yet now there is hope in Israel concerning this thing" (Ezra 10:2).

"But to this man will I look" (Isa. 66:2). For whom is God looking? Is He looking for the man who depicts an unauthorized encroachment upon His grace as "no big deal"? Is He looking for the man who would dare portray a Nadab and Abihu like intrusion into His holy presence as "no big deal"? Is He looking for the man who would describe a humanly devised act that renders worship vain as "no big deal"? (Matt. 15:9.) Is He looking for the man with the "no big deal" spirit of liberalism who would thrust into His presence an act of worship that has not been ratified and sanctified for acceptable use by the blood of Christ? Is He looking for the man who, motivated by the "no big deal" spirit of liberalism, would nullify the very nature of biblical faith by daring to come before Him with an act of worship void of a "thus saith God"? Is He looking for the man who, possessing the "no big deal" spirit of liberalism, would plant the seed of division into the body of Christ with mechanical worship? Is He looking for the man who would paint as "no big deal" the very piece of machinery that helped rend the church into pieces over a century ago and pave the road of apostasy? "But to this man will I look, even to him that is poor and of a contrite spirit, and trembleth at my word" (Isa. 66:2). Liberalism does not tremble.

2

Liberalism and the Past (Part I)

"For whatsoever things were written aforetime were written for our learning, that we through patience and comfort of the scriptures might have hope" (Rom. 15:4). There are numerous lessons in the Old Testament that God wants man to learn. Tragically, liberalism does not learn from the past. If those who have adopted the spirit of liberalism ever knew the lessons from the past, they have forgotten them.

The Old Testament is an attitude developer. It fine tunes the mind of man. It creates within the receptive heart a deep sense of reverence for God and His Word. It molds the heart in awe of things divine. It spiritualizes the mind. It negates self-will. It nullifies the argumentative spirit. It begets a trembling soul that stands with Moses at the foot of Sinai and affirms, "I exceedingly fear and quake" (Heb. 12:21). It prostrates man at the footstool of grace with a profound veneration for every word in God's revelation to man. It respects the silence of God's voice as well as the sound. It avers with Samuel, "Speak, for thy servant heareth" (1 Sam. 3:10).

Such a heart would no more view an unauthorized act of worship like the use of the mechanical instrument as "no big deal" than it would stand in the presence of God and shake its fist in His face. Yet, such is the spirit of liberalism. Liberalism is presumptuous. It reeks with arrogance. It is self-willed. It loves to experiment. It is constantly pushing the envelope.

It loathes the old paths. Relative thereto, it asserts with ancient Judah, "We will not walk therein" (Jer. 6:16). It has no respect for either the sound or the silence of God's voice. It only does what the Bible says in a given area because it happens to agree with the Bible on that point. At the first sign of conflict, it will have its own way every time. Liberalism does not learn from the past.

If liberalism possessed the ability to tremble, it would literally shudder to the core of its being at the sound of the names of Nadab and Abihu. This incident from the inspired past rises from the pages of inspiration like a giant monument, imploring man not to forget the powerful lessons contained therein. It longs to hang suspended over the spiritual landscape of the present, molding the minds of men into the highest possible state of esteem for God's Word, God's pattern for worship, God's will for man.

Like many today who have assumed the liberal spirit, Nadab and Abihu had a rich spiritual background. They were eye witnesses to the exhibition of God's wrath upon Egypt, one of the greatest and most extraordinary acts of divine judgment ever to befall humanity. The presence of God's indignation in Egypt left such a keenly felt impression on the world that four centuries later, it was yet being contemplated by the idolatrous Philistines. Endeavoring to encourage their leaders to manifest proper respect for the ark of God, the priests and diviners of Philistia declared,

> Wherefore then do ye harden your hearts, as the Egyptians and Pharaoh hardened their hearts, when he had wrought wonderfully among them, did they not let the people go and they departed? (1 Sam. 6:6).

Moreover, these two brothers observed God's continual presence in a cloudy pillar by day and a fiery pillar by night (Exod. 13:21). They watched as God partitioned the waters of the Red Sea, felt the miracle of dry land under their feet as they crossed to safety, and gazed intently as the waters returned to its abode and destroyed the powerful army of

Egypt in its depth (Exod. 14). They saw God use a tree to sweeten the bitter waters of Marah (Exod. 15:25) and beheld the earth blanketed with manna and quail (Exod. 16) and marvelled as water gushed from a rock (Exod. 17:6).

No doubt they echoed Moses' "fear and quaking" sentiments as they viewed the majesty of God on Mount Sinai (Exod. 19). Then God extended to them a blessing enjoyed by only a select few in the whole of humanity. They joined Aaron their father, and Moses their uncle, and seventy elders of Israel in ascending Sinai in order to behold a special manifestation of God that words could not describe.

So little is said about this unique incident that one is reminded of John who was on the verge of writing the amazing things that he had heard, when suddenly a voice from Heaven declared, "Seal up those things which the seven thunders uttered, and write them not" (Rev. 10:4). The record affirms,

> And they saw the God of Israel; and there was under his feet as it were a paved work of sapphire stone, and as it were the body of heaven in his clearness. And upon the nobles of the children of Israel he laid not his hand; also they saw God and did eat and drink (Exod. 24:10-11).

What an extraordinary revelation of God, a meal in the very presence of God. What an ineffable scene this must have been. One would think that such an experience would have left such an indelible impression upon their minds as to render totally impossible the tragedy for which Nadab and Abihu are remembered.

Following the sad spectacle of their father's carving an image of gold in violation of the commandment just recently thundered from Sinai, these two brothers witnessed a mighty display of divine wrath. Surely, they must have looked with horror as fellow Levites unsheathed their swords and stained them with the blood of some three thousand men of Israel (Exod. 32:26-28).

The tabernacle was completed. The sacred furniture was in place. The "glory of the Lord filled the tabernacle" (Exod.

40:34). The sacrificial system was revealed (Lev. 1-7). Aaron and his sons were washed, clothed, sanctified, and consecrated (Lev. 8-9). Portions of the atonement offerings were placed on the altar. The last recorded scene to transpire before the eyes of Nadab and Abihu was the entrance of their father and uncle into the tabernacle, a blessing pronounced from them upon the people, the appearance of God's glory before the nation, and fire emanating from the presence of God to consume the offerings upon the altar (Lev. 9:23-24).

Surely, in view of such phenomenal experiences from Egypt to this moment, these consecrated priest of God would approach God's presence with the greatest degree of reverence, caution, and trepidation. But such was not to be. The spiritual mind is ill-prepared for what follows.

> And Nadab and Abihu, the sons of Aaron, took either of them his censer, and put fire therein, and put incense thereon, and offered strange fire before the Lord which he commanded them not. And there went out fire from the Lord, and devoured them and they died before the Lord (Lev. 10:1-2).

The mind of the man molded by truth divine has great difficulty understanding this incident. In the name of reason, how could this have happened? Did Nadab and Abihu not learn anything from the past? From a practical perspective, had God's miraculous intervention in Israel's life, from Egypt to the consumption of the offerings by fire, have been so expunged from their minds as to have no impact upon their thinking? Whatever additional factors may have been involved, one thing is certain: they had somehow developed the liberal "no big deal" attitude toward God's pattern of worship. Had Nadab and Abihu ever had and thus maintained the frame of mind, "it's a very big deal," toward even the most meticulous aspect of God's revelation, the fire of Leviticus 10:1 would have been authorized fire, not strange fire.

There is as much New Testament authority for the use of machinery in worship as there was Old Testament authority for the fire which Nadab and Abihu used. Wherein lies the difference in unauthorized strange fire and unauthorized strange music? If God refused to accept the very element He had requested because it was secured from an unauthorized source, is it not presumptuous of liberalism to assume that God will accept a totally different kind of music from that He has authorized? Paul affirms that there are lessons to be learned from Nadab and Abihu (Rom. 15:4). What has liberalism learned? That entering into the presence of God with unauthorized acts of worship is "no big deal"? God obviously viewed what Nadab and Abihu did as a "very big deal."

Nadab and Abihu died without mercy (Heb. 10:28) for intruding into God's presence with strange fire. "Of how much sorer punishment, suppose ye, shall he be thought worthy who hath trodden under foot the Son of God, and hath counted the blood of the covenant wherewith he was sanctified, an unholy thing, and hath done despite unto the Spirit of grace" (Heb. 10:29) by daring to presumptuously intrude into God's presence with strange music? Attempting to approach God in worship with the unauthorized mechanical instrument, viewed by liberal thinking as "no big deal," is a proud, high-handed, presumptuous act of vanity (Matt. 15:9) and of self-will worship (Col. 2:23), thus a sin against God. Liberalism does not learn from the past.

3

Liberalism and
the Past (Part II)

The book of Deuteronomy constitutes Moses' final sermon to the nation of Israel. Moses had one month to live. He filled that month preaching to the nation, endeavoring to prepare their hearts to enter Canaan and serve God faithfully in love and gratitude. Moses knew that such faithfulness was dependent upon their refusal to forget the lessons of the past. Consequently, one of the key words in the book is *remember.* This word, or its equivalent, is used repetitiously throughout the book.

This principle is so significant in maintaining reverence for God, the authority of His Word, and faithful submission thereto, that on occasions, Moses would tie two terms or phrases together in order to press this point. For instance, in Deuteronomy 9:7, the text states, "Remember and forget not." A failure to remember the mistakes of the past is the seed for the inevitable duplication thereof.

Following Moses' death and thirty days of mourning over his passing, Joshua led Israel into Canaan. Having conquered the land and settled therein, God reminded Israel in repetitious form, "There failed not ought of any good thing which the Lord had spoken unto the house of Israel; all came to pass" (Josh. 22:45). Faithfulness characterized Israel during the days of Joshua "and all the elders that outlived Joshua which had known all the works of the Lord, that he had done for Israel" (Josh. 24:31). They remembered Moses' sermon.

They refused to forget the past. They learned well from the mistakes of that first generation that came up out of Egypt.

God wants the minds of His people steeped in the past. "For whatsoever things were written aforetime were written for our learning, that we through patience and comfort of the scriptures might have hope" (Rom. 15:4). Every time man opens the Old Testament and commences to read, God is saying, "There are some things I want you to learn from this reading." In 1 Corinthians 10:5-12, Paul enumerates five Old Testament occurrences, and then affirms, "Now all these things happened unto them for ensamples, and they are written for our admonition, upon whom the ends of the world are come" (1 Cor. 10:11).

Jereboam was the first king of the northern kingdom of Israel. He made four changes in God's pattern of worship (1 Kings 12:25-32): He changed the object of worship from God to two calves of gold; He changed the place of worship from Jerusalem in the south to Bethel and Dan in the north; He changed the priesthood from the tribe of Levi to various other tribes; and He also changed the date for the Feast of Tabernacles from the authorized seventh month to the unauthorized eighth month.

It is not possible to exaggerate the destructive nature of these deviations from God's worship pattern for the nation of Israel. These changes served to undermine the spirituality of the northern kingdom and ultimately served as its destroyer. At the commencement of his reign, Ahijah the prophet informed Jereboam's wife, "And he shall give Israel up because of the sins of Jereboam, who did sin, and who made Israel to sin" (1 Kings 14:16). Two hundred fifty years later, the national light of Israel was snuffed out in Assyrian captivity.

The sights and sounds of this calamitous moment in Israel's history surely must have weighed heavily upon their minds for many years. As they were being led from their homeland, never to return as a nation, punctuating the woeful lamentations were the words from God ringing in their ears,

And Jereboam drove Israel from following the Lord, and made them sin a great sin. For the children of Israel walked in all the sins of Jereboam which he did; they departed not from them; until the Lord removed Israel out of his sight, as he had said by all his servants the prophets. So was Israel carried away out of their own land to Assyria unto this day (2 Kings 17:21-23).

Consequently, at the beginning and at the end of Israel's national life, God pointed to Jereboam's tampering with His pattern of worship as the basic reason for the spiritual deterioration and ultimate destruction of the nation. Moreover, sandwiched between these two momentous statements is another amazing truth. Eighteen kings followed Jereboam to the throne of Israel. Void of a single exception, every king continued to lead the nation down the road of ruin by following Jereboam's perverted form of worship. However, most significantly, fifteen times the inspired record makes a specific statement to this effect. Only in the reigns of Elah, Shallum, and Hoshea is the statement omitted. Thus, repetitiously, at the accession of fifteen kings of Israel, the Bible affirms, "He walked in the way of Jereboam and in his sin wherewith he made Israel to sin."

When Jereboam altered God's pattern for entering into His presence for worship and fellowship, the priests and Levites left the northern kingdom of Israel and made their homes in the southern kingdom of Judah (2 Chron. 11:13-14). Following them was a significant number from all the remaining tribes who had "set their hearts to seek the Lord" (2 Chron. 11:16). The number and influence of these Levites and those from the other tribes who joined them was so substantial that "they strengthened the kingdom of Judah and made Rehoboam strong those years; for three years they walked in the way of David and Solomon" (2 Chron. 11:17).

There was a righteous remnant who remained in Israel. When Elijah was viewing himself as the only one yet faithful to God, God reminded him of that remnant when He said, "Yet I have left me seven thousand in Israel, all the knees which have not bowed unto Baal, and every mouth which hath not kissed him" (1 Kings 19:18). There were also the schools of the prophets who, no doubt, wielded a weighty influence with this remnant and others whose hearts were yet sensitive to truth. Moreover, these prophetic schools often worked in conjunction with the ministries of Elijah and Elisha. However, relative to the nation as a whole, this combined influence of the righteous remnant and the prophets was scarcely felt.

Consequently, Jereboam's actions left the northern kingdom void of sufficient righteous influence to make a difference as the nation commenced its uninterrupted journey to national destruction. Jereboam's decision was fueled by his recognition of the unifying power of worship that submits to God's pattern. He feared the possibility of Israel's reuniting under Rehoboam's rule if annual pilgrimages were made to Jerusalem for various worship and feast activities as ordained by God (1 Kings 12:27).

However, the core spirit that served as the basis for Jereboam's conduct was his liberal "no big deal" attitude toward God's Word, will, and way. This despicable spirit inheres in every departure from God's standard. It is an integral part of every apostatizing step. Had Jereboam possessed and sustained a trembling reverence for every jot and tittle of God's law, he would never have contemplated, much less embarked upon, such a disastrous course.

Furthermore, Jereboam's total alteration of God's design for Israel's worship paved the way for a second major step in their abandonment of God's will. Ahab, the seventh king to succeed him on the throne of Israel, took the baton of apostasy from the hand of Jereboam and flooded the nation with the worship of Baal. The very wording of 1 Kings 16:31 is most significant: "And it came to pass, as if it had been a light thing for him to walk in the sins of Jereboam the son of Nebat, that he took to wife Jezebel the daughter of Ethbaal king of the Zidonians, and went and served Baal and worshiped him."

Israel's downward plunge into total apostasy left it void of the ability to discern between simple right and wrong (Amos 3:10).

As a result, Jereboam's liberal, self-willed, change-agent mentality wreaked catastrophic consequences on the northern kingdom of Israel. From the past, Jereboam screams to the present, urging man to give the strictest of heed to God's pattern of worship. Extreme caution in following the "due order" (1 Chron. 15:13) is implored. The highest degree of reverence for God's order is entreated.

What has liberalism learned from Jereboam's tragic error? That there is no such thing as a pattern for approaching God in worship; that grace covers deviations from God's will; that feeling that something is right makes it right; that worship experiences that fail to stimulate the flesh are not spiritual; that old ways of worship must bow to new ways if we are to attract a crowd; that placating the flesh with worship that feels good is more important than glorifying God by yielding to His will; that approaching God in worship with unauthorized acts is "no big deal"? Are these the lessons that God intends for man to learn from the incessant biblical emphasis on Jereboam's transgressions embracing two hundred fifty years of history? Tragically, liberalism does not learn from the past.

4

Liberalism and
the Past (Part III)

Saul was one of the most tragic figures among the leaders of Israel. Inspiration gives an early hint of the low priority of spiritual concerns in Saul's life by noting his unawareness of Samuel (1 Sam. 9:18-19). Saul's lowly servant was far more solicitous of spiritual things, having to inform his master of Samuel's presence in Zuph, the honorable nature of his life, and the certainty of fulfillment of his prophetic announcements (1 Sam. 9:5-6). Saul's lack of reverence for God's means of approaching Him in worship, a basic tenet of the spirit of liberalism, was manifested by his usurpation of priestly functions (1 Sam. 13:9-13). Samuel informed Saul that God had rejected him and would replace him with a man "after his own heart" (1 Sam. 13:14).

However, no statement points more clearly to the void of concern for God's will in Saul's life and reign than does the assertion of 1 Chronicles 13:3, "And let us bring again the ark of our God to us; for we inquired not at it in the days of Saul." The ark of the covenant was the most sacred piece of furniture in Judaism. It symbolized the presence of God with the nation of Israel. The top of this oblong chest was a slab of pure gold, and it was called the mercy seat (Exod. 25:17-21). When David gave Solomon the blueprint for the temple, he referred to the Most Holy Place as the "place of the mercy seat" (1 Chron. 28:11). On the Day of Atonement, the high priest entered the Holy of Holies and sprinkled atoning blood on the mercy seat (Lev. 16). God said, "And there I will meet with thee, and I will commune with thee from above the mercy seat" (Exod. 25:22). Thus, Saul's apathy regarding the ark of the covenant was a manifestation of his indifference toward atonement, the very heart of redemption.

When David succeeded Saul to the throne of Israel and had reunited the nation, he was eager to return the ark of the covenant to Jerusalem. Accompanied by thirty thousand distinguished men of Israel and a great host of people from throughout the nation, David journeyed to the house of Abinadab in Kirjathjearim where the ark had been for many years. They placed the ark of God on a new cart drawn by oxen and led by Ahio and Uzzah.

> And when they came to Nachon's threshingfloor, Uzzah put forth his hand to the ark of God, and took hold of it; for the oxen shook it. And the anger of the Lord was kindled against Uzzah; and God smote him for his error; and there he died by the ark of God (2 Sam. 6:6-7).

Even David, a man after God's own heart, possessing acute insight into God's nature and matters of the spirit, viewed God's action on this occasion as exceeding the bounds of justice (2 Sam. 6:8). However, his thinking was temporary and soon corrected by proper reflection and study. He quickly regained his mental composure and realized, as before, that God does not think like man thinks; that sin is always far worse than viewed by man; that sincerity is not the sole criterion for determining divine acceptability; that God means what He says; that God's way is the only way; that God's pattern for all things is to be revered, respected, and followed; and that sin deserves swift and immediate punishment.

David learned what liberalism never learns. Liberalism would heartily concur with David's initial reaction to God's execution of Uzzah. If liberalism were honest, it would admit that it views every such act of divine judgment as excessive with regard to justice, incompatible with grace, a handcuff on the hand of mercy, and nullification of love. Many who have drunk long and deep at this stream of spiritual and mental pollution hesitate not to thus brand such acts of God.

Furthermore, David soon realized where the real problem lay. God had given stringent instructions for the transporting of the ark of the covenant. The Kohathites—descendants of Kohath, one of the sons of Levi—had full responsibility for the tabernacle furniture with its ministering vessels and coverings (Num. 3:29-31). Prior to their permanent placement in the temple, as the nation moved from place to place under divine direction, the high priest and his sons were instructed to cover each piece of furniture and its vessels with badgers' skins and cloths of scarlet or blue. The actual conveyance of these sacred items was the duty of the Kohathites. They performed their task under the sentence of death should one dare touch a single item (Num. 4:1-15).

Moreover, God's plan for moving the tabernacle and its furnishings called for the use of wagons and oxen. The Gershonites were accountable for the curtains and various coverings of the tabernacle. Hence, their assignment necessitated two wagons and four oxen (Num. 7:7). The Merarites were responsible for the framework; therefore, they were accorded four wagons and eight oxen (Num. 7:8). "But unto the sons of Kohath he gave none; because the service of the sanctuary belonging unto them was that they should bear upon their shoulders" (Num. 7:9).

David deviated from God's plan. He tampered with God's divine arrangement. There were no oxen and wagons in God's design for transporting the tabernacle furniture. God's way called for staves and shoulders. David substituted unauthorized oxen and a wagon for authorized staves and shoulders. He neglected to respect both the sound and silence of God's voice. His fatal error laid the foundation for Uzzah's death. David realized and acknowledged his grievous sin. The words of his confession are striking, "We sought him not after the due order" (1 Chron. 15:13).

"For whatsoever things were written aforetime were written for our learning, that we through patience and comfort of the scriptures might have hope" (Rom. 15:4). What has liberalism learned from David's error? That refusing to follow God's pattern—substituting one's own way for God's way, neglecting to walk by faith, acting without divine authority, refusing to respect both the sound and silence of God's voice, lacking reverence for His blood-sealed covenant, and intruding upon His grace by mishandling the very object that served as a symbol thereof—is "no big deal"?

Liberalism is not concerned with God's due order. Liberalism is too consumed with its own order. It mocks the "shoulder and staves" aspect of God's will. It stares incomprehensibly at anyone who would attach any significance to something so minor as moving from the shoulder to a wagon. It cannot discern the difference between "shoulder" affairs and "wagon" affairs. From its lofty, self-erected tower of spiritual superiority, it casts an eye of pity toward anyone who would view "shoulder and wagon" affairs as "salvation issues." Liberalism does not learn from the past.

5

Liberalism and Grace

Grace is God's unmerited favor divinely bestowed upon sinful humanity. Life apart from grace is fantasy, not reality. Grace is not a lifeless attribute of deity. It is active, perpetually manifesting itself to man in countless ways. The wardrobe of grace is variegated and is as vast as eternity. James pointed to God as the source of all good things (James 1:17). A portrait encompassing every good thing on earth is a portrait of grace. Incessantly, God exhibits His grace toward man by giving him "rain from heaven and fruitful seasons, filling our hearts with food and gladness" (Acts 14:17).

Man owes his very existence to God's grace. Even in the paradisaical world of Eden, man was a recipient of the grace of God. Did man deserve to be created? Even in a world of perfection and innocence, can the creation deserve even a solitary gift from the hand of the Creator? Prior to sin, could the first human pair look toward Heaven and stamp even the smallest blessing as merit? God forbid!

God is not in debt to man. God does not owe man anything. The very nature of grace stamps man as an eternal debtor. If man could live a million years, he could never perform enough good deeds to place God in his debt. In spite of all the notable works that he might accomplish, the term *unprofitable* is irrevocably attached to every man's name (Luke 17:10). Whatever God does for man is based on grace, not merit.

The moment Genesis 3:6 became a reality, grace took on new meaning—Genesis 3:6 is the introduction to sin. When sin became a reality, the cross became a necessity. At the first appearance of sin, God headed toward Calvary. Sin rendered man spiritually impotent. Severed from the work of Christ on Golgotha's height, man is as helpless as a straw in the wind. Every step he takes is a backward step. He is lost today, lost tomorrow, and lost forever.

If man is ever to be saved, it will be by the grace of God. "Being justified freely by his grace through the redemption that is in Christ Jesus" (Rom. 3:24). It is the "grace of God that bringeth salvation" (Titus 2:11). Salvation by human effort and merit is unthinkable. Apart from grace, the presence of just one sin in a man's life forever seals his doom. In the salvation process, man must look to God and His grace, not to himself.

However, man's reception of God's gifts is not the work of grace alone. Man must cooperate with God in order to benefit from the rich provisions of grace. This principle embraces both physical and spiritual matters. Physical sustenance is a gift of grace; yet, a tremendous amount of human effort must be exerted by the farmer in order to receive this gift. The consumer must then match the farmer's effort with sufficient work to accumulate the funds necessary to purchase the food grown and harvested by the farmer.

Relative to spiritual matters, grace is the basis of man's acceptability with God. However, grace does not exclude the obedience of faith (Rom. 16:26). God cannot manifest grace by saving those who refuse or neglect to submit to His will. Jesus clearly identified the saved as those who "do the will of my Father which is in heaven" (Matt. 7:21). Jesus is the author of eternal salvation, but only for those that "obey him" (Heb. 5:9). Purification from sin by grace through blood is the result of "obeying the truth" (1 Pet. 1:22). Therefore, salvation is "by grace through faith" (Eph. 2:8) and that faith is the "obedience of faith" (Rom. 16:26) that "works by love" (Gal. 5:6).

The majesty, greatness, and grandeur of God transcends human expression. The very term *God* punctures the mind with rivets of inexpressible awe. The mind reels and staggers under the load of this single thought. One might as well attempt to squeeze the universe into a thimble as to endeavor to compress God into the mind of man. The vastness and complexity of the universe defies human understanding. If every man were a Solomon and had a trillion lifetimes to devote entirely to research and study, he could not commence to unlock the secrets or solve the mysteries of the universe. However, with a simple "God said," everything external to Himself came into existence (Gen. 1).

God is absolute holiness. God is so holy that He "cannot look on iniquity" (Hab. 1:13). Thus, when Israel sinned at the feet of Aaron's golden calf, Moses had to position the tabernacle "afar off from the camp" (Exod. 33:7). Because of Judah's grievous sin, God is pictured as vacating the temple, leaving Jerusalem, and ascending to the top of the mountain to oversee the city's destruction (Ezek. 11:22-23). God's holiness will not allow Him to dwell where sin dwells.

What is worship? Worship is an expression of grace. It is grace as it works in man's behalf. It is grace as it reaches out to man and allows him the unspeakable privilege of coming into the sublime presence of the holy God. Worship is man in mental prostration at the footstool of grace, clothed in reverential awe and wonder, expressing love and gratitude in divinely ordained acts. In view of the vile, odious, grotesque insanity of sin, it is a powerful testimony to the amazing grace of God that His holy name should even be allowed to move across the sinful lips of humanity, much less for permission to be granted for man to come into His august presence for worship and fellowship.

Grace teaches. Grace instructs man regarding things to do and things not to do (Titus 2:11-12). Grace teaches man to enter God's presence with biblical instruction, prayers, congregational singing, Sunday contributions, and participation in the Lord's supper (1 Cor. 11-16). Consequently, grace has provided a pattern whereby man might approach God with authorized acts of devotion. Following the pattern is man's responding to grace in the obedience of faith. It is man's walking by faith in appreciation of God's grace. It is man's honoring God's choices of grace. It is man's expressing love for God by obeying the commands of grace. It is man with a teachable spirit, a willing recipient of the instructions of grace. It is man's listening and yielding to the marvelous grace of God. Respect for the pattern is respect for the grace that provided the pattern.

Liberalism preaches a grace that it does not understand and to which it will not listen. Grace furnishes a pattern for entrance into God's presence, but liberalism denies even the concept of a pattern. Grace teaches, but liberalism will not learn. Grace tugs at man's heart, imploring him to move in harmony with its melody, but liberalism is too busy marching to the beat of its own drum. If liberalism were teachable it would cease to exist.

Grace entreats sinful man to wash in the fountain of blood and then come with trembling awe and reverential fear into the majestic presence of the God of all holiness with authorized offerings of spirit–and–truth worship. Reverence for grace, the instruction of grace, the demands of grace is Abel with the authorized sacrifice (Heb. 11:4); Abraham at the altar of faith (Heb. 11:17); David's finally following the "due order" (1 Chron. 15:13); and the remnant of Israel "trembling" at God's Word (Isa. 66:2).

The spirit of liberalism is Cain's receiving the "grace of God in vain" (2 Cor. 6:2) at the altar of self-will (Gen. 4:5); Nadab and Abihu's nullifying grace with "strange fire" (Lev. 10:1-2); Jereboam's sinning against grace with a perverted pattern of worship "devised of his own heart" (1 Kings 12:33); and the Pharisees' spurning grace with humanly contrived "vain worship" (Matt. 15:9).

The brazen, unauthorized liberties of the grace of liberalism include audible prayers of women in the presence of men; the efforts of a choir, soloist, or praise team to draw attention to itself and fostering entertainment; an expensive playground called a "Family Life Center"; and childish activities such as clapping, hand raising, and swaying that intrude upon the solemnity of spirit and truth worship.

The grace of liberalism is man's standing in the august presence of the omnipotent God, pointing to a mechanized piece of strange music and pompously affirming, "It's no big deal." The shameless grace of liberalism is man's promoting what God hates (Mal. 2:16) by attempting to nullify one of His most effective laws of prevention (Matt. 19:9). The arrogant grace of liberalism is man's holding forth the church for which Jesus died before an assembly of sectarians as an object of ridicule and derision. The end of the grace of liberalism is the destruction of exclusive New Testament Christianity in a given community and full fellowship with the Billy Grahams of the world. The grace of liberalism is alien to the grace of the Bible.

6

Liberalism and the Cross

Genesis 1 and 2 constitute a portrait of the world prior to the entrance of sin. The theme of Genesis 1 is not the physical universe. It is not the profusion of light that drove darkness from hovering over the face of the deep. It is not the cleaving of the waters of the earth with the firmament. It is not the emergence of dry land from the womb of the sea. It is not the earth's being wrapped in a blanket of green. It is not the orbs deposited in the heavens to rule over the day and the night. It is not innumerable chandeliers of light being strewn across the universe in galaxies far removed from earth and human sight. It is not the moving of water giving birth to creatures of the sea, nor the symphonic songs of birds in flight. It is not convulsions of the earth as it produces companions of living things. It is not man's coming forth from dust, or woman's coming from a rib in his side.

The theme of Genesis 1 is "God." God is mentioned by name thirty-two times in thirty-one verses. The fourth word of the first verse of the first chapter of the first book of divine revelation introduces the greatest Being in all of Heaven, in all of the universe, and all that ever has been or ever will be. If the universe could rest on the mind of man, its weight would be feathery in contrast to the single thought of God.

The theme of Genesis 2 is "man." God takes man back to the sixth day of creation and informs him of some truths about himself that are not revealed in Genesis 1. The last verse of

Genesis 1 points to the perfection of creation. The last verse of Genesis 2 points to the innocence of man. Consequently, "God, perfection, man, and innocence" is a portrait of the world prior to the entrance of sin. It was an immaculate world. God's relationship with man was consummate. Man's relationship with man was impeccable. Adam was a perfect husband; Eve was a perfect wife. Man's relationship with the physical and animal world was void of a single flaw. There were no natural disasters to mar the perfection of God's creation. Neither man nor animal was carnivorous, hence defacing God's creative work with bloodshed and death (Gen. 1:29-30). The world of Genesis 1 and 2 was a world of perfection and innocence.

Commencing with Genesis 3:6, the story of the Bible is the story of redemption. God had done all the work that was essential for man's every need in the first six days of Genesis 1. However, sin left God with no alternative. He had to go back to work. God's second work on man's behalf was redemptive in nature. Thus, redemption through Christ and Calvary is the theme of the Bible. Man's problem is sin. God's solution is the cross. Following the entrance of sin into the world, every book, chapter, verse, and letter in the Bible is related to this theme. The cross is the pivot of the biblical record. Every verse bleeds.

Subsequent to the giving of the law on Sinai, Moses sprinkled the blood of animals on the book, the people, the tabernacle and its vessels, declaring, "This is the blood of the testament which God hath enjoined unto you" (Heb. 9:19-22). Therefore, the Old Testament was dedicated by blood (Heb. 9:18). Accordingly, by means of blood, Moses ratified and sanctified everything connected with Judaism. The book of the law was thus confirmed and set apart as God's only mandate for the nation of Israel. By blood, the seed of Abraham was sanctified to function as the womb of the Messiah. The tabernacle and all of the vessels utilized in conjunction with worship were consecrated by blood.

Correspondingly, Judaism was a blood-sealed religion. Employing blood, God hallowed the Old Covenant and everything therein. To alter God's plan even to the slightest degree would be a presumptuous action, an expression of irreverence for God's sacred seal of His will to the Jewish nation. Not even a knife, pot, or pan could be added to the vessels associated with tabernacle worship, for such items would not have been ratified and sanctified by blood. Thus, when Nadab and Abihu sought to modify God's divine order, they were destroyed by the very element they misused. There was no blood on their strange fire.

In the words of Hebrews 9:14, "how much more" has the New Testament been ratified and sanctified by the blood of Christ. Jesus said, "For this is my blood of the new testament, which is shed for many for the remission of sins" (Matt. 26:28). The blood of God's Son is the "blood of the covenant" (Heb. 10:29), thus serving as God's sacred seal, His divine stamp of approval on every tenet of the New Testament. Every law and authorized action in the New Covenant has been validated by the blood of Christ. Consequently, whether intended or not, any law written, institution established, or action performed external to the New Testament is a presumptuous, defiant act, a manifestation of contempt for the blood of Jesus Christ and the covenant consecrated by that blood.

The Book of Mormon, the Koran, and the Watchtower have not been ratified and sanctified by the blood of Christ. The catechism of Catholicism and the manuals and creeds of denominationalism have not been ratified and sanctified by the blood of Christ. There is not a drop of the blood of God's Son on these humanly devised documents. They were contrived in the spirit of liberalism. Having usurped God's legislative prerogative, they are forgeries, attempting to supplant God's blood-sealed covenant. They are enemies of truth and expressions of disdain for the blood of Christ.

The church of Christ is the prophesied "kingdom" of Daniel 2:44; the "house of the Lord" of Micah 4:1; the church that Jesus promised to build of Matthew 16:18; the product of the one gospel of Acts 2; the "saved" of Acts 2:47; the "one body" of

Ephesians 4:4; the only sphere of reconciliation of Ephesians 2:16; the only institution with Christ as its head (Eph. 1:22-23) and its foundation (1 Cor. 3:11); the only institution in which man can glorify God (Eph. 3:21); the object of the love of Christ (Eph. 5:25); and the only institution purchased by the blood of Christ (Acts 20:28). Moreover, membership in and allegiance to the church is evidence of man's love for God, love for truth, and reverence for the blood that Christ shed on Calvary.

The spirit of liberalism loathes the exclusive church of the New Testament. The liberal spirit detests the very concept of exclusiveness. Every humanly devised religious institution on earth is a monumental lie, a product of the spirit of liberalism's intent on having its own way, a counterfeit for the real thing, and an enemy of the cross of Christ. Not a drop of the blood of Christ was shed for Islam, oriental mysticism, Catholicism, or denominationalism. Reverence for the blood of Christ, the New Testament ratified and sanctified by that blood, and the church purchased with that blood would bring an end to their existence in a mere moment of time.

The present apostasy of the church for which Jesus died is the result of the infamous, insatiable spirit of liberalism and its lack of reverence for the blood of God's own Son. Every spirit of error and overt act of error presently prevailing in many congregations is a demonstration of irreverence for the blood of Christ and the stringent and restrictive power of that blood as set forth in the New Testament. There is not a trace of the blood of Christ on any doctrine or action extraneous to the New Testament. It is not possible to express veneration for the cross while teaching a doctrine or engaging in an action not taught or authorized in God's blood-sealed covenant.

There is no blood on the mechanical instrument. There is no blood on clapping, praise teams, choirs, and solos. There is no blood on family life centers—empty substitutes for the home, and exhibitions of parental neglect. There is no blood on the act of women's praying audibly in the presence of men.

There is no blood on the dedicating of babies, theatrical performances, and non-Sunday days for partaking of the Lord's supper. There is no blood on second marriages following a divorce, void of fornication and an innocent party. If strange fire unconfirmed by the blood of animals brought death, what of strange music, teaching, and actions unstamped by the blood of Christ?

The "no big deal" spirit of liberalism is a playground for man's self-will. It is an invitation for men to "cease not from their own doings, nor from their stubborn way" (Judg. 2:19). It is a license for man to elevate feelings above objective truth. It destroys spirit and truth worship. It nullifies the distinctiveness of the church. It is the path to total apostasy from New Testament Christianity. Indeed, it is an adversary of the cross of Jesus Christ.

7

Liberalism and Love

Man talks much about loving God. Where lies the evidence? The proof is not in folded hands and a pious look, a coffee table graced with a family Bible, or a "honk if you love Jesus" bumper sticker. Love is not mere sentiment. It is not emotion running wild. It is not unrestrained affection. Love centers in the mind, the thinking, reasoning, knowing part of man. Thus, man is to love God with all his "heart, soul, and mind" (Matt. 22:37).

Love and knowledge are inseparable. Paul speaks of love abounding in knowledge (Phil. 1:9). Growth in one's knowledge of God's nature, ways, and works leads to a continual maturing of love and gratitude that subsequently is exhibited in willing submission to God's law. The nature of both man and love necessitated a law in Eden. Eliminate Genesis 2:17 and man is reduced to a robot of flesh, divinely programmed to perform certain tasks void of choice. However, the presence of law provided choice which inheres in free will and also a means whereby man could display his love for God.

Additionally, the absence of law nullifies the very nature of man, for both free will and love demand choice and a means of expression. Viewing divine law as being hostile to love and grace is ludicrous. Having given laws to promote man's happiness and well-being is God's way of saying, "I love you," in addition to providing a basis for man to respond in kind. There is, therefore, an irrevocable connection between love for God and compliance with His law. It is wholly impossible to express love in any other way.

The first generation of Abraham's descendants that came out of Egypt thought that God hated them and had determined their destruction by the hands of the Amorites (Deut. 1:27). Moses spent the last month of his life endeavoring to correct that misconception of God. He pressed upon the minds of the second generation that God loved them even as He loved their fathers and was deeply desirous of their love and commitment to His will.

Incessantly, he tied their love for God to their submission to the law of God. Moses reminded them that God showed mercy to "them that love me and keep my commandments" (Deut. 5:10). Moses stated what Jesus later described as the supreme commandment (Deut. 6:5; Matt. 22:37), and then immediately tied that love for God to keeping and teaching His Word (Deut. 6:6-9). Moses pointed to the faithfulness of God "which keepeth covenant and mercy with them that love him and keep his commandments" (Deut. 7:9). "And now, Israel, what doth the Lord thy God require of thee?" Moses answered that question with, "Love God and keep his commandments" (Deut. 10:12-13).

The principles by which God relates to man are immutable. Thus, one should not be surprised to hear Jesus say, "If ye love me, keep my commandments" (John 14:15). "If a man love me, he will keep my words" (John 14:23). "He that loveth me not, keepeth not my sayings" (John 14:24). John affirmed, "For this is the love of God that we keep his commandments" (1 John 5:3). The friends of Christ are those who obey the commandments of Christ (John 15:14). Therefore, any man that claims to love God and refuses or neglects to comply with any aspect of His law "is a liar, and the truth is not in him" (1 John 2:4).

Every false religion on earth is an adversary of biblical love. If Islam loved God it would never have elevated Mohammed above Jesus Christ, nor supplanted the Bible with the Koran. Those who planted the initial seeds of corrupt, apostate Catholicism left their "first love" (Rev. 2:4) and never returned to it. Every basic maxim of denominationalism is a denial of love for God. It is not possible to express love for God while holding membership in a spurious religion that God did not plant but shall uproot and destroy (Matt. 15:13). If David were alive today, he would say, "I love the people and desire their salvation, but denominationalism, as a system, I hate" (Ps. 119:128).

Liberalism feigns love for God while combating love at every turn. The direction of liberalism is ever downward, and the love it alleges is denied every step of the way. Was Cain's offering a sacrifice of love? (Gen. 4.) With which law of God did he comply as an expression of his love? Did Jeroboam enter God's presence through the door of love? (1 Kings 12.) To what aspect of God's authority did he submit as a demonstration thereof? Was Nadab and Abihu's strange fire an act of love? (Lev. 10:1-2.) Was Uzziah's attempt to enter God's presence in the temple an indication of his love for God? (2 Chron. 26:16.) Was David's oxen and cart a manifestation of his love and reverence for God and His law that governed the transporting of the ark of the covenant? (2 Sam. 6.)

When Israel clamored for a king so they could be "like all the nations" (1 Sam. 8:20), was that a manifestation of their love for God and respect for His rule over them? Is the call for change that would enable the church to blend in with the religious environment evidence of love for God and a venerate spirit for the one church of Christ for which he died? (Eph. 5:25.) When a man stands before an assembly of sectarians and holds up the church of the New Testament as an object of ridicule and derision, is that love at work? Can a man love God without loving that which God loves?

When one, driven by the spirit of liberalism, endeavors to play a mechanical instrument in the presence of God as an act of worship, is that a display of love for God? To which command of God in the New Testament is he adhering as proof of his love? When one describes unauthorized strange music in the presence of the Holy God as "no big deal," is that a demonstration of love for God and trembling reverence for His Word? By what other choice of words could a man exhibit a greater sense of irreverence for God's authority, pattern of worship, Word, will, or way?

Paul speaks of the "labor of love" (1 Thess. 1:3). Are elders laboring to demonstrate love for God and His will by allowing women to pray audibly in the presence of men? What passage can be cited that negates the principle of 1 Timothy 2:12 that embraces both testaments, thus serving as an authoritative basis to which man can yield as an expression of his love?

Jesus said, "If ye love me, keep my commandments" (John 14:15). What command of God is being obeyed when one strives to enter the presence of God with choirs, solos, and praise teams as opposed to the principle of reciprocity demanded by Ephesians 5:19 and Colossians 3:16 and expressed in congregational singing? What command is being obeyed when the church constructs elaborate air conditioned and heated playgrounds for fleshly appeasement? To what command can one appeal for partaking the Lord's supper on non-Sunday days? Where lies the authority for love to express itself in the replacement of simple gospel preaching with theatrical performances?

Is clapping a manifestation of love for God? If so, where is New Testament authority that would allow love to be thus expressed? Is love for God at work when man attempts to abrogate Mark 16:16 with John 3:16, or annul God's effort to preserve the marital state in Matthew 19:9 with 1 Corinthians 7? Is love for God and His Word driving a man when he denies plain Bible teaching on eternal punishment or the authority of elders?

One may certainly comply with various imperatives of God's will without love. He may even ascend to the pinnacle of self-sacrifice by devoting all his material wealth to the poor or suffering a martyr's death and "have not love" (1 Cor. 13:3).

However, it is not possible to love God without yielding to the will of God. Love cannot function in the absence of law. It has no where else to go. Its life's blood courses through the veins of law. "Where there is no law, there is no transgression" (Rom. 4:15), and where there is no law, there is no love. Sin must have a law to transgress, because that is what sin is (1 John 3:4), and love must have a law to obey because that is what love does (1 John 5:3).

Love sings, prays, and remembers Christ in the Lord's supper every Sunday. Love teaches the truth, gives propor-tion-ately to that received, and submits to civil laws that are consistent with divine law. Love obeys parents, provides for one's family, and refuses to forsake the assembly. But love does not—yea, cannot!—worship God with a mechanical instrument, remember Christ in the Lord's supper on non-Sunday days, substitute a denomination for the one church that belongs to Christ, refuse to be baptized for the remission of sins, dedicate babies as a religious act, replace preaching with drama, clap, or manifest itself in any other way for which there is no "thus saith God." Love can no more "prove its sin-cerity" (2 Cor. 8:8) without law than man can see without eyes.

Thus, through law, an expression of God's love for man, God has provided a means whereby man might express his love for God. The spirit of liberalism nullifies the very nature of biblical love.

8

Liberalism and Faith

Divine revelation is the basis of faith. "So then faith cometh by hearing and hearing by the word of God" (Rom. 10:17). Where there is no word from God, there can be no exercise of faith. "For we walk by faith, not by sight" (2 Cor. 5:7). In the absence of a "thus saith God," one cannot walk, worship, or act by faith. The execution of faith demands divine authority. One can no more operate by faith where God has not spoken than he can breathe without lungs. To argue for a religious practice based on the absence of a "thou shalt not," is to argue against faith. It is not possible for man to express the "obedience of faith" (Rom. 16:26) in the absence of a word from God for faith to obey.

Paul speaks of the "law of faith" (Rom. 3:27). The law of faith of Romans 3:27 is equivalent to the faith of Romans 4:16 and Ephesians 2:8 that appropriates grace; thus, inspiration clearly combines law with grace, something which liberalism claims is never done in scripture. Furthermore, one of the two key elements in faith is obedience, and obedience necessitates law; therefore, in severing law from grace, liberalism has severed faith from grace.

Paul also speaks of the "law of works" (Rom. 3:27). The law of works is a legalistic system of self-trusting, human merit that nullifies grace and faith and produces a self-righteous, boasting spirit. It was this very kind of works that Paul had in mind when he said, "Now to him that worketh is the reward not reckoned of grace, but of debt" (Rom. 4:4); and again, "Not of works, lest any man should boast (Eph. 2:9).

Conversely, the law of faith rivets man's attention on God's great love, grace, and mercy and the provisions thereof in Christ and the cross. The law of faith is man's trusting in God and not in self. The "law of faith" (Rom. 3:27) is the "obedience of faith" (Rom. 16:26) looking to the cross for redemption. The law of faith is man's submitting to God's law, God's will, God's way, God's conditions for salvation, God's pattern of worship, while placing the totality of his trust in God, His grace, and the blood of Christ. The law of works is a proud Pharisee's trusting in self (Luke 18:11-12). The law of faith is a penitent publican's trusting in God (Luke 18:13).

As a result, biblical faith loves divine law. God's law is an extension of God's grace, providing faith, a means by which it can be expressed. Faith cannot function external to divine law. Removing God's law from faith is like extracting gas from an automobile. Divine imperatives are to faith what sunshine is to flowers. Faith draws the law of God to its bosom as a mother would a child. The psalmist affirmed, "And I will delight myself in thy commandments, which I have loved" (Ps. 119:47). That is what faith does. Faith anticipates with delight every opportunity to demonstrate its genuineness by complying with what God has instructed it to do. Faith delights in the law of God.

Abel listened to God and did what God told him to do (Gen. 4:1-7). Why? Because that is the nature of faith. Thus, Abel's offering was "by faith" (Heb. 11:4). God instructed Noah to build an ark. Noah listened attentively to God's instructions and "according to all that God commanded him, so did he" (Gen. 6:22). Hence, his construction of the ark was "by faith" (Heb. 11:7). Noah cooperated with God by responding to His will in obedient faith. He was characterized by the "work of faith" (1 Thess. 1:3). He possessed a "faith which worketh by love" (Gal. 5:6). Noah did not trust in the ark, or his construction thereof for his salvation. He did not rely upon his own efforts. His trust was in God and His grace. Yet, he knew that his salvation by God's grace could not be a reality apart from his obedience of faith. It is futile to plead for the display of grace apart from the exercise of faith. "And why call ye me Lord, Lord, and do not the things which I say?" (Luke 6:46).

God commanded Abraham to leave his home and proceed toward an unspecified land (Gen. 12:1). Only because God had thus ordered could Abraham embark upon his journey "by faith" (Heb. 11:8). When God foretold the judgment to befall Egypt in the death of the firstborn, His announcement was tempered with grace. He promised to spare the firstborn in every house where the blood of the lamb had been applied to the door post (Exod. 12:13). Had not God so directed, Israel could not have responded "by faith" (Heb. 11:28). God promised Israel the city of Jericho as a gift of grace (Josh. 6:2). However, reception of the gift depended upon marching around the city thirteen times over seven days, blowing the trumpet and shouting (Josh. 6:3-5). Submitting to God's will, Israel received Jericho as a gift of grace "by faith" (Heb. 11:30).

Therefore, biblical faith is based foursquare on "God said." Faith is wholly dependent upon a word from God. Faith has nowhere else to go. Its life's blood flows through the veins of divine authority. It owes its very existence to a "thus saith God." Thus, faith repents (Luke 13:3). Faith confesses Christ as God's Son (Matt. 10:32). Faith is baptized for the remission of sins (Acts 2:38). Repentance, confession, and baptism constitute faith at work; faith's respecting the "teaching" of grace (Titus 2:11-12); faith's obeying God; faith's submitting to the will of God; faith's responding to God's grace by complying with God's Word, while looking to Calvary for redemption.

Faith prays (1 Thess. 5:17). Faith remembers Christ and Calvary in the Lord's supper every Sunday (1 Cor. 11; Acts 20:7). Faith gives, every first day of the week, in proportion to that which has been received (1 Cor. 16:1-2). Faith preaches the Word (2 Tim. 2:4). Faith sings (Eph. 5:19). These are God's choices for expressions of worship. Faith honors these choices. These choices inhere in the "law of faith" (Rom. 3:27). Acceding to God's choices for worship is faith's respecting grace and the pattern that grace has provided for entrance into God's presence. It is faith's honoring the blood of Christ for sanctifying these choices as the authorized means of approaching God.

Faith accepts the oneness of the church (Matt. 16:18); God's pattern of worship for the church (1 Cor. 11-16); the organization of the church (1 Tim. 3; Titus 1); and the mission of the church (Mark 16:15). Faith submits to God's prohibition regarding women (1 Cor. 14:34-35; 1 Tim. 2:12). Faith yields to God's effort to preserve the sanctity of the marital state (Matt. 19:9). Faith honors the home as God's family-life center (Gen. 2:21-24; Matt. 19:3-9). Biblical faith has a trembling reverence for every word of God.

Conversely, faith knows nothing about Catholicism, Islam, denominationalism, or Oriental mysticism. These false religions are not even a part of Faith's vocabulary. Attempting to talk with faith about such concepts is like trying to talk with a machine about God. Faith does not possess the ability to understand anything extraneous to the Word of God.

Faith cannot agree to disagree on matters essential to its own nature. Faith flees when men strive for unity in diversity and therefore refuse to abide "in the doctrine of Christ" (2 John 9). Faith cannot remember Christ in the Lord's supper on non-Sunday days. Faith cannot dedicate babies. Faith cannot clap. Faith cannot sing a solo or join a choir. Faith is not in the same room where women pray audibly in the presence of men. Faith vacates a class when a woman rises to teach when men are present. Faith cannot divorce a mate for any reason other than fornication and remarry. Faith can talk intelligently about immersion, but faith has no knowledge of sprinkling or pouring. Faith cannot function in a Christmas or Easter ceremony. Faith cannot play an instrument in a worship assembly. Faith has zero tolerance for strange music. Faith would no more stand in the presence of God, point to an unauthorized piece of machinery and exclaim, "It's no big deal," than it would shout, "I hate God and love the devil!"

Liberalism has no hesitancy embracing everything that faith refuses. Liberalism views the old ways of faith as out-dated, moldy, and stuffy. Regarding the old paths that faith treads, liberalism exclaims, "Behold, what a weariness is it" (Mal. 1:13). Liberalism has a propensity for things new and exciting. Liberalism loves change, and the changes generated by liberalism abrogate faith. Liberalism lacks the ability to discern genuine spirituality, because genuine spirituality grows out of faith, and liberalism does not understand faith. Liberalism's "no big deal" attitude toward divine authority and fundamental principles of divine revelation destroys the very foundation upon which faith is constructed. The spirit of liberalism nullifies the very nature of biblical faith.

9

Liberalism and Law

God loves man. God's love for man is unfathomable, even by the combined genius of the Solomons of the ages. Though man is beyond merit, often unlovable, and generally found in opposition to truth and right, God's love for him is unquenchable.

Man needs God. In spite of his boasting, without God man "can do nothing" (John 15:5). Apart from divine revelation, every step that man takes is void of purpose and hope, for "it is not in man that walketh to direct his steps" (Jer. 10:23). Man needs a divine pattern for human behavior to prevent his self-ruin.

The existence of law is God's way of saying, "I love you." Parents operate on the basis of this same principle. Therefore, they lovingly encircle their children with laws (rules of conduct) in hopes of preventing their participation in activities that would destroy their happiness and general well-being and fill them with life-long sorrow and regret.

The divine prohibition relative to fornication is God's way of promoting purity and self-respect, preventing venereal diseases and human misery, and assuring one of marital happiness as either a present reality or a future prospect. Such is true of every law that God has ever given. Every divine statute, positive precept, prohibition, restraint, and restriction has God's love and concern for man written all over it.

Sin results when man transgresses the law of God (1 John 3:4). Since God's law promotes man's happiness and well-being, when man sins, he is robbing himself. He is his own thief. Were Adam and Eve happy as they hid from God's presence among the trees of Eden? Was the prodigal son happy and content in the hog pen of the far country? Was Judas happy with the thirty pieces of silver?

Ancient Israel was surrounded by heathen nations with a propensity for idolatry and an insatiable appetite for all the sins inherent therein. God's law was designed to serve as a divine protectorate, preserving Israel from the corrupting influences of those pagan nations (Lev. 18:30). Instead of being a cold, legal system, there was a warmth to God's statutes as He sought to draw Israel unto Himself and make them exclusively His.

God has never encased man in the cold bands of law, severed from grace and love. Though such was often the Jewish perspective, as illustrated by the Pharisee in Luke 18:10-13, that was their problem, not God's. From Eden onward, God has expressed His grace and love by clothing man in blessings divine when man, motivated by love, submitted to His will in the obedience of faith. Every "thou shalt" and "thou shalt not" of the gospel is a manifestation of the warm, benevolent heart of Jehovah beating in man's best interest. There is a gentle, caring warmth to divine law.

Accordingly, God's relationship with man has always involved law and grace. The concepts are inseparable. Divine law is a gift of grace, a demonstration of God's great love and concern for man, a means of securing man's soul for time and eternity. Consequently, the law of God contains "wondrous things" (Ps. 119:18), all penned in man's best interest.

Salvation involves grace and faith (Eph. 2:8). This faith has obedience and trust as its nature and love as its motivation (Gal. 5:6). One cannot obey that which does not exist. Thus, the "obedience of faith" (Rom. 16:26) necessitates law. Apart from law, faith would have no means of expression.

The object of faith's trust is God, not the act of obedience. Trusting in one's own obedience transforms works of faith into works of merit. It converts the "law of faith" into the "law of works" (Rom. 3:27), resulting in the nullification of both grace and faith. Works of faith trust in God. Works of merit trust in self. Works of faith declare, "Look what God has done." Works of merit exclaim, "Look what I have done."

By grace, God has made abundant provisions for man's salvation through Christ and the cross. However, in order to benefit from God's grace, man must respond to God's law in the obedience of faith, for salvation is by grace "through faith" (Eph. 2:8). Search in vain for a single biblical example of any spiritually blessed man, apart from his obedient faith.

Relative to spiritual matters, human compliance with divine law activates grace. God forgives by grace through blood when man submits to His will by faith (Acts 2:38). God continues to cleanse man of sin by grace through blood as man walks in the light by faith (1 John 1:7). Apart from divine law and compliance therewith in the obedience of faith, man would be void of any means of appropriating the rich provisions of grace in Calvary to his soul.

The desire for liberty is universal in its scope. The Declaration of Independence acknowledges liberty as an inalienable right, divinely bestowed upon all humanity. Ironically, freedom is not free. America's freedom was purchased by the blood of countless thousands. The supreme price of liberty was paid by Jesus Himself. Sin finds its remedy in the blood of Christ, and the shackles of spiritual slavery vanish in the presence of the cross. "If the Son therefore shall make you free, ye shall be free indeed" (John 8:36).

There is an unalterable affinity between law and liberty. Freedom disappears in the absence of law. A community without law to govern and restrain human behavior would result in utter chaos. Every man would be his own law, the strong would prey upon the weak and the knife would reign supreme in this lawless jungle of humanity.

Absolute freedom is a contradiction of terms. Eluding the power of one restraint only places one in the grasp of another.

Having escaped the law of gravity, the astronaut finds his activities and freedom more restricted than ever. Drug addicts, drunkards, murderers, and thieves have negated personal freedom and placed themselves in chains by their refusal to honor God's laws of constraint relative to human conduct.

Law promotes liberty. Freedom cannot exist or thrive except in the presence of law, submission thereto, and enforcement thereof. Sin is a violation of God's law (1 John 3:4). Thus, sin nullifies liberty and results in slavery. "Whosoever committeth sin is the servant of sin" (John 8:34). Man needs God's "perfect law of liberty" (James 1:25).

Law regulates liberty. Law informs liberty of its bounds and its sphere of operation. Every liberty man has is accompanied by a divine law or principle to control its employment. Even the liberty to do things right within themselves is governed by divine precept (1 Cor. 8). The "all-grace, no-law" theory encourages sin and abrogates liberty, the very thing that it is intended to promote. The reality of liberty is dependent upon the presence of divine law and man's respect for it and submission to it out of love for Him who gave it.

Liberalism loathes law. Liberalism views law as its enemy. Law restricts. Liberalism has no patience with restrictions. Divine law limits music in New Testament worship to singing, to making melody in the heart (Eph. 5:19), not on a machine. Liberalism discards God's restrictive law, points to the use of an unauthorized piece of machinery and presumptuously avers, "It's no big deal."

Divine law manifested its restrictive power in the "except" of John 3:5 and Matthew 19:9. Liberalism in denominationalism has never respected the "except" of John 3:5, and liberalism in the church has never esteemed the "except" of Matthew 19:9, thus abandoning both and formulating patterns for salvation and marriage more to its liking.

Divine law restricts the church to "one"; the organization of the church to "one"; the means of raising funds for the work of the church to "one"; the pattern of worship to "one"; the plan of salvation to "one"; and the means of expressing faith and love to "one." Liberalism detests these limitations. Liberalism has its own humanly devised substitutes for every restrictive element of God's law.

Divine law restricts the Lord's supper and the collection to Sunday, singing to congregational, assembly leadership to men, dedication to accountability, and fellowship to those who abide in the doctrine of Christ. Liberalism has a strong aversion to these constraints.

Divine law is God's saying, "It's my way or no way." Liberalism shouts, "It's no big deal" toward every limitation of divine law. Liberalism is intent on having its own way. The spirit of liberalism nullifies the very nature of God's law.

10

Liberalism, Gospel, and Doctrine

Liberalism draws a distinction between *gospel* and *doctrine*. Liberalism limits the gospel to the death, burial, and resurrection of Christ as set forth in 1 Corinthians 15:1-4. Liberalism views all teaching external to these three core facts as *doctrine*. Liberalism, as a result, asserts that the gospel cannot be preached to the church in view of the church's having already obeyed the gospel, and doctrine cannot be proclaimed to the world because the world has yet to submit to the gospel. Thus, liberalism views Matthew, Mark, Luke, and John as pure gospel, Acts as second-rate gospel, and Romans through Jude as no gospel at all. Moreover, liberalism regards gospel truths as matters of faith, and doctrinal truths as matters of judgment. This allows liberalism to open the door of fellowship to all those who acknowledge the death, burial, and resurrection of Christ regardless of their views concerning other matters of biblical teaching. Perhaps no tenet of liberalism points to its inane nature any more than this humanly devised theory.

Jesus forever negated this fatuous notion when He said,

All authority hath been given unto me in heaven and on earth. Go ye therefore and make disciples of all the nations, baptizing them into the name of the Father and of the Son and of the Holy Spirit; teaching them to observe all things whatsoever I have commanded you; and lo I am with you always, even unto the end of the world (Matt. 28:18-20 asv).

The terms *baptizing* and *teaching* are present tense participles pointing to the means by which disciples are made. Therefore, disciples are made by hearing the gospel (1 Cor. 15:1-4) and responding thereto in the "obedience of faith" (Rom. 16:26), embracing repentance (Acts 17:30) and confession (Rom. 10:10), and the culminating act of baptism (Acts 2:38). In addition, disciples are made by submitting to all things commanded by Christ, hence embracing the totality of the gospel, teaching, or doctrine of Christ as set forth in the New Testament. It is plainly evident that the gospel encompasses far more than the truths regarding the death, burial, and resurrection of Christ.

God has only one blueprint, pattern, or plan for man's salvation. This plan is variously described in Scripture. It is designated as "the gospel" (Rom. 1:16); "the word of this salvation" (Acts 13:26); "the truth" (John 17:19); "the word" (2 Tim. 4:2); "the new testament" (Heb. 9:15); "the law of the spirit of life" (Rom. 8:2); "the law of Christ" (Gal. 6:2); "the perfect law of liberty" (James 1:25); "the law of faith" (Rom. 3:27); "the word of his grace" (Acts 14:3); "glad tidings" (Acts 13:32); and "Jesus" (Acts 8:35). Though not an exclusive list, these terms or phrases demonstrate the variety of ways God's one plan for man's redemption is identified in Scripture. God does not have two plans or systems, one for saints and one for sinners. He has one gospel, or divine message, full of good news for both the saved and the lost.

Paul and Barnabas preached the gospel to Sergius Paulus in the city of Paphos on the island of Cyprus (Acts 13:6-12). In the course of six verses, inspiration identifies the gospel in five different ways: "the word of God" (v. 7); "the faith" (v. 8); "righteousness" (v. 10); "the right ways of the Lord" (v. 10); and "the doctrine of the Lord" (v. 12). Irrefutably, in spite of liberalism's intense denial, the doctrine or teaching of the Lord can be preached to the lost. Moreover, the gospel can be preached to the church, the saved. In writing to the church at Rome, Paul affirmed, "So, as much as in me is, I am ready to preach the gospel to you that are at Rome also" (Rom. 1:15).

While in Antioch, Peter and his Jewish brethren ate with the Gentiles. However, upon the arrival of certain Jews from James, Peter "withdrew and separated himself, fearing them which were of the circumcision" (Gal. 2:12). Peter's hypocrisy was so detrimental that "the other Jews dissembled likewise with him; insomuch that Barnabas also was carried away with their dissimulation" (Gal. 2:13). Paul described such conduct as being inconsistent with the "truth of the gospel" (Gal. 2:14). Peter and his Jewish brethren had not denied the triune truth of 1 Corinthians 15:1-4. Their hypocrisy, though, resulted in a violation of the truth of the gospel just as surely as if they had disavowed the death, burial, and resurrection of Christ.

What is the difference in the "any other gospel" of Galatians 1:8 and "no other doctrine" of 1 Timothy 1:3? There is no difference. Both constitute warnings against teaching anything contrary to God's revelation to man as is set forth in the New Testament, the "whatsoever I have said unto you" of John 14:26, and the "all truth" of John 16:13. This truth is reinforced in the context of 1 Timothy 1. Following the warning regarding "no other doctrine" in verse 3, verses 10 and 11 interchange "sound doctrine" and "the glorious gospel of the blessed God." Thus, the sins enumerated in verses 9 and 10 are at variance with the "gospel of Christ" and the "doctrine of Christ," both of which refer to the same body of divine truth.

Paul preached the gospel to the Thessalonians (1 Thess. 1:5). In receiving the gospel, they "received the word of God" (2:13). Paul reminded the Thessalonians that the gospel he preached to them contained an exhortation to "walk worthy of God" (2:12). The gospel would establish them in their faith (3:2). It would "establish their hearts unblameable in holiness" (3:12). Though much can be accomplished through an epistle, Paul desired personal contact with them so as to "perfect that which is lacking in your faith" (3:10). Faith comes by hearing the word of God (Rom. 10:17). Deficiencies in faith can be corrected only by instruction from the source of faith.

A gospel that encourages a worthy walk with God stabilizes and strengthens faith, compels a heart toward holiness, and corrects inadequacies in faith involves far more than "death, burial, and resurrection" truth. Though "all truth" (John 16:13) is irrevocably connected to these core truths, these fundamental verities do not exhaust the "all truth" of the gospel.

In addition, Paul reminded the Thessalonians that the gospel he preached to them (1:5), constituting the word of God, which they received (2:13), contained imperatives regarding sanctified living that abstained from fornication (4:2-5). He also stirred their memories concerning the "call" they had received (4:7) through the gospel (2 Thess. 2:14). The call of the gospel prohibits "uncleanness" while demanding "holiness" (4:7). These are the very truths that Paul said "grace teaches" (Titus 2:11-12). Therefore, by grace, through the gospel, God affirms that "without holiness, no man shall see the Lord" (Heb. 12:14). Emphatically, the gospel of Christ embraces the totality of New Testament teaching, the design of which is to provide redemption by "grace through faith" (Eph. 2:8) in view of the provisions growing out of the death, burial, and resurrection of Christ.

Having set forth the heart of redemption, (Matthew through John), the New Testament proceeds to answer two questions: How does one get into Christ (Acts)? and how does one stay in Christ (Romans through Jude)? Matthew, Mark, Luke, and John constitute grace: God, by grace, making provisions for man's redemption through Christ. Acts is grace: God, by grace, providing a plan whereby man might access His grace and enjoy the blessings inherent in the death, burial, and resurrection of Christ. Romans through Jude constitute grace: God, by grace, providing a second plan which enables man to "continue in the grace of God" (Acts 13:43) allowing him to enjoy perpetual cleansing of sin by the blood of Christ. Revelation is grace; God announcing ultimate victory for those who "receive not the grace of God in vain" (2 Cor. 6:2) by faithful continuance in the will of God until death (Rev. 22:14).

Matthew, Mark, Luke, and John comprise the gospel, the good news of redemption through Christ. Acts is gospel, the good news of God's plan whereby man might appropriate the provisions of grace in Calvary to his soul stained by sin. Romans through Jude constitute gospel, the good news of God's means of staying connected to Calvary by continual manifestation of the "faith which worketh by love" (Gal. 5:6) in complying with the doctrine or teaching of grace "that denying ungodliness and worldly lusts, we should live soberly, righteously, and godly in this present world" (Titus 2:11-12). Revelation is gospel, the good news of the sovereignty of God and the demonstration of that sovereignty in the salvation and preservation of those in great adversity who responded to God's grace in the obedience of faith and who "washed their robes, and made them white in the blood of the lamb" (Rev. 7:14).

Of what value is the knowledge of the good news of the work of Christ culminating in His death, burial, and resurrection as set forth in the four accounts of the gospel apart from the knowledge of the good news of God's plan enabling man to benefit from His redemptive work as revealed in Acts? Suppose every accountable person on earth believed the triune truth of 1 Corinthians 15:1-4 but, by choice, embraced eternity without obeying "from the heart that form of doctrine" (Rom. 6:17). Inspiration describes such people as objects of divine vengeance "who shall be punished with everlasting destruction from the presence of the Lord, and from the glory of his power" (2 Thess 1:7–9).

Peter preached the good news regarding the death, burial, and resurrection of Christ in Acts 2:22-36. In Acts 2:38, Peter announced the means whereby his audience could enjoy the benefits of these marvelous truths in the forgiveness of their sins. Would anyone deny that the three thousand on Pentecost viewed Acts 2:38 as gospel or good news? In Acts 9:4-5, Jesus confirmed to Saul the truth regarding Himself. In Acts 22:16, Ananias informed Saul of the culminating act of gospel obedience that would enable him to contact the blood of Christ and have his sins washed away. Would anyone argue against Saul's viewing Acts 22:16 as gospel or good news? Is preaching Jesus good news? In preaching Jesus, Philip preached baptism (Acts 8:35-39). Is baptism good news? Inspiration answers in the affirmative.

In its consummated form, liberalism demands Jesus void of His plan by which men are saved. Liberalism cries for the "Man," but decries the "plan." God unites them, and liberalism divides them. Peter preached the Man in Acts 2:22-36 and the plan in Acts 2:38. Since the Ethiopian eunuch progressed from ignorance of both to knowledge of both, Philip preached the Man and the plan in Acts 8:35. Jesus preached Himself in Acts 9:4-5, and Ananias preached His plan in Acts 22:16. Peter preached the Man in Acts 10:34-43 and the plan in Acts 10:47-48. Suppose the three thousand on Pentecost, the Ethiopian eunuch, Saul, and Cornelius had believed the good news about the "Man," but rejected the good news about the "plan." Would they have been any better off than the demons who confessed Jesus as the Son of God (Mark 5:7), the Jews who "believed on him" (John 8:30), but refused to obey Him, or the chief rulers who "believed on him; but because of the Pharisees, they did not confess him, lest they should be put out of the synagogue"? (John 12:42-43.)

The death, burial, and resurrection of Jesus Christ constitute the heart and core of redemption. Its significance is incomprehensible. No thoughtful person would dare equate the plan with the Man. However, from a practical perspective, relative to the act of salvation, of what value is one without the other? "Come unto me" is God's invitation through the gospel. Of what value is it to proclaim God's "come" without God's "how"? Where is the merit in preaching on God's grace without informing man how to respond to grace in the obedience of faith? How effective are sermons on the cross apart from advising man how to appropriate the provisions thereof to his soul by complying with the conditions of the gospel? Why extend God's invitation without instructing man as to God's means of responding to the invitation?

Of what benefit is Acts 2:22-36 without Acts 2:38? Why preach the "Man" of the cross without announcing the "plan" that permits man to profit therefrom? Did Jesus rebuke Saul for inquiring about a plan? (Acts 9:6). Did He refuse to answer his question? God sent Ananias to Saul with Acts 22:16. Every penitent believer needs to hear the answer that Ananias gave Saul. Cornelius needed to hear "all things that are commanded thee of God" (Acts 10:33). "All things" embraced the death, burial, and resurrection of Christ (Acts 10:39-40), and baptism (Acts 10:48), the Man and the plan. It's God's Son and it's God's plan. Both are good news, and that's what the gospel is. Only liberalism would be so presumptuous as to part asunder what God hath joined together.

What is Romans through Jude? Is it good news or bad news? Romans through Jude constitutes the gospel. It is God's good news of how to remain attached to Calvary. It is a divine commentary on how to "walk in the light" (1 John 1:7) in order to enjoy perpetual cleansing by the blood of Christ. Paul pronounced a blessing upon the man against whom God will not impute sin (Rom. 4:8). Who is the man against whom God will not impute or mark up sin? He is the man of 1 John 1:7. Who is the man of 1 John 1:7? He is the man who, having submitted to the Man (Matthew, Mark, Luke, and John) by obeying the plan (Acts), faithfully follows the good news of Romans to Jude, while manifesting a penitent spirit for failures along the way.

Once saved, it is not necessary for a man to ever be lost. Denominationalism teaches unconditional security. The Bible teaches conditional security. Can the man of 1 John 1:7 be lost? No. Why? Because he is walking in the light of divine truth and the blood of Christ continually cleanses him from sin. He is in a state of forgiveness as denoted by the perfect tense "are forgiven"—past action with continuing results—of 1 John 2:12. Can a man cease walking in the light? Yes. But should such become a reality, he is no longer the man of 1 John 1:7. He is now the one of Luke 8:13 who "in time of temptation fell away"; the unfruitful "branch" of John 15:6; the "castaway" of 1 Corinthians 9:27; the one of Galatians 5:4 who has "fallen from grace"; or the "shipwrecked faith" of 1 Timothy 1:19.

Who is the man against whom God will not impute or mark up sin? He is the sheep of John 10:27 who continually listens to and follows Christ. Can the man of John 10:27 be lost? Concerning such men Jesus said,

> And I give unto them eternal life and they shall never perish, neither shall any man pluck them out of my hand. My Father which gave them me is greater than all, and no man is able to pluck them out of my Father's hand (John 10:28-29).

Can a man desist from heeding and following Christ? Most assuredly. However, should he thus choose, he ceases to be the man of John 10:27 and can no longer claim the promises of spiritual security in John 10:28-29. He is now the one who has developed "an evil heart of unbelief in departing from the living God" of Hebrews 3:12; the one who has "crucified the Son of God afresh" of Hebrews 6:6; the one who has become "entangled again" in the "pollutions of the world" of 2 Peter 2:20; or the one whose name has been removed from the "book of life" of Revelation 22:19. This is the very thing that God is endeavoring to prevent in Romans through Jude.

The intent of Romans through Jude is to encourage the redeemed to walk in the light. The majestic truths from the mind of God contained in these books are intended to enable man to have "promise of the life that now is, and of that which is to come" (1 Tim. 4:8). Through these truths, God is striving to secure man's soul for time and eternity. These divine tenets aspire to serve as a barrier between the saved and the tragic state of apostasy. Is this not good news?

What is Romans through Jude? It is the love of God working in man's best interest. It is God's great love making provisions for man's inadequacy since "it is not in man that walketh to direct his steps" (Jer. 10:23). It is divine love as it seeks to bind man's heart to God with chords of truth. It is the wondrous love of God as it implores man to "abstain from fleshly lusts which war against the soul" (1 Pet. 2:11). It is gentle, caring love from on High, beseeching man to "walk in truth" (3 John 4) and allowing him to enjoy "all spiritual blessings" emanating from the death, burial, and resurrection of Christ. Is this not good news?

What is Romans through Jude? It is a work of grace. It is the marvelous grace of God tugging at man's heart with words, rules, and laws of love from God's heart. It is God's matchless grace pleading with man to array himself in the "beauty of holiness" (Ps. 29:2) by submitting to divine truths that promote holiness. It is grace divine imploring man to behold the "wondrous things" to be found in the "law" of God (Ps. 119:18). It is grace beseeching man to store in the heart the truths contained therein as a preventive to sin (Ps. 119:11). It is the "teaching of grace" relative to refraining from "ungodliness and worldly lusts," and practicing "sober, righteous, and godly living in this present world" (Titus 2:11-12) in order to enjoy victory in Christ as promised in the closing book of God's revelation to man. Is this not good news?

Of what eternal profit is it in being the man of Matthew, Mark, Luke, and John who accepts the core truths of the gospel and the man of Acts who appropriates the benefits of those truths to his soul in gospel obedience and then neglects or ceases to be the man of Romans through Jude who "abides in Christ" (John 15:4-6) by faithful adherence to the will of Christ? The effort to make a distinction between *gospel* and *doctrine* is arbitrary, unscriptural, and damnable. Only something as imprudent as liberalism could ever have arrived at such an inane conclusion. The gospel of Christ and the doctrine or teachings of Christ are one and the same, and liberalism is its enemy.

11

Liberalism Is Progressive

"It's no big deal." One would be hard pressed to find a better summation of the spirit of liberalism than these three words. This is the very essence of the liberal spirit. It was this attitude toward the authority of the Word of God that drove a wedge in the church over a century ago. This spirit constituted the womb of the Christian Church. This spirit is the womb of every denominational church on earth. Replace this odious spirit with a trembling reverence toward the absolute authority of the Word of God, and denominationalism would perish in a heartbeat, leaving in a standing-alone posture the church that Jesus said, "I will build." This church is characterized by pristine beauty and a divinely ordained pattern of worship, plan of salvation, organization, and work.

This vile attitude toward the Word of God did not originate with the preacher who expressed this sentiment, nor with the thousands of others in the church today who are marching to the tune of this song. This very attitude accompanied Satan in his entrance into the Garden of Eden. Inherent in Satan's approach to Eve was the "no big deal" spirit of liberalism toward what God had said. If Eve had remained convinced that what God had said was the truth, constituting a *very* big deal, she would never have succumbed to Satan's temptation. Tragically, Eve's adoption of the spirit of liberalism destroyed her innocence and postured the world on the road to ruin (Gen. 3:1-6).

God gave Cain and Abel a pattern for worship. Abel took God at His word and did what He said. That is what faith does. Faith obeys God. Faith submits to God. Faith does not insist on its own way. Faith trembles. "By faith Abel offered unto God a more excellent sacrifice than Cain, by which he obtained witness that he was righteous, God testifying of his gifts, and by it, he being dead yet speaketh" (Heb. 11:4). Conversely, Cain's liberal "no big deal" attitude toward God's divinely ordained means of entering into His presence nullified Cain's worship and opened the door to Abel's murder (Gen. 4:1-8).

The extreme wickedness of the world as described in Genesis 6:5 was the inevitable result of the continual and consistent application of the "no big deal" philosophy relative to the will of God. Obviously, not everyone reaches the state of depravity that characterized the world of Noah's day. There are degrees of apostasy. However, inherent in every degree is the "no big deal" spirit toward God's will for man. This attitude will not allow man to stand in one place. The spirit of liberalism is progressive. Like a physical disease that grows progressively worse, every man compelled by this disposition is on a constant downward course.

Some in the church today have applied the spirit of liberalism to praise teams, solos, choirs, and clapping. The gradual accruement of this spirit commences by allowing these unauthorized acts to lie gently on the heart. The elders who sat before Ezekiel had "idols in their hearts" (Ezek. 14:3). However, Ezekiel could not have known this had not God informed him. Even so, the idols of self-will can be in the heart of a man to the awareness of no one but himself and God. Others have progressed with the spirit of liberalism to the point of transferring these unauthorized acts from the heart to the overt act.

Some have appropriated this spirit of laxness toward biblical authority to children's church, family life centers, dedicating babies, and the observance of religious holidays, hence creating a zone of comfort for these unauthorized actions in the heart. Others have moved on to make these feelings of the heart apparent in life. Some have embraced the spirit of liberalism to the degree of allowing the mechanical instrument in the heart. Others have advanced in the spirit of leniency to the actual act. There are some in the church who have encompassed the Lord's supper in their flaccid spirit of looseness toward the authority of the Bible, having discarded the exclusive first day of the week for participation therein.

Traveling on the road of apostasy are some who view biblical teaching on God's role for women from a "no big deal" perspective. Acting upon this attitude, they presumptuously allow for women the very thing God forbids (1 Tim. 2:12). There are others who have attacked the most basic unit of society—marriage, the home—with the abhorrent spirit of casualness toward divine authority, leaving open the door to multiple acts of adultery (Matt. 5:32; 19:9). Some have deviated to the point of attaching this abominable principle to the oneness of the church and God's plan to redeem man from sin. The detestable spirit of liberalism will not allow man to maintain a stationary posture. It will not be satisfied until it has removed every vestige of truth from the mind of man.

Billy Graham is one of the most notorious false teachers the world has ever known. Multiplied millions have been posited on the road to perdition as a result of his fallacious teaching. For the whole of his preaching life, he has arrayed himself in opposition to some of the most basic tenets of biblical truth. Jesus said, "1 will build my church" (Matt. 16:18). That church burst upon the scene of time with the proclamation of the gospel of Christ and man's compliance with the conditions thereof (Acts 2).

The one gospel of Christ produced the one church of Christ. The gospel of Christ can no more beget the chaos of denominationalism than can the principles of capitalism give girth to communism. That church is the "one body" of Ephesians 4:4. It is the only sphere of reconciliation to God (Eph. 2:16). It is the only church to which the saved are added (Acts 2:47). It is the only church of which Jesus is the Savior (Eph. 5:23).

It was purchased by the precious blood of God's own Son (Acts 20:28). It is the only church that shall be delivered up to the Father to walk those streets of gold when time comes to its inevitable end (1 Cor. 15:24).

However, Billy Graham does not believe a word of this simple, yet vital truth of God. For sixty years he has fought the oneness of the church while avidly promoting the divisions of denominationalism, one of the most monumental evils known to man. It is human in origin and divisive in nature. It is one of the most potent weapons in Satan's arsenal of barriers to truth. For fifteen centuries, denominationalism has been blinding men to the singularity, beauty, and simplicity of the church of the Bible. This cyclopean adversary of truth has never enjoyed a more ardent advocate than Billy Graham.

God's plan to redeem man by grace through blood involves baptism. Jesus said, "He that believeth and is baptized shall be saved" (Mark 16:16). Believers were commanded to "repent and be baptized for the remission of sins" (Acts 2:38). A penitent believer was instructed to "arise and be baptized and wash away thy sins" (Acts 22:16). Baptism is faith's responding to grace while appealing to the blood of Christ for forgiveness. Baptism is faith's reaching for the cross. Baptism is the culminating act of gospel obedience that enables man to appropriate to his sin-stained soul the rich provisions of grace in Calvary. Baptism is man's acknowledgement of the sovereignty and transcendence of God.

Baptism is an expression of man's acceptance of the supreme authority of God and His Word over his life. Baptism is trembling reverence for God's commandment. Baptism is man void of pride. Baptism is a demonstration of man's refusal to bow in homage at the shrine of human reasoning. Baptism is man in full agreement with God as He affirmed, "For my thoughts are not your thoughts, neither are your ways my ways, saith the Lord" (Isa. 55:8). Baptism is a manifestation of man's utter loathing for sin. Baptism is man's embracement of the cross as his only hope. Baptism is man's crying for grace. Baptism is love for God—obeying God (John 14:15).

For over six decades, Billy Graham has defied this commandment from the mouth of God. By such egregious action, he has dethroned God and enthroned himself. He has usurped the legislative prerogative of God. He has perverted the gospel of Christ. He has nullified biblical faith. He has prevented his hearers from reaching the blood of Christ. He has erected a barrier to the provisions of grace in the cross. The harm that this proponent of error has done to the cause of Christ is inestimable. The souls that have embraced eternity without hope because of his influence are incalculable. In response to man's greatest question, "What must I do to be saved?" Billy Graham has quoted the words of Jesus in Mark 16:16 and purposefully omitted the word *baptized*. He has quoted the words of Peter in reply to that same question and has intentionally excluded the word *baptized*. What presumption! What contempt for the truth! What unmitigated effrontery!

John's baptism was temporary. It looked forward to an act yet to be accomplished, and it was not performed in the name of the resurrected Christ; yet, those who refused it "rejected the counsel of God against themselves" (Luke 7:30). The baptism of the great commission is permanent; it looks back to an accomplished act and it is performed in the name of the resurrected Christ. If those who spurned John's baptism were rejecting the counsel of God, how much more are the Billy Grahams of the world rejecting God's counsel by repudiating the baptism of Jesus Christ? Billy Graham has spent the whole of his life in rebellion to the counsel of God.

The summer of 2000 was a summer of infamy for the church eternally purposed by God, foretold by the prophets, prepared for by John, promised by Christ, and purchased by His blood. In at least three cities, elders, preachers, and churches of Christ played a leading role in helping to implement a Billy Graham crusade. In the name of sanity, how could this be? The answer is not hard to find. For years, these pseudo-leaders in the church have persistently and consistently applied the "no big deal" spirit of liberalism to the Word of God. This heinous attitude toward the Bible has led them to repudiate totally the exclusiveness of New Testament Christianity and draw to their bosoms one of the most fervid champions of error of our generation. Such is the progressive, erosive power of the spirit of liberalism.

Among the leaders in one of these crusades was Rubel Shelly and the Woodmont Hills Church of Christ in Nashville, Tennessee. Some three decades ago, brother Shelly wrote a powerful article for the *Spiritual Sword* (July, 1972, vol. 3, p. 30) entitled, "What about the Ecumenical Movement?" This cogent article now serves as his own personal rebuke along with his many colleagues in error who are determined to convert the one church of the New Testament into just another sect among sects. In view of his present tragic state, the following verbatim quotation is irony in its most extreme sense:

> The fact of the matter is that the Ecumenical Movement has been spawned by liberalism and is only one more weapon in its arsenal to destroy true Christianity. Ecumenism is seeking harmony and peace at the expense of revealed truth. It is an attempt to reconcile differences by means of a deliberate deviation from the will of God. It is condemned in scripture and must be resisted by the people of God!
>
> There are trends toward ecumenism among the churches of Christ which make the study of this movement especially crucial at this time. Some among us are contending that we have unduly restricted our fellowship. They are urging that we "recognize Christians of other denominations" as our fellow-laborers in the vineyard of the Lord.
>
> The suggestion of the Ecumenical Movement (which has been taken up by some brethren) that we should seek union by agreeing to disagree on the doctrinal content of Christianity is fundamentally erroneous! The spirit of ecumenism is an utter repudiation of scriptural authority. Whereas God would have men to be united in their mutual submission to His Word, liberalism's Ecumenical Movement offers union apart from a biblical norm or standard.

Brother Shelly correctly identified liberalism as the foundation upon which the Ecumenical Movement has been constructed. Tragically, he has now embraced the very spirit of liberalism he once so strongly condemned and has influenced thousands of others to join him to the ruin of their faith. Those in the church today who have espoused this infamous philosophy should be objects of pity and prayer, not praise and emulation.

Methodism is unknown to the Bible. Its origin is traced to the work of John and Charles Wesley early in the eighteenth century. It is steeped in Calvinism's total depravity and direct mystical work of the Holy Spirit. As is characteristic of almost all religions, Methodism can rightfully boast of people with high moral and ethical character. However, relative to its teaching, it is corrupt from its core outward. The Methodist Discipline avers, "Faith only is a most wholesome doctrine and very full of comfort." There is nothing wholesome and comforting about a doctrine so patently false and so injurious to the soul. Faith only is an insurmountable barrier to grace and an insuperable obstruction on the road to the cross. One cannot reach grace and the provisions thereof in the cross by faith alone. Faith only would have left Enoch on earth, Abraham in Ur, Moses in Pharaoh's court, Israel in Egypt, Rahab in Jericho, Ruth in Moab, Hannah childless, and Naaman a leper. Faith only leaves a man outside of Christ, isolated from His cleansing blood, imbued with sin, hopeless in death, and lost in eternity.

Methodism does not respect the Bible. Its very existence is proof of its total lack of esteem for God's revelation to man. If Methodism were to suddenly develop a deep, trembling reverence for the Word of God, it would cease to exist at that moment. In a recent conversation with a Methodist minister, he made this startling admission, "The Methodist church has weakened and socialized scripture." Every four years, Methodist leaders and representatives convene for the World Methodist Council. There is no practice in Methodism that more clearly demonstrates its disdain for God's will than the conduct of this Council. Any local Methodist church can submit a petition for the Council to vote on some aspect of biblical teaching. There is no biblical subject so sacred, fundamental, or vital to the life of Christianity as to be viewed off limits. As one Methodist minister said, "Everything is up for grabs." In the last twenty-four years, they have voted six times on the ordination of homosexuals. The number in favor of this action has grown with each vote. The spirit of liberalism in this Council breathes the air of Sodom and Gomorrah. For fallible, mortal men to sit in judgment on the Word of the Almighty God is inexpressible presumption. No man or religion that possesses even the slightest degree of reverence for the eternal truths of God would ever entertain such a notion.

On a world-wide television program, the pulpit preacher for the Frazer Memorial Methodist Church in Montgomery, Alabama, one of the largest Methodist churches in the nation, exhibited toward the Lord's supper the spirit of liberalism that permeates Methodism. In a casual, cursory fashion, he implored the television audience to join him in partaking of the Lord's supper with a piece of loaf bread and a cup of water or any other like items they could find in the house. He made an absolute mockery of the greatest memorial known to man. He utterly debased the only divinely ordained means of remembering in some special way what Jesus did for man on the brow of Golgotha. He disparaged the body and blood of Jesus Christ. His manner was crude. His deportment was indefensible. His conduct was devoid of any trace of reverence for this most sacred act of worship. Methodism does not respect the Bible.

In February, 2001, the Frazer Memorial Methodist Church sponsored a seminar on "Personal Holiness in Times of Temptation." Concern for holiness and moving ever closer to viewing homosexuality as an acceptable lifestyle are hardly consistent, but consistency is not something that one expects to find in error. The totality of God's revelation to man thunders forth with incessant warnings against joining ranks with any man, group, movement, or institution whose teaching and practice are rooted in error instead of truth. In years past, no congregation of the Lord would have dared transgress the express will of God relative to this matter.

Consequently, it may have come as a surprise to some to read in the *Montgomery Advertiser* a list of eight other denominational churches serving as co-sponsors of this event, culminating with the "Landmark Church of Christ." However, the surprise quickly dissipates upon the realization that the preacher for this church is the author of the "no big deal" statement regarding the use of the unauthorized mechanical instrument in worship. There are other churches of Christ with this same repugnant attitude toward biblical authority who have done likewise. Such is the progressive, erosive spirit of liberalism.

12

Liberalism and Preaching

The pulpit plays a major role in setting the spiritual tone of a congregation. There is no such thing as a strong church and a weak pulpit. God's view of congregational strength demands a pulpit that echoes with the sound of God's voice, not man's. The prophets were Bible-centered preachers. God told the prophet of tears, "Behold, I have put my words in thy mouth" (Jer. 1:9). Twenty-four times in thirty-eight verses, Haggai declared, "Thus saith the Lord." Twenty-five times in four brief chapters, Malachi pointed to God as the source of his message.

Peter's sermon on Pentecost was the first gospel sermon ever preached, as an accomplished fact, under the world-wide commission in the name of the resurrected Christ (Acts 2). It served to inaugurate New Testament Christianity in the world. Strikingly, half of the sermon was composed of direct quotations from the Old Testament. The success of the Restoration Movement was tied to Bible-centered preaching. Those grand restorers of the Jerusalem gospel knew, believed, and preached the book. Void of frills and fleshly trappings, they heralded the gospel with clarion simplicity. They were spokesmen for God, not Shakespeare, Plato, or Whitman.

Apostasy is rampant. The pulpit in many congregations is a spiritual disgrace. Jokes, personal experiences, political statements, and perpetual excursions in philosophy and human wisdom are empty substitutes for a "thus saith God." It is God's design that His Word be made known "through preaching" (Titus 1:3). Many preachers are nullifying God's will by their failure to preach the Book. They are robbing the pulpit of its power. The power is in the gospel, not the preacher. They are negating God's power to save, instruct, and edify by substituting the word of man for the Word of God. The pulpit is to function as a launching pad for the gospel, not a course in the humanities.

"To the law and to the testimony; if they speak not according to this word, it is because there is no light in them" (Isa. 8:20). "If any man speak, let him speak as the oracles of God" (1 Pet. 4:11). "Teach me, O Lord, the way of thy statutes" (Ps. 119:33). "Preach the word" (2 Tim. 4:2).

Bible-centered preaching is distinctive preaching. It sounds different because it is different. The preaching of Jesus rang with uniqueness because He "taught them as one having authority" (Matt. 7:29). Book, chapter, and verse preaching is authoritative. It is absolute, demanding, and binding. Some men speak and some men preach. There is a difference. Preachers "preach the word" (2 Tim. 4:2). A man may be a great orator and a poor preacher. Real preachers inform man as to what God has said. They are microphones through whom God speaks. They proclaim the Bible, not the various *ologies* of humanity. God told Ezekiel, "Thou shalt say unto them, thus saith the Lord God" (Ezek. 2:4).

There are preachers who have majored in Bultmann and Barth and minored in Peter and Paul. They can quote the theologians, but not the Bible. Preachers preach what they are full of. With the setting of Sunday's sun, the preacher does not have to inform the audience as to what he has been studying during the course of the week. The pulpit is secure in the hands of a man who has saturated his mind with what the Bible teaches on every subject.

A great pulpit is a Bible-based pulpit. A great preacher is a preacher that preaches the Word. A great sermon is a sermon that is permeated with what God says. Every preacher must study and prepare so as to enable God to say, "Behold, I have put my words in thy mouth" (Jer. 1:9). A biblically weak pulpit is a plague on the church. It stifles spirituality, suppresses commitment, nurtures apathy, and encourages sin. It blinds the church as to its purpose and mission. Such a preacher ought either to repent or resign.

Preachers of the past were Bible-quoting preachers. They knew what the Bible said and where it said it. Every point was verified with scripture. Their preaching was distinctive. It rang with authority. Under such preaching, the church grew and prospered. Conversions were more numerous and sin was less prevalent. Their preaching was powerful because it was biblical. People listened because there was something worth hearing. They were instructed in mind, cemented in conviction, stirred in emotion, and renewed in heart. Such preaching was a ceaseless reminder that it does make a difference what one believes and how one lives—that it's God's way or no way.

Some of our schools have made major contributions to the dying pulpit. Professors therein have obtained their degrees from denominational institutions. They have sat for years under the incessant sound of modernism. Many received their degrees with scarred convictions. Their students then graduate as parrots and mount our pulpits with dull swords. From their lofty, pedantic platforms of intellectualism, they view with disdain the "book, chapter, and verse" preacher while proclaiming spiritually insipid sermons that appease the flesh but numb the spirit.

Every sermon should begin, continue, and end with what God has said. The crux of the lesson is the verse that substantiates the point, not the point itself. Apart from the text, there is no point. Peter quoted more scripture in one sermon on Pentecost than many preachers quote in a month of preaching. Wearied by a lesson solely on the life of a secular historical figure, a brother on the mission field arose and said, "Enough of this foolishness; let us hear a word from God." Every pulpit needs a Micaiah who affirmed, "What the Lord saith unto me, that will I speak" (1 Kings 22:14).

Preaching is serious business. It is a life or death matter. It involves souls on the road to eternity. It must "reprove, rebuke, exhort with all longsuffering and doctrine" (2 Tim. 4:2). Nothing will avert the present apostasy like getting the "book, chapter, and verse" preacher back into the pulpit. There is no substitute for Bible-centered preaching.

With the exception of seven years during the transition between Saul and David, the nation of Israel was united for one hundred twenty years under three kings. When Solomon's son, Rehoboam, ascended to the throne, God divided the kingdom as an act of judgment due to idolatry on the part of Solomon and the nation (1 Kings 11). Two hundred fifty years later, having exhausted God's forbearance, the northern kingdom lost its national identity in Assyrian captivity (2 Kings 17). Over a century later, the southern kingdom was carried into Babylonian captivity for seventy years.

At the end thereof, Cyrus lifted the gates of captivity and some fifty thousand Jews returned to Jerusalem to rebuild the temple. Having laid the foundation, the Samaritans, a people of mixed race and religion, began to frustrate their efforts until finally they ceased building altogether. For sixteen years the work on the temple lay idle. By ceasing their work, they negated the very purpose of their return.

At that point in Israel's history, Haggai appeared on the scene. Four years later the text reads, "And the elders of the Jews builded, and they prospered through the prophesying of Haggai the prophet and Zechariah the son of Iddo. And they builded and finished it, according to the commandment of the God of Israel, and according to the commandment of Cyrus and Darius, and Artaxerxes, king of Persia" (Ezra 6:14). Haggai 1:14 affirms that God so stirred their spirits that all the people "came and did work in the house of the Lord of hosts."

Consequently, the people prospered under Haggai's preaching. Their hearts were "stirred up" by the power of Haggai's preaching. What kind of preaching did Haggai do to dissolve sixteen years of indifference toward the temple of God and skewed priorities? It was preaching based foursquare on the Word of God. It was an incessant emphasis on what God said. In repetitious form Haggai thundered, "Thus saith God." This is the basis of all successful preaching.

God does not want scholarly expositions of philosophical ideas. There is no power in human wisdom to create faith, incite penitence, and compel a man toward God. Funny stories and personal experiences will not motivate a man to ask, "What must I do to be saved?" Human interest stories are powerless to provoke sober reflection on one's condition before God. A pulpit occupied by an intellectual exhibitionist will not encourage spiritual growth or stir man's heart in concern for the lost. All of the devices of man combined cannot resurrect man from the ashes of apathy and foster spiritual action.

What difference does it make what man thinks, likes, or wants? Naaman almost allowed what he thought to prevent him from reaching the water of Jordan and the cleansing power of God (2 Kings 5:11). Balaam pursued his wants instead of God's will and died on the field of battle in rebellion to God (Num. 31:8). Preaching that conforms to human desire instead of need will never extract man from the world or erase the Laodicean spirit from the church.

Every preacher should be able to say, "But as we were allowed of God to be put in trust with the gospel, even so we speak; not as pleasing men, but God, which trieth our hearts" (1 Thess. 2:4). From the sermon's introduction to its conclusion, every pulpit ought to resound with what God says. Strong pulpits and strong churches are inseparable companions. The preaching that prospers is preaching that is based on a "thus saith God." There is no substitute for Bible-centered preaching.

Liberalism knows that it has no adversary with more potential for nullifying its desired end than a Bible-centered pulpit. A pulpit that proclaims "all the counsel of God" (Acts 20:27) is an anathema to the spirit of liberalism. Therefore, liberalism has assailed the pulpit. Tragically, its efforts have been far from vain. The pulpits in many congregations have been vanquished by its pernicious spirit.

A pulpit that has been converted from a Bible-centered pulpit to a liberal pulpit must begin anew its efforts in sermon preparation. Sermons heralded from its premises in times past must be discarded. The distinctive tone is gone. The new sound would be welcomed in any denominational church in town. Under the sound of its voice, Christmas and Easter programs appear. Open fellowship with churches alien to the Bible is encouraged. The outward look is replaced by the inward look. Some of the old faces are supplanted by new faces, and the new countenances are often more youthful in appearance. Elaborate recreational centers with an abundance of toys are constructed to pacify the new crowd. Youth ministers with degrees in fun and frolic are hired to entertain young people whose parents have vacated their parental responsibilities and whose homes no longer function as family life centers. Classes once devoted to Bible study now focus on "crisis management, financial planning, self-esteem, sharing sessions, testimonials, and Andy Griffith shows." Women's roles change. Worship practices change. Activities change. Everything changes.

A congregation in a southern city enjoyed a well-deserved reputation for steadfastness in the faith, contending earnestly for the faith, and abiding in the doctrine of Christ. The pulpit was occupied by a man whose knowledge of the Bible and ability to proclaim it is unique among men. Moreover, his sermons were saturated with biblical quotations. Almost every statement was reinforced with a "thus saith God." Unfortunately, a change was made and three preachers and several new elders later, the difference in "what was" and "what is" defies adequate depiction. The difference was summed up by a member whose brother is a Baptist preacher. He expressed concern for her spiritual welfare, fearing that she had joined a cult. She attempted to allay his fears. He asked her to provide him with some tapes of the preacher's sermons. Having listened to them, he said, "It's all right; he's one of us."

A liberal pulpit will never take its text from Genesis 4:1-7 and warn of worship practices adverse to God's pattern. An assembly in the presence of a pulpit with a penchant for liberalism will never hear the names Nadab and Abihu. A pulpit partial to liberal thinking will never take its text from Exodus 25-40 and press the need of following even the most minute aspects of God's will. A liberal pulpit will never cite 2 Samuel 7:7 and Hebrews 7:14 and urge respect for divine silence. A pulpit with a proclivity for liberalism would never consider preaching a sermon on Jereboam's grievous sin in 1 Kings 12 in an effort to show the disastrous results from human's tampering with God's arrangement for worship. Pulpits with an affinity for liberalism will not quote David's, "we sought him not after the due order" (1 Chron. 15:13), as a rebuke for unauthorized actions.

Liberal pulpits love to talk about Jesus, but only on a very selective basis. A pulpit with a preference for liberalism will never sermonize on Matthew 15:7-9 and alert the hearers regarding the unauthorized nature of mechanical instruments, praise teams, solos, clapping, and women in leadership roles invalidating the divine acceptability of worship. A pulpit with a liberal bias will shun the truth from Jesus in Matthew 15:13-14 concerning the inevitable destruction of false religions like denominationalism that have not been planted by God. A pulpit inclined toward liberalism has no use for the words from Jesus, pointing to the exclusive church of Christ (Matt. 16:13-19).

Pulpits with a liberal disposition do not believe the "whosoever" and "except" of Matthew 5:32 and 19:9. Therefore, such pulpits will not preach these marriage-preserving truths. If liberal pulpits were honest, they would acknowledge, "That is what Jesus said, but we do not believe it, and we are not going to preach it." Pulpits sympathetic to liberalism detest the stern, candid language of Jesus in Matthew 23. Even as prejudiced Jews from Judea would detour around Samaria to reach Galilee, so the liberal pulpit will circumvent

Matthew 23 unless it has the conservative mind as its target. A pulpit attracted to liberalism will not press for the "from heaven, or of men" (Matt. 21:25) principle to be applied to its teaching and practice.

The world is permeated with chaos and confusion. Sin is brazenly paraded on placards on public streets. The blood of innocent babies runs ankle deep as depraved physicians' hands convert the mother's womb into a war zone. The heart of man is filled with apathy toward truth and contempt for divine restraints while laced with warm affection for sensual pleasure. Homosexuality, fornication, drunkenness, pornography, lying, stealing, profanity, child abuse, divorce, and drug addiction are as common as the cold. The world is drunk on sin. The world has invaded the church, and some even in the leadership roles have serious sin problems that do not fall in the category of momentary acts of fleshly weakness immediately confronted with a broken and contrite heart. Numerous others are afflicted with biblical illiteracy, misplaced priorities, materialism, and the Laodicean spirit.

Preachers driven by the "no big deal" spirit of liberalism toward the Word of God are much to blame for the spiritually odious state of society and the tragic state of many in the church. Should one consider this to be an unfair assessment, just consider the Old Testament world and see if this is not the exact spot upon which the hammer of divine judgment often fell. Of Judah, God said, "Hear the word of the Lord ye rulers of Sodom; give ear unto the law of our God, ye people of Gomorrah" (Isa. 1:10). This one statement is more than a sufficient description of Judah's spiritual state. Jeremiah 23 and Ezekiel 13 are two entire chapters devoted to the corrupting influence of preachers whose preaching was based on contrivances of "their own heart, and not out of the mouth of the Lord" (Jer. 23:16), thus causing Judah to "err by their lies" (Jer. 23:32).

The dark clouds of divine judgment were hovering over the nation. Judah needed to hear sermons on the holiness of God, the ugliness of sin, and the need for penitence. They needed to see the door of grace closing and God mounting His chariot with an unsheathed sword in His hand. They needed to see the walls of Jerusalem in rubble, smell the smoldering ashes of the temple, and hear the clanging chains of captivity.

Instead, they were deceived by prophetic lies of peace and prosperity, the impregnability of Jerusalem, the perpetuity of the temple, and the impotence of the enemy's sword. Such preaching blinded the eyes of the nation to the character of God, the nature of sin, the necessity of judgment, and consequently, "strengthened the hands of the wicked" (Ezek. 13:22). When the heel of Babylon descended upon the neck of Judah, the blood of the nation was beheld dripping from the fingers of such prophets.

The masses of people in the world today do not love the truth. If they did, Matthew 7:13-14 would have been penned in reverse form. Men will perish "because they receive not the love of the truth, that they might be saved" (2 Thess. 2:10). Paul prophesied of a day when men would turn a deaf ear to the word of God and demand preachers who would tickle the ears with soft, unoffensive preaching (2 Tim. 4:3-4). Truly, that day has come, and such preachers are in plentiful supply.

The nation of Israel during Micah's day was saturated with sin. They were "incurable" (Micah 1:9). They lay upon their beds at night mapping out their evil schemes, eagerly desiring the first ray of morning light that they might convert their plans into realities (Micah 2:1). They hated good and loved evil (Micah 3:2). Conditions were so bad that Micah pictured the righteous as having "perished out of the earth" (Micah 7:2).

What kind of preachers did they want? "If a man walking in the spirit and falsehood do lie saying, I will prophesy unto thee of wine and of strong drink, he shall even be the prophet of this people" (Micah 2:11). They wanted positive messages assuring the nation of the presence of serenity and affluence. They wanted to be soothed, petted, and appeased. They had no trouble finding preachers to fill their pulpits.

Many modern preachers are like the beggar's monkey that dances to the tune of the one who holds the purse. Like those of Micah's day, they "divine for money" (Micah 3:11). They preach to please and not to convict. They have no desire to rock the boat or disturb the status quo. They are particularly careful not to offend those of wealth and social prominence. What the pew demands, the pulpit supplies. The dirt in the pew cannot be erased with soft soap in the pulpit. One does not become a spiritual giant on a diet of baby food. The desire to make a name for oneself, satisfy an ego, build and maintain a following, develop a clerical entourage, be the subject of praise and plaudits, and preach for the largest church in town demands a pulpit devoted to liberalism that blends in with the "we want to be like the churches around us" philosophy. People generally get what they want, but that seldom is what they need. Many pulpits are for sale if the price is right.

The world today is a replica of ancient Judah and Israel. Even many who claim to be religious have such a loose lifestyle as to make it difficult to discern any basic difference between them and those who claim no religion. Their religion is pomp and ritual with no genuine conviction and substance. Jesus said the lukewarm state of the Laodiceans made Him sick (Rev. 3:14-17). Surely, the liberal, divided, materialistic state of religion today is a stench in the nostrils of God.

To a great degree, present conditions in the world, the religious community, and the church have been created by preachers whose minds have been deceived, darkened, and dominated by the malignant spirit of liberalism. Many preachers have proclaimed such a watered-down version of the gospel as to give people little or no incentive to climb to higher ground. Such doctrines as "all grace and no law," "unity in diversity," "salvation by faith alone," "the impossibility of apostasy," and the "believe, teach, and do as you please" philosophy have shot holes in man's desire to study, know, grow, fight for the right, and contend for the faith. They have caused people to "trust in a lie" (Jer. 28:15). At the judgment bar of

God, the hands of such preachers will be stained red with the blood of their fellow man.

Strong faith, rock-solid convictions, unyielding courage, and true spirituality are not the fruits of a pulpit that undermines reverence and erodes respect for biblical authority with a "so what" attitude toward unauthorized activities and acts of worship. The lethal power of liberalism nullifies the divine nature and purpose of Bible-centered preaching.

13

Liberalism and Missionaries

He that goeth forth and weepeth, bearing precious seed, shall doubtless come again with rejoicing, bringing his sheaves with him (Ps. 126:6).

The fruit of the righteous is a tree of life; and he that winneth souls is wise (Prov. 11:30).

And he said unto them, Go ye into all the world, and preach the gospel to every creature (Mark 16:15).

Therefore they that were scattered abroad went everywhere preaching the word (Acts 8:4).

These verses set forth the mission of the church of Jesus Christ on earth. What is the mission of the church? Viewed negatively, the mission of the church is not to preach a social gospel. A social gospel may tickle the ear, but it will not save the world. A social gospel may appeal to man's pride, but it will not redeem his soul. A social gospel may soothe the conscience, but it cannot conquer sin.

The mission of the church is not to so plan its work as to enhance its image in the community. It is true, if the church does its work well, it will have a good image in the community among those who are spiritually discerning. However, the concern of the church must not be the formulation of a plan that will elicit nods of approval from the community.

The mission of the church is not to entertain. Let those seeking entertainment go to an amusement park, a ball game, or a zoo. For those craving some cheap, superficial thrill, let them ride a roller-coaster. Aspirants of laughter can hire a comedian. The church, as designed by God, is not an entertainment medium.

Moreover, the church is not a bank. Some congregations have multiplied thousands of dollars tied up in savings accounts or CDs with no planned objective for its use. These funds have not been laid aside for the purpose of constructing a facility that would aid in some spiritual work of the church. Such funds have not been garnered with the aim of supporting some mission work. Overseeing these funds are elders who are often more concerned with the interest rate than the salvation of men lost in sin.

Neither is the church a school. Let the church support the teaching of the truth in any institution on earth. It would be a marvelous thing if the church could finance the proclamation of God's truth in all the Harvards, Yales, and UCLAs of the world. However, when it comes to reading, writing, arithmetic, football, baseball, and basketball, the church is not in the school business.

The mission of the church is to confront every accountable soul with the gospel of Jesus Christ. Man's problem is sin. "For there is not a just man upon earth, that doeth good, and sinneth not" (Eccles. 7:20). "For all have sinned, and come short of the glory of God" (Rom. 3:23). God's remedy for sin is the blood of His Son. Jesus affirmed, "For this is my blood of the new testament which is shed for many for the remission of sins" (Matt. 26:28). Peter negated the ability of silver and gold to procure redemption from sin and then announced that the exclusive power to thus obtain was in the "precious blood of Christ" (1 Pet. 1:18-19).

The only way to contact the blood of Christ is to obey the gospel of Christ. God's power to save resides in the gospel (Rom. 1:16). Paul pointed to the gospel he preached and affirmed, "By which also ye are saved" (1 Cor. 15:2). The gospel is the good news of God's provisions of grace at Calvary. Those who embrace death, having never obeyed the gospel, enter eternity void of hope (2 Thess. 1:7-9). As Aaron "stood between the dead and the living" (Num. 16:48) with the token of atonement, it is the mission of the church to stand between every accountable soul and death with the saving message of the gospel of Christ.

Jesus Christ entered the world to "seek and to save that which was lost" (Luke 19:10). The work of the early church was an extension of the work of Christ in the world. Publicly and privately, "they ceased not to teach and preach Jesus Christ" (Acts 5:42). When the church at Jerusalem was scattered by persecution, they "went everywhere preaching the word" (Acts 8:4).

One of the greatest needs in the church today is to recapture the zealous spirit that characterized those early Christians. Righteous zeal is one of the most powerful forces in the world. It was righteous zeal that motivated Noah to preach to the sin-bound people of his day for a hundred and twenty years. It was righteous zeal that drove Israel against the giants of Canaan. It was righteous zeal that compelled a simple shepherd boy to confront a giant man of war with a sling and five stones. It was righteous zeal that provoked Phinehas to enter the tent of Zimri with the javelin of death. With that same righteous zeal, the church of today could cover the earth with the saving message of the gospel of Christ.

The gospel must be preached to every accountable soul because God has thus commanded: "Go into all the world and preach the gospel to every creature" (Mark 16:15). That is sufficient for those who love God. "If ye love me, keep my commandments" (John 14:15).

The lost must hear the gospel because Christ is the only Savior men have. Jesus said, "I am the way, the truth, and the life; no man cometh unto the Father, but by me" (John 14:6). John Newton once said, "I am an old man and I don't remember many things. However, I do remember two things: I am a great sinner. Jesus Christ is a great Savior." One of the reasons many have never been zealous with the gospel is because they have never really been convinced that men are lost and hopeless apart from Jesus Christ.

The value of the soul demands that the gospel be heralded to the whole world. If a man could exchange his soul for all the wealth of the earth, he would have lost the only thing of any eternal value. "For what is a man profited, if he shall gain the whole world and lose his own soul? Or what shall a man give in exchange for his soul?" (Matt. 16:26). Every soul needs to hear the gospel because of the horrors of hell. Jesus Christ is the very personification of love; yet, he said more about hell than any other spokesman in the New Testament. "And fear not them which kill the body, but are not able to kill the soul; but rather fear him which is able to destroy both soul and body in hell" (Matt. 10:28). "Ye serpents, ye generation of vipers, how can ye escape the damnation of hell?" (Matt. 23:33). "And cast ye the unprofitable servant into outer darkness; there shall be weeping and gnashing of teeth" (Matt. 25:30). The gospel of Christ which contains the blood of Christ is man's only hope of escaping an otherwise certain descent into the eternal suffering of hell.

The gospel of Christ needs to be urged upon the world because of the glories of Heaven. There are mansions in that heavenly abode, prepared by Jesus Himself, awaiting the faithful (John 14:1-3). Jesus is the door through which man must enter in order to enjoy the blessings of that eternal home (John 10:9). Obedience to the gospel allows grace to open the door and grant possession of "an inheritance incorruptible, and undefiled, and that fadeth not away" (1 Pet. 1:4).

In Philippians 2:16 Paul affirmed, "Holding forth the word of life, that I may rejoice in the day of Christ, that I have not run in vain, neither labored in vain." The word of life is synonymous with the gospel. It is the word of life, the source of life, that which produces life. Jesus said, "It is the spirit that quickeneth; the flesh profiteth nothing; the words that I speak unto you, they are spirit, and they are life" (John 6:63). Peter averred, the word of life "liveth and abideth forever" (1 Pet.

1:23). Real living is wholly dependent upon the word of life being taught and received.

What is to be done with it? It is to be "held forth" to the world. It is to be proclaimed to every creature under heaven. It is to be taught privately and heralded publicly. It is to be shared on a street corner and shouted from the rooftop. God forbid that we should ever view the truth as our own private possession, convert the church into a monastery, and silence the sound of the blessed gospel of Christ among men.

The church is the "pillar and ground of the truth" (1 Tim. 3:15). Inherent in the term *pillar* is the idea of support. As a column serves to buttress a building, even so the church is to sustain the truth. The church is the support of the truth relative to its proclamation and its defense, for should the church neglect to "hold forth the word of life," there is no one left to do it.

Catholicism cannot preach the truth. This fraudulent religion worships the pope and spews forth an endless stream of error that has corrupted the minds of incalculable millions for fifteen centuries. Denominationalism cannot proclaim the pure gospel of Christ. This spurious religion is itself the product of a perverted gospel. Islam cannot herald the truth of God. This bloodletting religion is blanketing the world with its Christless message void of hope. Oriental mysticism cannot declare the message of redemption. These humanly devised religions wander aimlessly in the murky realm of feral imagination.

As the fable goes, when Jesus returned to Heaven, He was asked what arrangements He had made for the ongoing of His work on earth. He replied, "I left it in the hands of my followers." Inquiry was then made concerning additional plans should His followers fail to carry on with His work. Jesus replied, "I have no other plan."

There will be neither angelic intervention nor direct operation of the Holy Spirit in making known the truth. The word *go* needs to be put back into the word *gospel*. It is still "go or woe." Paul affirmed, "For though I preach the gospel, I have nothing to glory of, for necessity is laid upon me; yea, woe is unto me, if I preach not the gospel" (1 Cor. 9:16). The church must reach out or it will fade out. Every congregation is either a mission church or a mission field.

The early church took earnest heed to its mission. Jesus said, "Go ye into all the world and preach the gospel to every creature" (Mark 16:15). Some three decades later, the apostle Paul was able to affirm,

> If ye continue in the faith grounded and settled, and be not moved away from the hope of the gospel, which ye have heard, and which was preached to every creature which is under heaven; whereof I Paul am made a minister (Col. 1:23).

Without modern means of travel and communication, how were they able to accomplish what has not been duplicated to this very hour? The answer is in Acts 8:4: "Therefore they that were scattered abroad, went everywhere preaching the word."

We go! We are a people on the go. We go everywhere. We go to ballgames. We go on vacations. We go hunting, fishing, and shopping. We go everywhere "preaching." We can preach with the best. We preach sports, politics, world affairs, and the state of the economy. We can buttress every argument with facts and statistics. The early church went everywhere preaching the Word, and therein lies the difference.

Every Christian should be a missionary. There is something that every member of the church can do in seeking and saving the lost. Who cannot pray for the perishing of the world? Who cannot issue an invitation to the assembly of the saints for worship? Who cannot invite a neighbor to a gospel meeting? Who cannot offer some lost soul a Bible tract or correspondence course? Who cannot encourage some friend to listen to a gospel program on television or radio? It will take eternity to reveal the souls saved by these simple acts of concern.

Compelled by righteous zeal, some go to areas of this country that have never heard the pure gospel of Christ and where living conditions are often harsh and demanding. Still others leave their country, family, and friends and go into foreign lands where a strange language, people, and culture prevail. These missionary families are special people. They possess a love for God, reverence for truth, and concern for the lost that is unexcelled among men. As a result of their labors, faithful churches of Christ, products of the gospel of Christ, have been established all over the world.

Tragically, as Saul "made havoc of the church" (Acts 8:3), even so liberalism is having a calamitous influence on the church in mission areas all over the world. Liberalism is lazy. It seldom commences its own work. Liberalism is insidious. It had rather "creep" (Jude 4) in and steal a work established by the sacrifice and labor of faithful brethren or peel off sufficient numbers to begin with a good nucleus of their own.

Several years ago, an expression of grave concern regarding this matter was made to one of the most highly respected men in the church today. His response was frightening. He predicted, "In ten years, there will be congregations of the Christian church all over the mission field established by brethren of liberal thinking who were supported by sound, unsuspecting congregations of the church." Indeed, there are men laboring on mission fields whose doctrinal views are not consistent with the doctrinal soundness of the elders and congregations who support them. They possess the "no big deal" spirit of liberalism relative to the use of the mechanical instrument in worship. They do not believe in the verbal inspiration of Scripture. They do not accept the exclusiveness of the church of the New Testament. They would have no hesitancy extending fellowship to denominational churches. They believe the Holy Spirit exerts an influence on men separate and apart from the Word of God. They would experience no disturbance of conscience with women's leading prayer or serving communion in the assembly, or teaching a class in the presence of men. They would argue in favor of theistic evolution. They do not believe what Jesus taught on marriage, divorce, and remarriage.

Some of these brethren are permanent fixtures on the mission field. Others rotate back and forth, often carrying groups of people with them from one mission point to another. Frequently, their financial support comes from multiple congregations and/or individuals. These brethren know that their convictions are not compatible with those from whom they receive their support. They also know that if their convictions became known, their financial base would vanish. Is it honest for such a man to take money from faithful brethren, whose willingness to support him is based on their belief that they are "perfectly joined together in the same mind and in the same judgment"? (1 Cor. 1:10.) Is such conduct ethical, virtuous, and blameless, or deceitful and fraudulent? Suppose his convictions have changed since the initial agreement was made regarding his support. Does not honesty demand that he inform his supporters of his present doctrinal posture, hence allowing them the right to decide whether or not to continue his support? "Thou therefore which teachest another, teachest thou not thyself?" (Rom. 2:21).

Are elders not stewards of the finances given to God by members of the church who love the truth and who in good faith assume that they will properly dispense the funds in harmony with the will of God? Is it not the case that elders shall account to God for their responsibilities as stewards? Is it "required in stewards that a man be found faithful"? (1 Cor. 4:2.) Are elders faithful when they distribute God's money without inquiring of the recipients as to their convictions on fundamental matters of biblical teaching? Are elders accountable to God for error planted in the minds of men by missionaries whom they support?

Men who have surrendered to the spirit of liberalism are as sly as a fox. In answer to a question, they can so clothe a response as to make it appear candid and straightforward, but in reality it is as crooked as the slither of a serpent. They are verbal magicians. They can answer a question in more ways than it can be asked. They are masters at clothing their answers in terms that sound true to the Word. They have become proficient in what the political world identifies as spin. For example, in response to a question on divorce and remarriage, a person encased in the spirit of liberalism may say, "I believe Matthew 19:9." That would be equivalent to a Baptist preacher affirming, "I believe Mark 16:16." However, what they believe about these texts is not based on the actual truth's being taught, but only their perspective of it. Ascertaining liberalism's convictions on any Bible subject demands very specific questions that leave no room for equivocation.

A man reveals much about himself in the manner in which he deals with questions. For many years, a congregation had been faithfully supporting a missionary who made frequent trips to various foreign mission points. Having received word that his convictions on a vital matter of biblical teaching were not in accord with truth, they sent a questionnaire in hopes of determining exactly what he believed. Instead of respectfully answering the questions in compliance with divine imperative (1 Pet. 3:15), and as an expression of appreciation for many years of faithful "fellowship in the gospel" (Phil. 1:5), he branded the questions as an "insult to his integrity." He declared, "No preacher, elder, or any person will force me to answer such a questionnaire." It is incomprehensible that any Christian would refuse to give what he believes to be God's answer to any Bible question. Such a man is not worthy of support from the people of God.

There are various reasons for elders' refusing or neglecting to make inquiry as to the doctrinal positions of those they support or of those requesting support in order to assure proper use of funds under their stewardship. Though difficult to conceive, there are elderships who are yet unaware of the global flood of apostasy sweeping over the church. Some are willfully blind and resent any efforts tended to enlighten. There are some who lack motivation to thus act due to an absence of reflection upon the matter. There are others whose reticence is based on timidity. Moreover, it is sad but true that some elders are so deficient in Bible knowledge and un-informed regarding the doctrinal problems plaguing the church as to render them incapable of coping with such situations. A few well-chosen, well-worded, and persistent questions on vital matters of truth, enabling elders to discern the pretense in the minds of some of their missionaries, followed by a cessation of support would bring a swift end to much of the liberalism presently flourishing on the mission fields of the world.

14

Liberalism and
Youth Ministers

The son of promise, he was but a youth when his father
informed him of a trip to a distant mountain. In the early
dawn, Abraham commenced what surely must have been
three of the longest days of his life. Accompanied by two young
servants, he and Isaac departed for the land of Moriah and
an appointment with God on a mountain of His choosing.
Every step was akin to walking on hot coals. If a thousand
questions consumed his mental activity, not one saw the verbal light of day. Every question would have to return to one
inescapable conviction, God will "raise him up, even from the
dead" (Heb. 11:19).

On the third day, the most horrific scene of his life burst
upon Abraham's sight. He "lifted up his eyes and saw the
place afar off" (Gen. 22:4). Abraham had climbed many mountains in the course of his life, but never a mountain like the
one in Moriah. Instructing the two young men to proceed no
further, Abraham affirmed, "I and the lad will go yonder and
worship, and come again to you" (Gen. 22:5). What faith! Just
as surely as they both ascended the mountain, Abraham
believed they would descend the mountain.

Wood, fire, and a knife—Isaac knew that something was
missing. "Where is the lamb for a burnt offering?" he asked
(Gen. 22:7). Isaac had felt the assuring sound of his father's
voice many times before, and this time was no different as he
heard him say, "My son, God will provide himself a lamb for a

burnt offering" (Gen. 22:8). Having reached the designated place, Abraham constructed the altar and carefully laid the wood thereon. What did Abraham say before he bound his son, the only son of his beloved Sarah, the son of promise? Can there be any doubt but that he expended no little effort in trying to help Isaac grapple, even as he was, with the most phenomenal circumstance in the history of human experience involving a father and his son? Surely, this must have been the case.

Perhaps he took Isaac's mind back to the days of his own youth, the idolatrous environment into which he was born and reared (cf. Josh. 24:2) and his journey of faith to the one true God. Conceivably, he informed his son of God's call to Canaan, his promise of seed, a nation, and blessings to all the families of the earth (Gen. 12:1-3). Possibly, he spoke of his failure of faith, hence the birth of Ishmael. Undoubtedly, he endeavored to calm Isaac's fears and his own with the unwavering promise of God,

> Sarah, thy wife shall bear thee a son indeed, and thou shalt call his name Isaac; and I will establish my covenant with him for an everlasting covenant, and with his seed after him (Gen. 17:19).

Among Abraham's final words must have been, from his perspective, the only answer to this dilemma: "God will raise you from the dead." As far as the record is concerned, Isaac never raised a finger or word of resistance to his father. What faith! Abraham was willing to offer his son as a sacrifice. Isaac was willing to be that sacrifice.

He was only seventeen years old. A multicolored coat draped his shoulders, a sign of his father's favoritism. "And when his brethren saw that their father loved him more than all his brethren, they hated him and could not speak peaceably unto him" (Gen. 37:4). The twin sins of hatred and envy were fueled by Joseph's dreams. While tending their flocks, Jacob sent Joseph to inquire of his brothers' welfare. Observing his approach from a distance, they plotted to kill him, but Reuben's intervention saved his life. Stripped of his coat, he was placed in a pit and, in Reuben's absence, sold to a band of Ishmaelites for twenty pieces of silver. Upon reaching Egypt, Joseph was sold a second time to Potiphar, captain of Pharaoh's guard.

As Joseph conducted business in Potiphar's house, he began to experience seductive overtures from Potiphar's wife. Resisting her relentless efforts, she finally "caught him by his garment, saying 'Lie with me'; and he left his garment in her hand and fled" (Gen. 39:12). An accusation of attempted rape resulted in Joseph's imprisonment. Having interpreted the dreams of Pharaoh's butler and baker, Joseph implored the butler to remember him before Pharaoh when he was restored to his former position. "Yet did not the chief butler remember Joseph, but forgot him" (Gen. 40:23). The butler's ingratitude cost Joseph two more years in prison. Pharaoh's two successive dreams and the inability of the wise men of Egypt to reveal their meaning led the butler to exclaim, "I do remember my fault this day" (Gen. 41:9). Joseph's appearance before Pharaoh and the interpretation of his dreams by the power of God, induced Pharaoh to place Joseph in a position of authority "over all the land of Egypt" (Gen. 41:43).

She was an unnamed maiden in a foreign land. A band of Syrians had severed her from her country, family, and friends and imported her into an alien land to serve as a slave (2 Kings 5:2). It was a heathen land where gods were carved from wood and stone. It was a strange country with strange customs, culture, and language.

One would normally expect such extraordinary hardships in the tenderness of youth to produce an embittered spirit; hatred for her captors, contempt for life, and indifference toward God. However, adversity only served to fuel her faith. Her affection and concern for her master was voiced as she said, "Would God my lord were with the prophet that is in Samaria, for he would recover him of his leprosy" (2 Kings 5:3)

This simple expression of faith and concern initiated a chain of events that culminated in Naaman's physical healing, for "his flesh came again like unto the flesh of a little child"; and his spiritual conversion, for he declared, "Behold, now I know that there is no God in all the earth, but in Israel" (2 Kings 5:14-15). In the springtime of youth, this maiden helped to light another candle to dispel the darkness in a pagan land.

She was lovely in countenance, and she was lovely in life. Prior to becoming the queen of Persia, Esther had at least four major hurdles to cross. First, she lost her parents at an early age. For a young girl to lose her parents in the tender years of youth is a tragedy of immense proportions. Though obviously grateful to be clothed with the love of Mordecai, her cousin, that was no substitute for the joy of growing up in a home where her father and mother loved her and each other.

Second, she was reared in a pagan environment. Esther's presence in Persia was the result of the idolatry of her ancestors, leaving God with no alternative but to bring judgment upon Judah by means of the Babylonians, who were later conquered by the Persians. The nature of her Persian environment can best be seen in the king's response to Haman's inconceivable proposal. When Haman proposed the annihilation of the entire Jewish race, Ahasuerus coldly and unhesitatingly declared, "Do with them as it seemeth good to thee" (Esther 3:11). Immediately, orders were dispatched to the various provinces to "destroy, to kill, and to cause to perish all Jews, both young and old, little children and women in one day" (Esther 3:13), after which "the king and Haman sat down to drink" (Esther 3:15).

Third, she was denied a normal life. The triune goal of every Jewish girl was marriage, family, and a home of her own. No doubt, Esther had often dreamed of those very joys of womanhood. Instead, she was placed in the harem of a king. In pagan society it was not unusual for an undesired woman in the king's harem to exist in virtual solitude. Even as queen, Esther informed Mordecai on one occasion that she had not been with Ahasuerus for thirty days (Esther 4:11).

Fourth, she was compelled to sacrifice her virginity to a pagan king. For a young woman like Esther, virginity would be among her most treasured possessions. It would be something she would guard with her life until she could give herself in marriage to the man of her choice. Instead, she was taken from her home and given to Ahasuerus like some kind of material object, a man whom she had scarcely seen and for whom she had no love or feeling.

Such experiences would normally produce a woman angry with the world—possessing an intensely bitter spirit and sour disposition—who felt cheated by life, hence manifesting a negative attitude toward everything and everyone. But equally acute were the temptations she faced as queen of the most powerful nation in the world. Following the death of Haman, all of his immense wealth was given to her (Esther 8:1). As a result, Esther lived daily with some of the most potentially destructive forces with which man has ever had to contend: power, enormous wealth, and worldly fame. From these molds one would expect to behold an individual characterized by arrogance, egotism, and feelings of self-sufficiency. Esther's sterling character stands out in bold contrast to the massive difficulties and temptations with which she had to struggle.

Esther defied conventional wisdom. Unlike the majority who would find themselves in her situation, Esther exhibited an humble and submissive spirit. Choice young virgins throughout the kingdom were assembled in Shushan the palace from which Ahasuerus would choose one to be queen of Persia. These women were among the most beautiful in the kingdom. No doubt, most of them came from homes of the socially elite, women who had been pampered, petted, and catered to all of their lives. For the most part, such women would be vain, arrogant, and demanding. Prior to spending the night with the king, each one issued her demands and received whatever she desired (Esther 2:13). In contrast, Esther "required nothing but what Hegai the king's chamberlain, the keeper of the women appointed" (Esther 2:15).

She also possessed a lovely personality. "And Esther obtained favor in the sight of all them that looked upon her" (Esther 2:15). Providence? Yes, but respecting man's free will, even providence must have something with which to work.

She manifested a respectful and obedient spirit. Even after the royal crown adorned her head, the record declared, "Esther did the commandment of Mordecai, like as when she was brought up with him" (Esther 2:20). She was queen of mighty Persia. She was powerful, wealthy, and famous. How easy it would have been to forget Mordecai, even to view him with contempt.

Additionally, she was willing to sacrifice her life for her people. "I go in unto the king, which is not according to the law, and if I perish, I perish" (Esther 4:16). She was willing, not only to surrender her power, position, wealth, and fame, but even her very life. Esther is proof that an individual can recover from personal tragedy, rise above a pagan environment, conquer extreme trials, and be a blessing to the world.

These examples from the past confirm the springtime of youth to be a unique opportunity for faith and service, not fertile soil for an acceptable harvest of wild oats, or a time for justifying sin. It is not necessary to allow the ardor of youth to steal one's faith, integrity and purity. "Let no man despise thy youth, but be thou an example of the believers in word, in manner of life, in love, in spirit, in faith, in purity" (1 Tim. 4:12).

The neglect, misuse, and abuse of youth in the church today is a brotherhood tragedy. As the Moabites feared Israel would "lick up all that are round about us, as the ox licketh up the grass of the field" (Num. 22:4), even so, the spirit of liberalism has licked up a host of young people and deposited them on the road to spiritual ruin. Liberalism has performed much of its wicked work through youth ministers.

God has His youth ministers, and they are called parents. There are exceptions to the rule, but speaking generally, youth ministers are symbols of parental neglect. If parents were functioning according to God's design for the home, there would be no need for an employee of the church to minister to the youth. Elders have hired youth ministers to do the work that God has ordained for the home.

Some of God's greatest servants failed in their own homes. In spite of his well-known personal failings, David was a mighty man of God. However, his home was a disaster area. Polygamy and over-involvement in the affairs of state no doubt played major roles in his failure as a father. Regarding one of his sons, Adonijah, it is expressly stated that he was reared in the absence of discipline, having never been called into account for his improper conduct (1 Kings 1:6).

Relative to his personal righteousness, the biblical portrait of Eli is exemplary. During Israel's conflict with the Philistines, even as his grandson was near birth, his primary concern was with the ark of God (1 Sam. 4:17-19). However, his failure as a father led God to say, "For I have told him that I will judge his house forever for the iniquity which he knoweth; because his sons made themselves vile, and he restrained them not" (1 Sam. 3:13). It was Samuel who delivered this tragic news to Eli, yet his sons fared no better. "And his sons walked not in his ways, but turned aside after lucre and took bribes and perverted judgment" (1 Sam. 8:3). It is possible that Samuel was often an absentee father (1 Sam. 7:16), therefore allowing his sons to grow up in a home frequently vacant of strong fatherly presence and influence.

"Latch-key kids" is a phrase of recent invention to describe children who come home from school to an empty house. Regarding intimate, emotional, conversational, biblically instructive contact with children, many of the homes of members of the church are parentally uninhabited. Both parents work, come home weary, and allow toys created by technology to baby-sit their children until bedtime. Saturdays are catch-up and fun days with parents and children often going in opposite directions. Many devote an hour on Sunday to perfunctory worship, lease the remainder of the day to leisure, and start the whole process all over again on Monday.

Consequently, the stage has been set for youth ministers. Youth ministers are "gap fillers." They are hired by elders to fill the gaps in the lives of children left by parents in regard to spiritual and social activities. Concerning the latter, they are professionals. In most cases, elders hire a youth minister who himself is a youth. Being only a few years at best out of his teens, he has intimate knowledge of fun and frolic. There are no gaps in his monthly social calendar. Youth ministers often know more about the young people under their youthful oversight than the parents, because they spend more time with them.

Regarding spiritual activities and biblical instruction, youth ministers are frequently spiritual catastrophes. Their biblical knowledge is diminutive, and what little they know is so dominated by the spirit of liberalism as to render them the most dangerous influence in the lives of these young people. Deficient in Bible knowledge, they are unable to discern the exclusiveness of New Testament Christianity. Their "no big deal" spirit toward various tenets of inspired teaching renders useless the whole concept of biblical authority. If their life depended upon it, they could not articulate the difference in the church that cost Jesus His blood and some denomination void of a divine right to exist. They do not believe there is any difference.

Youth rallies are significant events in the lives of youth ministers and those committed to their care. Many of these gatherings are nothing more than Pentecostal pep rallies. The speakers are professionals in creating an emotional climate. They are full of jokes and stories. They are comedians, not preachers; entertainers, not spokesmen for God; actors, not teachers of truth. Attentive minds and calm reflection on faith-building, biblical truths are supplanted by clapping, swaying, and displays of emotion. The participants return home in touch with their feelings, but not with God through the enlightenment of distinctive Bible truth.

One of the most popular and well-attended youth rallies is Winterfest. Headquartered in Edmond, Oklahoma, the

Winterfest organization is a money-making enterprise that is void of deep reverence for the majesty of God and the authority of His Word. In their rally in Gatlinburg, Tennessee, February 16-18, 2001, they featured during a Sunday morning worship service, a slovenly dressed actor portraying Jesus' partaking of the Lord's supper. For some forty-five minutes, carrying a bottle of liquid and two loaves of bread, he traipsed about the stage and through the audience, quoting scripture, eating bread, and passing out pieces for some in the assembly. Elders who allow the young people under their oversight to be influenced by such spectacles of blasphemy shall surely answer to God in the Judgment. Moreover, on their website, Winterfest promotes a CD entitled "Radical Praise Movement," and then proclaims, "We need a worship revolution." It is crystal clear as to what this detestable organization is endeavoring to do to the minds of youth.

Youth ministries are often emblematic of pastoral neglect. It is the responsibility of pastors to oversee the flock. Their duty demands intimate knowledge of every sheep. They shall account to God for every one (Heb. 13:17). Some elders employ youth ministers as though they were maintenance men. Cursory attention is given to the young man's convictions on essential matters of biblical teaching. Little emphasis is placed on his depth of Bible knowledge. In spite of their lacking a thorough knowledge of his position on all matters of faith, they proceed to place under his youthful oversight the precious souls of young men and women for whom they are accountable before God. Unknowingly, due to their own neglect, they have often employed a young man in whose veins flows the diseased blood of liberalism.

"And they were scattered because there is no shepherd; and they became meat to all the beasts of the field, when they were scattered" (Ezek. 34:5). The shepherds of Israel had no concern for the spiritual welfare of the sheep. Without a shepherd, the sheep were no match for the savagery of nature. In like manner, manifesting little concern for the spiritual lives of the lambs, such elders commit them to the care of a young wolf in sheep's clothing. They are soon devoured by the wild beast of liberalism and planted on the road to eternal ruin.

Youth ministries frequently exemplify an eldership's misuse of deacons. There are congregations where the work of a deacon amounts to no work at all. They have a title, but no tasks. They wear a designation that connotes service, but they do not serve in any specific way. Some of these men are biblically knowledgeable and extremely capable of effective service, but wander aimlessly under elders who, regarding directive ability, are either derelict or incapable.

Moreover, some of these men have grown up with the youth of the church and have their love and respect. There are many good works in which the talents, enthusiasm, and vigor of youth can be usefully employed. Indisputably, even though parents have the primary responsibility in this regard, there is a time and place for youthful congregate social and recreational activities external to parental involvement. What better work for these deacons to perform than to have such youth, work, and activities placed under their oversight. One congregation in particular comes to mind in which deacons have been appointed, under the oversight of the elders, to coordinate the activities of the pre-teens and teens. Among these activities are regular nursing home visits; young people are paired with elderly members of the congregation who become their adopted grandparents; intense study sessions are conducted in order to prepare for an area-wide annual Bible-bowl competition; and regular outings are planned involving wholesome recreational activities. As a result, these young people form a cohesive, close group, well-grounded in biblical truths. The retention rate of these youths has been remarkable.

Most youth ministers are young, single, married with no children, or married with small children. Hence, they are not seasoned in age, marriage, or parenthood. Even when sound in the faith, through no fault of their own, due to their youth, they are deficient in the meat of Bible knowledge, in wisdom, and in life's experiences. They themselves are yet in need of adult guidance. However, they are often employed, furnished good salaries, and given free rein with priceless young souls, with little to no direction from even the elders. Is this sound judgment when in the same congregations are deacons, matured in age, marriage, family, life's experiences, wisdom, and Bible knowledge, who would give freely of their time and talents to the youth of the church?

For every biblically sound youth minister in the church today, there are twenty-five whose minds have been contaminated by the defiling spirit of liberalism. These young men are deficient in understanding some of the most fundamental principles of biblical teaching. "Desiring to be teachers of the law, understanding neither what they say, nor whereof they affirm" (1 Tim. 1:7). If remunerated for their services, they would be just as content in some denominational church as in the church of the New Testament. They love to talk about grace. Their countenance swells with pride as they pontificate thereon as though they had plumbed the depths of the subject and unlocked all of its mysteries. To hear them speak, one would tend to think they had followed Paul's path into the third heaven and been enlightened on matters not revealed in the Bible. Ignorance and pride are joined at the hip, and they walk lame with both. They have been robotized by those well-matured in liberal thinking and parrot their foolishness in mechanized form. They are a continual blight on the cause for which Jesus died and have made major contributions to the present apostasy of the church.

There are, however, a few young men presently serving as youth ministers who are sound in the faith. They love the truth and tread the old paths with ardor and delight. They understand and esteem biblical authority. They possess a trembling reverence for every word of God. The pivot of their labor is spiritual and not a continuous stream of activities that mollify the flesh. They share an attitudinal kinship with the young man who affirmed, "I am a gospel preacher who just happens to work with the youth of the church." However, even these young men should not be allowed free and unfettered access to the minds and lives of young people. Such an arrangement is not in their own best interests, nor that of the young people under their guidance. They themselves would generally prefer the guiding and assisting hand of some older, knowledgeable, spiritual leader in the church. Even so, it would be far more consistent with the will of God to utilize the zeal and talents of these young men as personal evangelists in the community, with a much smaller portion of time devoted to youth work, while encouraging parents to be the youth ministers of their own children.

15

Liberalism and Christian Schools

The Christian school concept finds its origin in the schools of the prophets that first appeared on the pages of inspiration during the time of Samuel. When Samuel anointed Saul as the first king of Israel, he gave him three signs to verify the divine nature of his appointment. The third sign pointed to his meeting a company of prophets and joining them in prophesying (1 Sam. 10:5-6). When the sign became reality the people inquired, "Is Saul also among the prophets?" (1 Sam. 10:11). Their query attests to the well-established nature of the prophetic schools in the life of Israel.

God ruled over the nation of Israel during the period of the judges. However, Israel grew weary of God's rule and demanded a king, "that we also may be like all the nations" (1 Sam. 8:20). Samuel viewed Israel's request as personal repudiation of his leadership. God informed Samuel, "They have not rejected thee, but they have rejected me, that I should not reign over them" (1 Sam. 8:7). God proceeded to apprise Samuel that Israel's rebellious spirit and proclivity for idolatry had characterized them from "Egypt even unto this day" (1 Sam. 8:8).

Consequently, Samuel was a pivotal leader in Israel's history. He was a transitional figure through whom Israel moved from God's rule through the judges to a king like the nations about them. This arrangement was not in harmony with God's design for the nation. The fuel of liberalism is self-will, and it was that very spirit that compelled Israel to insist upon a king. Centuries later, God reminded Israel of that spirit that had ruled their lives for the whole of their national history and then declared, "I gave thee a king in mine anger, and took him away in my wrath" (Hos. 13:11). It is, therefore, highly probable that during this time of transition, by divine design, Samuel established these prophetic schools to help teach and educate the nation in spiritual verities during the tumultuous years under the rule of the kings.

When David fled from Saul, he met Samuel and informed him of all that Saul had done to him. When messengers from Saul arrived in Naioth to arrest David they "saw the company of the prophets prophesying, and Samuel standing as appointed over them" (1 Sam. 19:20). This passage testifies to Samuel's leadership role with regard to these prophetic bands. To whatever degree these schools were active during the reign of David, the text focuses on the prophets Nathan and Gad. It was Nathan of whom David inquired concerning the construction of the temple (2 Sam. 7:2). It was Nathan whom God sent to rebuke David for his sin (2 Sam. 12). Moreover, Nathan was with David in the last days of his life and joined Zadok the priest in anointing Solomon king over Israel (1 Kings 1).

The prophet Gad came to David's aid during a time of great need. On the run from Saul, David had just left his parents in the care of the king of Moab when Gad appeared with needed instruction (1 Sam. 22:5). He is described as "David's seer" in 2 Samuel 24:11. He rebuked David for numbering Israel (2 Sam. 24:12-14) and is mentioned in conjunction with Samuel and Nathan in writing a history of David's life (1 Chron. 29:29).

When Jereboam changed God's pattern of worship for the northern kingdom (1 Kings 12), the Levites and their priests expatriated from the north to the south (2 Chron. 11:13-14). "And after them out of all the tribes of Israel such as set their hearts to seek the Lord God of Israel came to Jerusalem, to sacrifice unto the Lord God of their fathers" (2 Chron. 11:16).

Ahab, Israel's seventh king, followed Jereboam's disastrous influence with his own by introducing and flooding the nation with the worship of Baal (1 Kings 16:31-33). Refusing to give up on the nation, God raised up Elijah to counteract the evil influence of Jereboam and Ahab (1 Kings 17:1). Assisting Elijah were "sons of the prophets" (1 Kings 20:35), prophetic descendants of the schools of the prophets. When Jezebel commenced her bloody rampage against these very prophets, Obadiah, the governor of Ahab's house, saved a hundred of them by hiding them in caves and feeding them with bread and water (1 Kings 18:4). From among these prophets came word to Ahab of a victory over Syria (1 Kings 20:13), a second victory (1 Kings 20:28), and a final defeat (1 Kings 20:35-43). There was a school of these prophets at Bethel, one at Jericho, and another at Gilgal (2 Kings 2:1-4; 4:38-41).

When Elijah was transported into heaven, the mantle of prophetic leadership fell upon Elisha after which the sons of the prophets "came to meet him, and bowed themselves to the ground before him" (1 Kings 2:15). He miraculously aided a widow and two sons of one of these prophets by furnishing sufficient oil to pay her debts with money remaining for future needs (2 Kings 4:1-7). He detoxified a poisonous communal meal in the prophetic school at Gilgal (2 Kings 4:38-41), and as Jesus would do with a few loaves and fish, he multiplied food which was barely adequate for twenty to feed a hundred prophets, with food left over in what appears to be that same school (2 Kings 4:42-44). Moreover, Elisha commissioned one of the "children of the prophets" (2 Kings 9:1) to anoint Jehu the tenth king of Israel and mandate him with the destruction of Ahab's descendants as an act of divine judgment for the "blood of my servants the prophets, and the blood of all the servants of the Lord, at the hand of Jezebel" (2 Kings 9:7). Amos had reference to these very prophetic schools when he said, "Neither was I a prophet's son" (Amos 7:14). He was pointing to his occupation as a common laborer when directed by God to preach to Israel as opposed to being trained in one of the prophetic schools under a father figure like Samuel, Elijah, or Elisha.

The Bible is not a history of the Jewish race, much less a chronicle of Gentile nations. The theme of the Bible is redemption. Genesis 3:6 to John 21:25 answers one basic question: How did God get from man's sin to His solution in Christ and the cross? Many other questions are answered along the way, but they all relate to this core question. A failure to keep this truth fresh in one's mental storehouse will result in a minimizing of the great role these prophetic schools played in the life of Israel and the nations about them.

One can select any book, chapter, incident, or personage, and relative to the information revealed, in most instances, it is but a microscopic portion of what actually transpired. Abraham was the one to whom the promises were made concerning a great nation, their inheritance of Canaan, and redemption through Christ (Gen. 12:1-3; Gal. 3:16); yet, the story of his life is covered in just thirteen chapters. Isaac was the son of promise, one of the great patriarchs through whom the promise of redemption continued its flow. However, following Abraham's death, just two chapters are needed to cover the major portion of his life. Most of the earthly life of Jesus Christ Himself is passed over in silence. Though hyperbolic, John affirmed,

> And there are also many other things which Jesus did, the which, if they should be written every one, I suppose that even the world itself could not contain the books that should be written (John 21:25).

God has given just enough to weave together the marvelous story of redemption in a form more wonderful than words can describe.

Moreover, this answers the question as to why so little attention is devoted to the Gentile nations in contrast to the nation of Israel. Even members of the church have been heard expressing doubt regarding God's concern for anyone outside of Israel, even to the point of doubting the possibility of their salvation. Lamentably, they have missed the very thrust of the Old Testament. The Bible is about redemption, and redemption was made possible through the seed of Abraham. The world was immersed in idolatry. God needed a man through whom He could continue the "seed of woman" (Gen. 3:15) toward Calvary. God needed a man of faith. That man was Abraham. Out of Abraham came Isaac, Jacob, Judah, David, and Mary, "of whom was born Jesus, who is called the Christ" (Matt. 1:16).

Israel, therefore, was the womb of the Messiah. The seed of human conception grows and develops in the mother's womb for nine months to the point of physical birth. The seed of Genesis 3:15 was planted in Abraham, thus the nation to come from his loins. As a result, the period from Genesis 12 to Matthew 1:15 might well be viewed as a figurative nine months in which that seed of redemption grew and developed until it burst forth in the person of Jesus Christ. Hence, the major portion of Old Testament history and teaching focuses on the nation of Israel through whom God would become incarnate.

However, from Genesis 3:6 onward, God in His great love has desired "all men to be saved, and to come unto the knowledge of the truth" (1 Tim. 2:4). God has never been "willing that any should perish, but that all should come to repentance" (2 Pet. 3:9). God's concern for Potiphar in Egypt, Balak in Moab, Agag in Amalek, Goliath in Philistia, Hiram in Tyre, Benhadad in Syria, and Cyrus in Persia was just as great as His concern for Abraham, Isaac, Jacob, Moses, and David. No man has ever been conceived, born, lived, or died external to the love of God. Once sin becomes a reality in one's life, no man can enjoy the spiritual benefits of God's love apart from obedience to His will, but that does not mean that God does not love him.

Even though little is said concerning the great work, effective influence, and positive results of the schools of the prophets in Israel, much less in nations outside of Israel, it would be a grave mistake to assume that their influence for God, truth, and right was inconsequential. Elijah and Elisha were both leaders in the prophetic schools. God instructed Elijah to "anoint Hazael to be king over Syria" (2 Kings 19:15), and Elisha, through tears, said to Hazael, "The Lord hath showed me that thou shalt be king over Syria" (2 Kings 8:13). Of the writing prophets, Daniel lived and labored in the courts of Babylon, Obadiah announced judgment against Edom, Jonah preached to Nineveh, and Nahum foretold its destruction. Isaiah uttered oracles against heathen nations. Zephaniah pronounced God's judgment on Philistia, Moab, Ammon, Ethiopia, and Assyria (Zeph. 2:4-15). "The word of the Lord which came to Jeremiah the prophet against the Gentiles" (Jer. 46:1), embraces six chapters. It is reasonable to conclude that men from the schools of the prophets were often commissioned to preach and teach among the Gentiles.

Much of the preaching of the prophets was done in such spiritually turbulent times as to make positive results of their efforts appear small. Their preaching often ensued in persecution and even death. There was only one Nineveh, and that remarkable penitent response enjoyed a unique sign (Luke 11:30). The masses of humanity from the beginning have never been concerned about God, truth, and righteousness. The miraculous ministries of Elijah and Elisha found the nation of Israel continuing in Jereboam's corrupt worship and Ahab's idolatry. Jesus Christ and the gospel were proved divine by mighty wonders and signs, but both were rejected by the majority, and so shall it ever be (Matt. 7:13-14). Thus, viewing man as a whole, positive consequences from efforts exerted for God and His will have always been small.

However, the value of the world is incomparable to just one man's soul (Matt. 16:26). Therefore, encouraging the ever-present righteous remnant and snatching a few souls "out of the fire" (Jude 23) along life's journey, are acts of great significance in the sight of God. As evidenced from Samuel onward, the prophetic schools played a significant role in the spiritual life of Israel. They were a stabilizing influence in the nation. They proclaimed the one God to a people with a penchant for idolatry. They called for a return to God's pattern of worship for those mimicking Jereboam. Their very lives rebuked the evil of the day and served as a constant call to holiness. They helped constitute the righteous element essential for the preservation of a nation (Prov. 14:34). The southern kingdom was blessed with several righteous kings. However, the northern kingdom failed to produce a single pious ruler. Had it not been for the influence of the prophetic schools and their leaders, the national life of Israel would surely have been shortened considerably. They, no doubt, had an influence on the lives of individuals in the heathen nations about them. The schools of the prophets and their leaders were indispensable to the cause of God in the earth.

In like manner, the Christian schools have exerted a monumental influence for the cause of Jesus Christ. It is not possible to convey adequately the great good that these institutions have accomplished through the years. There is no way to measure the truth that has been taught, the Christian homes that have been formed, the lives of children that have been blessed, the congregations of the church for which Jesus died that have been established, the benevolent work that has been achieved, the wrecked lives that have been salvaged, the wounds that have been healed, or the souls that have been saved as a consequence of the marvelous work of these schools.

When these schools were first formed, and for years thereafter, love for the truth and the souls of men were their paramount concerns. Though exceptions exist to every righteous endeavor, the founders of these schools and those involved therein would have bathed in their own blood before they would have tampered with a jot or tittle of the law of God. A martyr's death would have been preferred over any effort to modify or dilute God's revelation to man. The fervor of these men for the truth of God matched that of the prophets of the Old Testament and the apostles of the New Testament. Modernism and liberalism were verbal objects of loathing. They would not have come within a million mental miles of the abhorrent spirit of liberalism.

These great men of God understood and possessed a deep and abiding reverence for the absolute authority of the Bible. They would have elected for their tongues to be severed from their roots before characterizing even the "mint, anise, and cumin" elements of biblical teaching as "no big deal." They understood the grace of the Bible and deplored the perverted grace of liberalism. They possessed a clear, unblemished perception of the exclusiveness of New Testament Christianity with its one standard of authority, plan of salvation, church, and pattern of worship. They viewed Catholicism, denominationalism, and their kindred as religious systems having no divine right to exist, monuments to religious error marching under the banner of self-will, potent weapons in the hands of Satan to blind the minds of men to the truth of the gospel, and destined to be rooted up and destroyed (Matt. 15:13).

These schools were founded and filled by men who understood that the power of their influence lay not in the architectural design of their buildings, but their commitment to the truth; not in academic degrees of their faculty, but their understanding of and loyalty to the one faith; not their acceptance in the community, but their dedication to the one gospel and its proclamation in the world; not the size of their endowment, but the strength of their character; not in their enrollment with the educational accrediting institutions, but their devotion to divine revelation; not in numbers of students, but in faithfulness to God.

The leaders in these schools abhorred the compromising spirit. They knew that the spirit of compromise would negate their distinctiveness, hence their reason for existence. They knew the purpose for their existence was not to offer instruction in English, science, history, math, or business. It would be obscene to beg money from Christians that could support the proclamation of the gospel, in order to teach secular subjects, when thousands of existing institutions were accomplishing this on a professional level. They understood that apart from the glorification of God in the communication of His truth, their doors had no right to be opened. Moreover, they were all aware that the first step in institutional apostasy would be taken in the shoes of compromise. They knew that the spiritual life of the school was dependent upon the pure blood of unadulterated truth's flowing through its veins. They would have joined Benaiah to fight a wild lion "in the midst of a pit in time of snow" (2 Sam. 23:20) before they would have compromised even the smallest tenet of biblical truth.

The founders, leaders, and instructors in these schools were men of great spiritual discernment. They could spot a whisker on the chin of liberalism a mile away. They knew that the spirit of liberalism and the spirit of compromise were conceived in the same womb, marched to the same tune, and were inseparable companions on the road to spiritual ruin. They understood that the gangrene of liberalism would commence when the spiritual blood supply of pure truth was obstructed by the spirit of compromise. If such were allowed to happen, they knew that the spiritual decay of the school was inevitable.

These godly men detested the spirit of liberalism with the whole of their being. They would have fought Goliath with a stick before allowing the destructive Goliath of liberalism to gain even the slightest toe-hold on the schools to which they were devoting their lives. They were well aware that no power on earth could destroy a Christian school with more swiftness and thoroughness than the wicked spirit of liberalism. They were spiritual sentries in the school's watchtower, constantly watching for the devouring wolves of liberalism that love to "creep in" (Jude 4) disguised as sheep.

When these men were looking for board members to serve the school, their chief concern was the depth of their love for the truth, not the depth of their pockets. They knew that the school was secure in the hands of men who loved God and truth supremely. They also knew that evil men, greedy for power and eager to pollute the pure water of truth with the poison of liberalism, would fill the school's coffers with large sums in order to attain a position of influence. They would rather have received five dollars from a widow who loved the truth, than five million from a man of means seeking favors for the cause of liberalism.

The Bible professors in these schools were men who loved the truth above their own lives. They held "fast the form of sound words" (2 Tim. 1:13). Their teaching was "wholesome" (1 Tim. 6:3) because it was the truth. Like the prophets of old, they listened to God and then spoke accordingly (Ezek. 3:10-11). The young, impressionable minds of their students were safe in their hands. They strove mightily never to utter a single word that would plant the slightest seed of doubt in their minds relative to the truth of God on any subject. Parents were comforted knowing that the faith they had endeavored to instill in their sons and daughters would be reinforced in these institutions. No student was ever encouraged to refrain from taking classes under a certain professor because of his proneness toward liberalism.

Moreover, these professors would never have attempted to clothe their convictions in an air of secrecy, because their convictions were based on the truth. They would have stood on a mountain and shouted their convictions to the whole world. They would never have entertained the thought of refusing to answer a Bible question coming from an honest inquirer. They would have viewed any attempt to do otherwise as a presumptuous act and a transgression of the law of God (1 Pet. 3:15). They would never have accepted a position on a Bible faculty under false pretense in hopes of gradually planting seeds of liberalism in young minds. They were honorable men whose lives were consistent with their teaching.

Except for a few non-members of the church among the student body, everyone associated with these schools, from board members to president to faculty to student, was of one mind on all fundamental matters of biblical teaching. There was no argument, debate, or wrangling on essential matters of revealed truth. Not a single shot was ever fired on the campus of a civil war between those treading the old paths and those intent on changing the church to adapt to the culture of denominationalism. The entire school glowed with a marvelous spirit of unity. If just one person had held forth the unauthorized, worship-defiling mechanical instrument and cried, "It's no big deal," he would have been denounced by every member of the church connected with the school.

The chapel and devotional experiences in these delightful, faith-building, spiritually enhancing schools were incessant sources of encouragement. Ask any student from those longed-for days of old, and he will have difficulty recalling a single instance when some strange sound was heard in those assemblies. Every lesson was solidly based on the unchanging Word of God. If a student had applauded the speaker in one of those gatherings, and thus, transferred the object of the assembly from God to man, he would have been summoned to the office of the president and censured. When a student skipped chapel or some devotional gathering, it was not for fear of being overcome with nausea because of some teaching or practice rendered foolish or silly by the contaminating spirit of liberalism.

When those remarkable institutions affirmed to the home and the church, "Lend us your sons, daughters, and young people for four years and we will return them with a greater knowledge of the Bible, a more matured faith, and a deeper level of spirituality," they were true to their word. Graduates of these colleges were a blessing to the home as designed by God, to the church as eternally purposed by God, and the teeming masses of humanity in need of the gospel. As did Jesus, they went everywhere "doing good" (Acts 10:38). They made great elders, preachers, husbands, wives, mothers, fathers, employers, and employees. Unwavering faith in the immutable Word of God made them powerful forces for truth and righteousness in a world drunk on error and sin.

Those schools majored in training men to preach and teach the gospel of Christ. They often boasted, and rightly so, of the large numbers of young men preparing to devote their lives to the proclamation of the truth. These young men filled pulpits all over the brotherhood. They believed the truth, loved the truth, lived the truth, and preached the truth. There were no strange or uncertain sounds in their preaching. Their allegiance to the truth made them a blessing to the cause of Christ throughout the world.

Relative to these schools, the difference in then and now literally defies description. The spirit of liberalism has swept over many of these institutions with hurricane force. Some have been so corrupted by this egregious evil as to render them a detriment to the cause of truth for which they were originally established. It would be a mighty blessing to the cause of God's Son on earth if the Bible departments in some of these institutions were eliminated and the schools totally secularized in their teaching and instruction. Those who have followed these universities closely know that this is not an exaggerated statement.

There are Bible—a misnomer!—professors in some of these colleges who do not believe that one can prove that God is, that the Bible is His Word, or that Jesus is His Son. Of what spiritual value to the minds of young men and women is such a professor? How can a man conscientiously offer instruction in spiritual and eternal truths that he does not believe can be proven? Is a thing really true if it cannot be authenticated? Does a man have a right before God to call upon others to accept his statements as truth when, by his own admission, he cannot supply the evidence to fully validate his assertions? One such professor was asked, "Does not honesty require that at the close of each class you affirm your personal belief in each statement made, but also your inability to prove a single one?"

There are professors teaching in the Bible departments of some of these universities who do not believe it is sinful to intrude into God's presence with the unauthorized mechanical instrument. They possess the "no big deal" spirit toward the use of machinery in spiritual worship to God. This is the very spirit and essence of liberalism. How can a man with such a wretched attitude toward biblical authority ever impress a young mind with the need of respecting the author- ity of the Bible on any subject? How can he conscientiously call for restraint regarding a single act not expressly forbid- den in the New Testament? If he allows for himself the "no big deal" spirit toward the instrument, does not consistency demand that he grant to all others the expression of that same sentiment toward any Bible subject of their choosing? What sane parent would pay for his son or daughter to sit at the feet of a professor with such an abominable attitude toward the authority of the Word of the sovereign God?

The Bible departments of some of the Christian colleges contain professors who manifest the "no big deal" spirit toward premillennialism. This contemptible doctrine perverts the scheme of redemption, the very heart and core of the Bible. It does not understand the spiritual nature of God's revelation to man. It reduces the church for which Jesus shed His blood to a temporary substitute for the real thing. Premillennial- ism beats with a materialistic heart. It is concerned with a physical nation, kingdom, king, and rule. It undermines the very essence of the biblical record. Is it wise to entrust educa- tional institutions with such disdain for clear biblical teach- ing with the immortal souls of youth who constitute an inte- gral part of the church of today and leaders of the church of tomorrow?

Some of the Bible professors in these colleges do not believe what Jesus said about the crucial subject of marriage, divorce, and remarriage (Matt. 5:32; 19:9). Was not marriage and the home the first institution ordained by God? Outside of one's relationship to God, is there a more intimate relationship known to man than the bond of marriage? Is not the home as designed by God the foundation upon which the whole of soci- ety is constructed? Does not God's restrictive law of love serve to promote the sanctity of marriage and preserve the permanence of the marriage bond? Are not Matthew 5:32 and 19:9 consistent with God's holiness and the manifestation of that holiness in His attitude toward divorce? (Mal. 2:16.) Is there any truth more vital to a man's earthly happiness and eternal security than God's truth concerning the marital state? Can a man live in persistent violation of God's law for marriage and die in hope of Heaven?

Christian colleges are full of young men and women seeking mates for life. A spiritual environment—numerous young people from similar backgrounds with concern for truth and spiritual things—furnishes a splendid setting for selecting a companion for life. This is one of the primary motivations for many young men's and women's preferring a Christian school over a state school. What greater evil could be done to the mind of a young man or woman than to plant the seed of error regarding marriage that produces the harvest of adultery? Extensive correspondence with a Bible professor in a Christian college involved in planting such seeds of error culminated in this amazing admission, "There are some things which are faith to me, but which I must put in the category of opinion in the interest of unity and fellowship." Is it not the summit of presumption for a mere man to take an admitted matter of faith and deposit it in the realm of opinion? Would he reserve for himself alone the right of such action? Granting to all men that same right would nullify all matters of faith and reduce the Bible to a divine suggestion book. In the course of a gospel meeting, this professor baptized a couple with six mates between them and then returned to the safety of his classroom, leaving behind a problem with which the elders had to contend. The president of a Christian college is on record affirming the right of couples to marry and divorce ten times and be allowed to remain with the partner they are with at the time of their baptism.[1] Is this statement consis-

---

1. Jack Evans, President of Southwestern Christian College, Terrell, Texas, Tape of sermon of questions and answers regarding marriage, divorce and remarriage, Dunbar, SC, 10 July 1998.

tent with God's holiness and the holiness that His very nature demands of His offspring? Is it compatible with God's attitude toward divorce? (Mal. 2:16.) Does this sentiment encourage or discourage that which God hates? It is frightening to think of standing in judgment before the God of all holiness who hates divorce and having to give account for a doctrine that Jesus said has not been true "from the beginning" (Matt. 19:8). Such is the villainous spirit of liberalism.

There are highly educated men who are offering biblical instruction in some of these universities along with others in leadership positions who look beyond the Word of the Spirit to the Spirit Himself as the source of spiritual direction and influence. Three such professors have written a book entitled *The Worldly Church,* painting a portrait of the direct work of the Holy Spirit with brushes borrowed from Calvinism and Pentecostalism. They criticize Alexander Campbell, Walter Scott, and those allied with them for virtually banishing the Holy Spirit as the living presence and power of God in the world. They depict Campbell and Scott as having been far more influenced in their view of the Holy Spirit's work through the Word of God by John Locke and the eighteenth-century enlightenment than the Bible itself. They write with an undiscerning spirit relative to the obvious fact that their own minds regarding this subject have been affected more by denominational theologians than the Bible. They affirm that the gospel of Christ, apart from the direct work of the Holy Spirit, is a secularized gospel. They further assert, "It is the indwelling Spirit who enlightens our minds to the things of God."[2] This is pure Calvinism.

This kind of teaching fosters subjectivism. It possesses the potential of positioning a soul on the road to eternal condemnation. This is especially true in view of the present climate of the church. A large percentage of the church today has only a meager knowledge of the Bible. They are subject

---

2. C. Leonard Allen, Richard T. Hughes, Michael R. West; "The Worldly Church," ACU Press, Abilene, TX, 1991.

to being "tossed to and fro, and carried about with every wind of doctrine" (Eph. 4:14). Lacking substantive biblical knowledge, they are often attracted by teaching that appeals to the flesh and the emotions.

Moreover, they frequently take such teaching far beyond that which was intended. Recently, on a foreign mission field, the term *Comforter* was used in conjunction with the present relationship of the Holy Spirit with the Christian. Some of the hearers, discerning the obvious connection between this term and the miraculous in John 14-16, now believe that God speaks to them through dreams and other means external to the Word of God.

One infant step beyond the Word of the Spirit in search of spiritual guidance and inspiration, already abundantly available in the Spirit's Word, is a reflection upon the Spirit Himself. Jesus promised the apostles that the Holy Spirit would be His replacement in their lives, and He would give them perfect memory of His personal instruction and furnish them additional truths which they were not yet prepared to receive, hence enabling them to possess all truth (John 14:25-26; 16:12-13). To accomplish this great task, the Holy Spirit searched the mind of God (1 Cor. 2:10). Having searched the infinite mind of the transcendent God, the repository of every truth of everything that is, He took every truth essential for the present and eternal security of man and through the pen of inspiration deposited it in the Bible (2 Pet. 1:20-21; 2 Tim. 3:16-17).

What does the Word of the Spirit do for man? It teaches, reproves, corrects, and instructs in righteousness (2 Tim. 3:16). It produces faith (Rom. 10:17). It sanctifies (John 17:17). It pricks and stirs the heart to obey God (Acts 2:22-41). It purifies the soul (1 Pet. 1:22). It produces the new birth (1 Pet. 1:23). It saves the soul (James 1:21). It is the means through which God's love is perfected in man (1 John 2:5). It is the basis of unity (John 17:20-21). It nourishes (1 Tim. 4:6). It generates spiritual freedom (John 8:32). It yields spiritual maturity (2 Tim. 3:16). It comforts (Rom. 15:4). It combats temptation (Matt. 4:1-11). It strengthens (Eph. 6:10-18). It builds up and supplies an inheritance (Acts 20:32). It will judge man when time ends (John 12:48).

If under an inferior covenant, ratified and sanctified by the blood of animals, the Word of the Spirit cleansed the path of youth (Ps. 119:9); served as a barrier to sin (Ps. 119:11); was a spiritual counselor (Ps. 119:24); was the source of spiritual strength (Ps. 119:28); provided liberty (Ps. 119:45); quickened or furnished spiritual life (Ps. 119:50); fostered gratitude (Ps. 119:62); afforded hope (Ps. 119:74); produced wisdom and understanding (Ps. 119:98-99); was the wellspring of joy (Ps. 119:111); effectuated spiritual light (Ps. 119:130); and served as a basis for praising God (Ps. 119:164); how much more does that same Word under the glorious covenant of Christ, ratified and sanctified by His own blood, furnish the totality of man's spiritual needs for the whole of his life? What spiritual need does man have that needs to be supplied directly by the Holy Spirit that He has not already bounteously provided in His Word?

It is the height of foolishness and futility to seek spiritual guidance, wisdom, and motivation from the Holy Spirit while an abundant supply thereof is readily accessible in His Word. The Holy Spirit did not leave any spiritual leftovers to be furnished by some direct action in addition to His Word (2 Tim. 3:16-17). Such teaching opens the door to the feeling, subjective religion of denominationalism. Though denying personal involvement, one such professor has removed the door itself and reinstated the spiritual infancy stage of the church declaring, "I am no longer willing to forbid the speaking in tongues."[3] It is frightening to think that the leaders of the church of tomorrow are being nurtured under the influence of such men.

There are professors of Bible in some of the Christian schools who deny biblical teaching on the role of women, eternal condemnation in hell, and the limitation of the observance

3. Carroll Osburn, lecture: "That Which Is Perfect," Abilene Christian University Lectureship, 24 Feb.1992.

of the Lord's supper to Sunday. Relative to the Lord's supper, one such professor delivered a speech to an assembly of students, primarily from denominational backgrounds, then joined them in observing the Lord's supper on Tuesday evening. Can such professors instill trembling reverence in young minds for every Word of God? Will students leave their classes with profound veneration for the absolute authority of the Bible? Will young men trained under their teaching and influence ascend to pulpits with a clear, distinctive, resolute presentation of the unchanging truths of God? There are professors in the Bible departments of some of these schools whose minds are so poisoned by liberalism and modernism as to render them unacceptable even by some of the seminaries operated by denominational churches.

Many of the preachers, coming forth from these institutions, are a curse to the cause of truth. They do not believe the truth on many matters of fundamental significance. Their preaching is not distinctive because it is not biblical. They are dramatic, comedic, poetic, theatrical, philosophical, and entertaining, but not biblical. They could exchange pulpits with the denominational preacher across the street, and no one could discern the difference. Such preaching enlivens the emotions, but numbs the spirit. It negates spirituality, because spirituality grows out of faith, and faith is based firmly on a "thus saith God." These preachers are spiritual counterfeits. They are a disgrace to preaching. They fill pulpits where elders and members ceased long ago engaging in serious Bible study. In turn, they have lost the power of discernment between truth and error. Consequently, in a surprisingly short period of time, they are able to influence a once faithful congregation to embark unwittingly on the road of apostasy. The spirit of liberalism is the spirit of evil.

The apostasy of a number of these schools has left a huge vacancy in training "faithful men who shall be able to teach others also" (2 Tim. 2:2). This void has been most capably filled by schools of preaching and like institutions established for the sole purpose of training men to preach the pure gospel of Christ. Some of these schools are patterned after the schools of the prophets and send forth men with a knowledge and love of the truth unexcelled by graduates of Christian universities.

The schools of preaching have a reputation for unwavering devotion to the truth. Unlike many of the Christian universities, their lectureships are composed of men whose doctrinal soundness is unquestioned. Also, many of the bookstores of Christian universities and the foyers and hallways of their lectureships are filled with books written by the best-known false teachers in the church. These books are satiated with damnable error. The leaders of these institutions are seemingly oblivious to their culpability and accountability for the souls of those people who are influenced and led astray by these tools of Satan. It is a deeply lamentable and undeniable fact that many of the Christian universities are more concerned with power, prestige, popularity, politics, money, and egos than faithfulness to the immutable truths of God.

Conversely, several years ago, at the Brown Trail School of Preaching in Bedford, Texas, permission was requested by an individual to set up a display of books and materials for sale during the lectureship. The request was granted upon the condition that not a single book of questionable soundness would be displayed. As the exhibit was being emplaced, word came to the elders of the Brown Trail congregation that a number of books being displayed were the works of well-known proponents of error. Immediate instructions were given to remove the entire display from the premises. There are Christian universities who would do well to imitate this action.

Speaking generally, state colleges and universities are dens of depravity. God, the Bible, and spiritual things are vilified. Drinking and fornicating are as common as breathing. A poll taken among students in a state university in a small, conservative city revealed that ninety-eight percent of the students regularly imbibed alcohol. Various forms of vile conduct are viewed as morally neutral. Humanism has been enthroned as God. There is often zero tolerance for those who desire to make a public stand for God, truth, and righteousness, and those who persist in doing so are defamed. It is terrifying to think of a young man or woman, deeply sensitive to truth and spiritual concerns, being thrust into an environment so antagonistic to everything they have been taught for the whole of their lives. One would be better served playing in a bed of rattlesnakes. Trying to find in such a milieu a spiritual mate who loves God and truth supremely would be comparable to searching for pearls in a landfill.

The sword that pierced Mary's soul (Luke 2:35) has lanced the heart of many a parent as they viewed their beloved son or daughter on graduation day: a diploma in one hand and a vacant faith in their heart. For what is a man profited, if he shall gain a degree from the most prestigious university in the land and lose his own soul? Proud parents sometimes point to a son or daughter with yet strong faith who has endured the rigorous trials of such an environment. However, the tragedy of war is not to be judged by those who return physically whole, but rather in those who return with missing limbs or do not return at all. Sadly, their mental and emotional wholeness seldom matches their physical wholeness. In like manner, if the truth were known, many of those who attended these secular institutions could confess as did one, "I still have my faith, but I have had doubts embedded into my mind that will follow me to my grave." Even for one who has maintained a degree of faith, that is a heavy price to pay for a diploma from a state school. The indisputable fact is, a weakened faith is an open door to the destructive power of liberalism and often buckles under the trials of life.

The spirit of liberalism is a highly progressive evil. Some Christian schools have been so decimated by liberalism and modernism as to render them equally dangerous to one's faith as a state university. In one sense, such schools are even more menacing to youthful faith because they are so insidious. The wicked men of ancient Judah were so intent on practicing evil that they were depicted as engaging therein with "both hands earnestly" (Micah 7:3). The prophet affirmed, "They all lie in wait for blood" (Micah 7:2).

The Bible departments of some of these schools are full of men who have sold their souls to the spirit of liberalism. They loathe the old paths. They view the ancient landmarks, meticulously laid in place by divine inspiration, as being stuffy, molded, and outdated. They arrogantly assert, "Behold, what a weariness is it" (Mal. 1:13). Wolves in sheep's clothing, they lie in wait to lay both hands on youthful minds in hopes of liberating them from the musty past and ushering them into the age of enlightenment.

Unwittingly, parents send their sons and daughters to such institutions, viewing them as safe havens for spiritual growth and development. Having not been forewarned and thus fortified against the assaults soon to be made upon their faith, they are slowly but surely reeled into the bosom of liberalism. Sometime later, while discussing the exclusiveness of Christianity with all of its attendant elements, the beloved fruit of the womb suddenly announces to the utter shock and dismay of the parents, "I no longer believe in those things."

Abortion is an evil so cataclysmic as to defy the combined languages of the world to depict its true nature. Abortion is man's declaring war on his own offspring. Abortion converts the womb into a bloody house of slaughter. Abortion is man's intruding into the workshop of God, extracting from His hands a work in progress (Ps. 139:13-15), and crushing out its life with tools of death. Abortion is man's inserting the poison of physical ruin into the veins of the innocent. As Manasseh "shed innocent blood very much till he had filled Jerusalem from one end to another" (2 Kings 21:16), even so, the streets of America run red with the blood of aborted babies. Abortion clinics are monuments to human depravity.

Liberalism is spiritual abortion. The Bible departments in Christian schools that have sold their souls to the spirit of liberalism have declared war with God's offspring. They transform youthful minds into playgrounds for error that will lead them down the path of eternal ruin. They bring to a tragic end a work of faith in progress. Obtrusively, they snatch from young minds divine truths that loving parents have worked diligently for the first quarter of their lives to instill. They insert the poison of liberalism into veins of faith. If abortion that brings physical death is a catastrophic evil, what must be the abortive power of liberalism that results in spiritual death? Is there anything more wicked than the destruction of faith built on a "thus saith God"? Professors in Bible departments who plant the destructive seeds of liberalism in youthful minds will face the "wrath of the Lamb" when time comes to its certain end (Rev. 6:16).

There are yet Bible professors in some of the Christian schools who love, revere, and teach the truth. Like those of old, these men would breathe their last breath in a martyr's death before they would compromise a single biblical truth. They would wish their voices to end in permanent silence before uttering a solitary syllable that would plant the slightest doubt in a young mind regarding the truth of God on any subject. They are acutely aware of their stewardship with regard to the young people under their influence. They have dedicated their very lives to reinforcing in youthful minds the tenets of New Testament Christianity that were taught by their parents and preachers and teachers in their home congregations. The eternal value of these honorable men to the cause of truth in today's environment cannot be exaggerated.

A Christian school with at least some men of this caliber offers an environment for spiritual growth and development and courtship opportunities with young men and women of like precious faith that constitutes another world from that to be found at a state university. The difference is literally immeasurable. A congregation in Tennessee conducted a study of one hundred thirty of their young people over a period of twenty-two years from 1976 to 1998. Out of the thirty-three who attended a state university, five had experienced divorce and only forty-five percent were faithful members of the church. Of the twenty-five who had attended a Christian school for at least two years, not a single one had tasted the bitter fruit of divorce and all twenty-five were faithful in their service to God. A similar study was conducted in a major state university of students from Christian homes from their freshmen to senior year. At the end thereof, only seven percent were faithful in their devotion to God and truth. A state university often proves to be a cemetery for youthful faith and concern for spiritual things.

Parents, looking for a safe spiritual educational environment for their sons and daughters, would be well advised to consider a Christian university, but to make a thorough investigation of the school under consideration. Some of these institutions have been so utterly consumed by the spirit of liberalism as to make them an adversary of a young person's faith. Others may have one, two, or several Bible professors that need to be marked and avoided (Rom. 16:17). Specific inquiries must be made in order to obtain sufficient information to make informative judgments for the spiritual welfare of one's son or daughter. There are occasions when no answer is all the answer one needs. Four letters to a Bible professor, from an avid supporter of a particular Christian school, seeking an answer to the question, "What are your convictions on marriage, divorce, and remarriage?" have been met with silence. His refusal to answer is itself an answer. Recent graduates or present students of a school are good sources of much-needed information. They generally know more about the overall spiritual status of the school than the individual instructors themselves. Moreover, they are candid. Employees of a school are often prone to withhold information or put a far better face on certain matters than the truth demands. If a young man or woman will select the right professors, the right friends, and the right congregation with which to worship, four years in a Christian school can make a positive impact of eternal significance upon their lives.

It is indeed a tragedy of immense proportions for such statements to have to be made, warnings given, and caution urged. There was a time in the not-too-distant past when such observations were wholly unnecessary. However, such are the sad and appalling consequences of the ruinous spirit of liberalism.

16

Liberalism and Marriage

Marriage is the foundational unit of society. It has its origin in the mind of God. God ordained it and regulates it. The heart of marriage beats smoothly when moving in harmony with divine instruction. The songs of marriage are melodic when the fingers of God's will are allowed to pluck the strings of man's spirit. The oneness of marriage is indestructible when the soul is in tune with divine directions. The happiness and success of marriage are assured when two hearts in unison exclaim, "Teach me, O Lord, the way of thy statutes; and I shall keep it unto the end" (Ps. 119:33).

God's will relative to matters essential to salvation are as clear and as easy to discern as the sun at high noon. Thus Paul said, "Wherefore, be ye not unwise, but understanding what the will of the Lord is" (Eph. 5:17). For centuries the seed of Abraham lived with misconceptions concerning the divine plan and relationship relative to God, Jews, and Gentiles; yet, Paul asserted that a simple reading of what God had revealed would suffice for a clear understanding thereof (Eph. 3:1-6).

Marriage is universal in its scope. It transcends racial, social, economic, and educational concerns. It embraces the literate and illiterate. Consequently, God has addressed the marital state in such a simple, elementary manner as to render foolish any rebuttal to its clarity.

Jesus set forth God's general law for marriage when He affirmed,

> Whosoever putteth away his wife, and marrieth another committeth adultery; and whosoever marrieth her that is put away from her husband committeth adultery (Luke 16:18).

To this agree the words of Paul,

> So then, if while her husband liveth, she be married to another man, she shall be called an adulteress; but if her husband be dead, she is free from that law; so that she is no adulteress, though she be married to another man (Rom. 7:3).

Therefore, the general formula for marriage is "divorce plus remarriage equals adultery."

However, to this general law, Jesus gave one exception:

> And I say unto you, whosoever shall put away his wife, except it be for fornication, and shall marry another, committeth adultery; and whoso marrieth her which is put away doth commit adultery (Matt. 19:9).

Thus, God's formula for marriage is "divorce, except for fornication, plus remarriage equals adultery." Therefore, all second marriages, following a divorce void of fornication and an innocent party, constitute a continual state of adultery relative to the sexual act. Paul described people who once "lived in fornication" and various other sins (Col. 3:5-7).

God's law for the marital state is strikingly simple. One who would argue against the clarity of Matthew 19:9 should have no difficulty understanding denominationalism's opposition to the simplicity of Mark 16:16. How can one conscientiously press for the acceptance of the obvious import of Mark 16:16 while refusing to acknowledge the same with regard to Matthew 19:9? The raging controversy over this matter is no more an argument against the lucidity of this text than is denominationalism's resistance to God's plan of salvation a legitimate case against the plainness thereof. If every man on earth were to raise his voice in unbelief regarding God's law for the one-flesh relationship, that would not change a thing. The problem is not understanding, the problem is acceptance.

Liberalism wants nothing to do with this subject. It is eager to apply its "no big deal" spirit to this aspect of biblical teaching. Liberalism views this whole matter with an air of impassiveness, intent on moving on to areas deemed more worthy of its time and attention. By such action liberalism undermines the principle of clarity that characterizes every fundamental tenet of biblical instruction. Matthew 19:9 and divine clarity are perfect compatible partners, and liberalism is the enemy of both.

The concept of divine stringency has never been in vogue with the masses. The permissive nature of man allows no room for a God who operates on the basis of law, restraint, and accountability. Maximizing grace and mercy to the near exclusion of holiness and justice has caused man to develop a casual attitude toward sin and a spirit of unbelief regarding divine rigidity and judgment. This disposition has invaded the church and presently serves as part of the basis for rejecting the exacting and universal nature of Matthew 19:9.

How strict is God? God is so strict that He barred the gate of Eden to Adam and Eve for eating a piece of forbidden fruit (Gen. 3); embraced Nadab and Abihu in fiery death for using unauthorized fire in worship (Lev. 10:1-2); commanded death by stoning to a man who gathered sticks on the sabbath (Num. 15); and denied Moses and Aaron entrance into Canaan for one act of rebellion (Num. 20).

God is so strict that He destroyed an entire family for a moment of covetousness (Josh. 7); wrapped Uzzah in the mantle of death for touching the ark of the covenant (2 Sam. 6); and deposited Ananias and Sapphira at the feet of Peter for lying (Acts 5). Divine stringency demands obedience to the one gospel (Gal. 1:8), membership in the one church (Acts 2), and faithful continuance in the one doctrine (2 John 9). A greater covenant with superior blessings and opportunities calls for weightier responsibilities and judgment. Consequently, "he that despised Moses' law died without mercy under two or three witnesses," but transgression under the law of Christ brings "sorer punishment" (Heb. 10:28-29). Grace and sternness are compatible principles.

Lax positions on the marriage issue that lift the restraining nature of law from the back of the masses, allow multiple reasons for marriages, and free both parties for future relationships are wholly inconsistent with the very nature of God. The concept of divine stringency demands the obvious import and universal application of Matthew 19:9 and kindred passages.

Liberalism and stringency are bitter enemies. Liberalism loathes stringency, branding it as narrow-minded, bigoted, legalistic, radical, and mean-spirited. Liberalism fears stringency, viewing it as a thief of its freedom. However, the stringent nature of the law of Christ governing the marital state is as natural and consistent with God's relationship with humanity from the sin of Genesis 3:6 to the final bestowal of grace in Revelation 22:21 as the closing of day with the darkness of night. Matthew 19:9 and divine stringency are perfect, compatible companions, and liberalism is the enemy of both.

God is independently, infinitely, and immutably holy. He sits upon the "throne of his holiness" (Ps. 47:8). He is of "purer eyes than to behold evil and cannot look on iniquity" (Hab. 1:13). Isaiah pictures the seraphim's flying about the throne of God crying, "Holy, holy, holy, is the Lord of hosts" (Isa. 6:3). God is absolute holiness. Not even the shadow of sin can dwell in His presence.

One of man's basic errors is the formation of God in human likeness. Man has attempted to pare God down to his own level. In essence, man has formed his own god, which feels and thinks just like he does. God's goodness and longsuffering are designed to provoke repentance (Rom. 2:4). However, while enjoying these traits of the divine nature during the practice of sin, some have confused them with the humanizing of deity. Having depicted His forbearance with man while on a course of sin, God exposed man's self-drawn conclusion saying, "Thou thoughtest that I was altogether such an one as thyself" (Ps. 50:21).

Certain physical substances appear fuzzy when viewed with the natural eye, but when seen through a microscope, their true nature becomes readily apparent. Even so, one of the most effective means of discerning error is through the disclosing power of the nature of God. Every fundamental religious error can be verified as such when viewed through the microscope of God's nature. By contrasting humanly devised doctrines with the character of God, one can easily perceive the error in the creative works of the human mind. This is true even of the new convert who does not yet possess the ability to produce specific passages exposing a particular error, or of a mature Christian who is unable to answer all the arguments made regarding a difficult passage at a given time.

Consider the well-worn doctrine of salvation by faith alone. This doctrine, while emphasizing God's grace, nullifies the concept of God's holiness. Advocates thereof have a one-sided perception of God. Grace is viewed as a panacea for man's ills apart from human response. During a fleeting moment, John Doe utters a profession of faith in God's existence and the deity of Christ. He proceeds to live a life of debauchery, and at death leaves behind a body ravaged by long years of sin, only to have some preacher attempt to secure his soul in the heavenly abode. Such a doctrine is blatantly inconsistent with the holiness of God.

The impossibility of apostasy dogma is equally offensive to God's nature. Consistency demands the position that one could die in the very bosom of the most vile sin known to man and immediately be bidden into that eternal realm of perfection by the outstretched arm of the Holy One Himself. Attempting to nullify biblical teaching on this subject, one preacher affirmed that he could not be lost even if he were swinging over the fires of hell on a "rotten potato vine, spitting tobacco juice in the devil's eye." This contemptible doctrine makes a mockery of the holiness of God. The Calvinistic concept of unconditional predestination and election is easily perceived by the unprejudiced mind as being utterly incompatible with the very essence of deity. Biblical scholarship is not a prerequisite for discerning the obvious contradictions between this tenet and God's holiness, love, mercy, and justice.

The premillennial theory has many defenders, but no defense. Though the novice might experience some difficulty contending for the faith relative to the specifics thereof, the basic incongruity between this doctrinal product of the finite mind and the nature of God is easily discernable. The mentality of the Judaizer has been resurrected in the premillennialist with his physical temple, kingdom, throne, and reign. This materialistic thrust is patently inconsistent with the spiritual nature of God.

Applying this same principle to the many and diverse errors presently being promulgated on the crucial matter of marriage and divorce aids immensely in discerning their erroneous nature. Every position that seeks to negate the obvious import of Matthew 19:9 and kindred passages is at variance with the holiness of God. Moreover, it is acutely antagonistic to God's attitude toward divorce and the necessity of holiness on man's part, both of which ensue from the holiness of God. Divine revelation and divine holiness are indubitably consistent. Any doctrine that is contradictory to the holiness of God is a false doctrine.

Illustrative of the many errors being taught on this subject is the limitation of God's law to marital relationships in which both partners are Christians. This is one of the most loathsome theories ever expounded within the confines of New Testament Christianity. This spurious theory confines Matthew 19:9 to covenant people—those who have submitted to the gospel and are in covenant relationship with God. Some even restrict this text to the covenant marriages of the Old Testament, thus totally removing Matthew 19:9 from the New Testament world.

This theory encourages the very thing God hates. "For the Lord, the God of Israel saith that he hateth putting away"

(Mal. 2:16). Indisputably, God hates divorce! The world's population stands at six billion. Of this number, a microscopic portion are Christians. Smaller still is the number of marriages in which both partners share in the faith of the gospel. Is it conceivable that our holy God who hates divorce would leave the teeming masses of humanity in pagan darkness severed from the restraining power of law to govern their sexual relationships? Are we to conclude that by divine design, the non-covenant world is allowed to wallow in the pit of sexual indulgence with as many partners as they wish until they submit to the gospel? By His permissive will in the absence of law, would not God be encouraging animalistic sexual behavior among His own offspring?

Consider the man whose daughter is married to a non Christian. Certain problems arise that threaten to dissolve their conjugal union. The concerned father who holds to the "non-covenant" theory approaches them with fervent hope of granting aid that would save their marriage. What is he going to say to them? On what basis will he plead for them to remain together, work through their problems, and expend the effort necessary to stymie Satan's attempt to "part asunder what God hath joined together"? He cannot refer to God's law for marriage, for he does not believe they are amenable to such law. Is it not obvious that his philosophy renders him impotent? His position on this vital matter will not allow him to make use of the most powerful means at his disposal to exhort his own daughter's faithfulness to her wedding vows.

We read much about grace, love, law, and obedience as though the principles were at war. Wherein lies the problem? Webster defines *law* as a "rule of conduct." Divine law is an expression of divine grace and love. The presence of God's law constitutes the basis for man to manifest his love for God. "If ye love me, keep my commandments" (John 14:15). Man's loving compliance with God's will is God's way of enabling man to appropriate to his life the rich provisions of grace and love.

The existence of law is God's way of saying, "I love you." Parents relate to their children on this same basis. Therefore, as an expression of love, they set in place certain laws—rules of conduct—as deterrents for behavior that would infuse their lives with grief and shame. In like manner, the stringent nature of Matthew 19:9 is God's way of preventing a mountain of woes from entering the marital state, thus aiding man in developing an intimate marital relationship, tightly bound by the strong cords of love, trust, and mutual respect.

As a consequence, the reality of divine law's governing the marital state is a manifestation of God's grace, love, and deep concern for those who become one flesh. Man's submission to God's laws results in holiness, the separateness from the very sins that could destroy the one-flesh relationship and man's enjoyment of the rich blessings of that most sacred state.

Are such expressions of divine grace, love, and concern denied to the inconceivable masses of humanity outside the church? Is God indifferent to their fidelity in marriage? Have they been left without rules of conduct to govern their sexual behavior? In the absence of law, according to this theory, have they not been encouraged in their wanton, lewd, and self-indulgent conduct? Can two non-covenant people marry and divorce multiple times with impunity? Can a Christian marry and divorce as many non-Christian partners as he desires until he finally enters a marital union with another Christian? Who can believe such foolishness? Yet, such is the inevitable result of the repugnant doctrine that would limit God's law to those marriages in which both partners are Christians.

This humanly devised doctrine is an odious affront to the holiness of God. It is as incompatible with the nature of God and as easily discernible as such as is the Calvinistic view of predestination and election or the impossibility of apostasy. This matter could not be more serious. This is not an ivory-tower theological debate on some abstract principle. It has eternal implications involving the souls of men and the purity and unity of the church. The principle of God's holiness is overwhelming evidence for the fallacious nature of this doctrine and those in kinship therewith and for the universal application of Matthew 19:9 and kindred passages.

Moreover, this execrable theory crumbles at the footstool of Matthew 28:18-20. Possessing all authority, Jesus utilized two present-tense participles, *baptizing* and *teaching,* in order to press the manner in which disciples are made. Disciples are made by submitting to the gospel, culminating in the act of baptism. In addition, disciples are made by complying with all things commanded by Christ, hence embracing the entirety of the teaching or doctrine of Christ set forth in the New Testament. In spite of the intense efforts of some brethren to remove it, Matthew 19:9 yet remains among the teachings of Christ. It is one of the truths by which disciples are made. Can a man be a disciple of Christ while rejecting Mark 16:16? No more than he can be a disciple of Christ while rejecting Matthew 19:9. Both constitute teachings of Christ by which disciples are made. Tampering with the teachings of Jesus Christ on any subject is an immense evil.

Liberalism is intent on modifying God's marriage laws in order to accommodate the massive number of divorces that characterize modern society. Liberalism is determined to include, not exclude. God's holiness, hatred of divorce, and love for man erects a barrier (Matt. 19:9) to keep marriages intact, promote sexual restraint, and warn of severe consequences for non-compliance. Discarding the barrier, liberalism breaks the shackles of sexual constraint, converts consequences into rights, ravages the sacred intimacy and oneness of marriage, and tramples upon the holiness of God. God's holiness, hatred of divorce, and love for man provides a law (Matt. 19:9) to promote holiness in marriage and prevent divorce. Liberalism removes the law and opens the door for sexual infidelity which nullifies holiness and fosters divorce. Matthew 19:9 and the holiness of God are perfect companions, and liberalism is the enemy of both.

What is Matthew 19:9? It is grace at work. It is grace's moving in man's best interest. It is grace's seeking to preserve marriage. It is grace's illustrating God's holiness and demand for holiness in man and marriage (1 Pet. 1:15-16). It is grace's training man's mind to understand the oneness and marvelous intimacy in God's spiritual marriage between each member and Christ (2 Cor. 11:2; Eph. 5:22-33).

Matthew 19:9 is grace "teaching us that denying ungodliness and worldly lusts, we should live soberly, righteously, and godly in this present world" (Titus 2:11-12). By divine design, there is nothing more characteristic of this present world than marriage. In contrast, there is nothing more typical of ungodliness and worldly lusts and more hostile to soberness, righteousness, and godliness than fornication, the very thing that Matthew 19:9 is endeavoring to prevent. Matthew 19:9 and grace are perfect companions, and liberalism is the enemy of both.

What is Matthew 19:9? It is love at work. "God is love" (1 John 4:8). Man's very existence is a manifestation of God's love. God created man in order that he might serve as the object of His love. God's love for man is deep and unfathomable. Between dew drops and Calvary lie a thousand expressions of God's love for man.

Marriage is a divine institution. God designed the marital state for man's happiness and well-being. The Bible constitutes God's pattern for conjugal joy and contentment. The degree of gratification attained by any married couple is directly proportionate to the degree of submission that they give to the principles of the Bible.

Therefore, Matthew 19:9 is an expression of God's love for those who have chosen to enter the marital state. It is love's promoting purity in marriage. It is love's putting a padlock on the door of the home. It is love's binding together in marriage one man and one woman until death. It is love's closing trust in and suspicion out. It is love's giving man a thousand reasons to ponder seriously the one-flesh relationship. It is God's love affirming to man, "I hate divorce." Matthew 19:9

and divine love are perfect companions, and liberalism is the enemy of both.

What is Matthew 19:9? It is a divine safeguard around the home. It is a potential impenetrable wall around marriage, constructed by God's grace and love in an effort to prevent the entrance of a third party. A man whose mind is tightly bound by the stringent nature of Matthew 19:9 will go a million miles in mental thought before allowing a third party to enter his home and destroy the love, trust, peace, joy, and contentment characteristic of marriage as fashioned by God.

There is no sin known to man with greater power for totally undermining the very foundation of the home than the sin of fornication. As contrasted with other sins, fornication is unequaled in its destructive impact upon marriage, upon the person of the guilty party, and upon the totality of man's being. "Every sin that a man doeth is without the body, but he that committeth fornication sinneth against his own body" (1 Cor. 6:18). This text affirms two great truths. First, relative to origin, sin is without—outside, not pertaining to—the body. Sin proceeds from the heart or mind. The body is merely a conduit through which the overt act of sin is committed (Rom. 6:13). Jesus confirmed this truth when He said,

> But those things which proceed out of the mouth come forth from the heart, and they defile the man. For out of the heart proceed evil thoughts, murders, adulteries, fornication, thefts, false witness, blasphemies (Matt. 15:18-19).

Second, fornication has a peculiar impact upon the body. Though various sins injure the body, fornication maims the body in a way characteristic of no other sin. This truth possesses an unfathomable depth. There is something mysteriously wonderful and incomprehensible about the one-flesh relationship in the marital state. Conversely, there is something uniquely injurious about the sin that severs that relationship.

This truth is observable even in the attitude of nonreligious people. It is quite common to hear people, wholly devoid of religious inclinations, state their willingness to endure almost any kind of conduct on the part of their mate with the single exception of sexual unfaithfulness. This is the proverbial straw that broke the camel's back for many people in unhappy and abusive marital relationships. Unknowingly, these secular dominated people are expressing their agreement with the very truth announced by an inspired apostle. This passage also sheds much light on Matthew 19:9. It provides insight into why Jesus specified fornication as the single exception to the general rule of second marriages subsequent to a divorce constituting adulterous relationships.

This divine truth also supplies some of the answers to the question as to why David could be so susceptible to the temptation to commit adultery with Bathsheba when he had numerous wives and concubines readily available to assuage his physical needs. The stringent, singular, exclusive nature of the marriage bond set forth in Genesis 2 and mirrored in Matthew 19:9 points to the core and essence of human sexuality. There is a profundity to this matter that greatly exceeds man's comprehensive powers. The very nature of the marital state as designed by God and the exacting laws governing that state are intended to keep sexual desire and expression in a state of confinement. Sexual activity external to marriage as ordained by God strikes a telling blow to the very center of man's sexual being. It goes to the heart of man's physical being and afflicts it in a distinctive and damaging manner. It weakens the very structure of man's sexual nature. Consequently, when David multiplied wives, he tampered with God's arrangement for marriage and so diluted his own sexual nature as to open the door for the act of adultery with the wife of Uriah.

Matthew 19:9 is a harbor of safety for man's sexual being. God designed this harbor to preserve the sanctity of marriage and to shield man from the turbulent sea of sexual sin. When a man leaves this refuge, he enters a world at war with his innermost self. When passion is spent and spiritual sanity is regained, his heart will lay shattered at his feet. The way home to forgiveness and spiritual wholeness is as certain as the promises of God, but the scars will follow him to his grave. Putting the mental and emotional pieces back together again is a long and arduous process.

Therefore, Matthew 19:9 is divine grace and love's working in man's best interest, endeavoring to prevent the severance of the one-flesh relationship by the entrance of a third party. It is God's protectorate of the home. Only a man and a woman bound by God have a right to the marital bed. When a third party intrudes into that realm, he does so as an alien. He has no right to be there. The inflexible nature of Matthew 19:9 with its severe consequences for non-compliance is designed to prevent that very thing from becoming a reality.

Matthew 19:9 is a friend of marriage, not an enemy. Efforts designed to either limit or eliminate this text have thus depicted it as an adversary of marriage instead of an ally. Such attempts compel one to view this divine law governing the marital state as the worst statement Jesus could ever have made concerning marriage. Liberalism in the church wants Matthew 19:9 and kindred passages removed from God's plan for marriage just as liberalism in denominationalism wants Mark 16:16 and kindred passages extracted from God's plan of salvation. Both constitute blatant intrusions into the exclusive realm of divine legislation where no man has a right to be, and both shall answer in the judgment for their follies.

The Pharisees borrowed the mind of liberalism in their effort to tempt and entrap Jesus concerning God's pattern for marriage. "Is it lawful for a man to put away his wife for every cause?" (Matt. 19:3). Liberalism answers in the affirmative. Liberalism demands a broad playing field, enabling its adherents to run with abandonment, carrying the ball of self-will. Liberalism abhors law that prevents, but delights in law that permits. It detests law that forbids, but revels in law that grants unfettered freedom to fleshly desire. Every effort to restrict or nullify the obvious truth of Matthew 19:9 is an act of concurrence to the question the Pharisees posed to Christ.

"Why did Moses then command to give a writing of divorcement and put her away?" (Matt. 19:7). Liberalism loves the looseness of Moses' era relative to marriage and divorce and demands a continuance thereof in the era of Christ. "Moses because of the hardness of your hearts suffered you to put away your wives" (Matt. 19:8). Liberalism's insistence on rendering invalid the stringency of Matthew 19:9 and opening the door to multiple sexual partners has identified itself with the unsavory disposition of hardness of heart.

Twice in this brief debate Jesus made reference to God's original pattern of marriage "from the beginning." Jesus pointed to the first marriage and affirmed God's cogent will for it and all subsequent marriages, "Wherefore they are no more twain, but one flesh. What therefore God hath joined together, let not man put asunder" (Matt. 19:6). God's prototype for the marital state was exceedingly stringent. It called for one man and one woman until death. Divorce and remarriage were as foreign to God's original plan for the home as sin is to righteousness. However, in view of man's stubborn spirit, God saw fit to relax His will for the marital state under Moses. This period of relaxation was not a part of God's original design for marriage. It was identical to the circumstances of 1 Samuel 8. God did not want a king in Israel, and God did not want divorce in marriage. However, respecting man's free will, He allowed both. Tragically, the Israelites suffered severe consequences for their hardness of heart in the nation and in the home.

What is Matthew 19:9? It is a divine commentary on God's original intent for all marriages for all time as enunciated in Genesis 2:21-24. The significance of this truth cannot be overstated. What is the restoration plea relative to New Testament Christianity? It is an adjuration to go back behind denominationalism and Catholicism and restore the one church that Jesus said, "I will build" (Matt. 16:18), which is the product of the one gospel that commenced on Pentecost of Acts 2.

What is Matthew 19:9? It is a move backward in order to go forward with God's original design for marriage. It is a move back behind the "hardness of heart" of Moses' era in order to restore God's original pattern for marriage and the home. Therefore, any attempt to eradicate, limit, or modify Matthew 19:9 constitutes human tampering with God's blueprint for marriage "from the beginning." Matthew 19:9 and God's original plan for the marital state are perfect companions, and liberalism is the enemy of both.

Liberalism's workshop boasts of many models for wedlock. Having no trembling spirit, liberalism thrusts itself into that exclusive legislative realm and proceeds to dismantle God's pattern for matrimony and constructs one of its own. Liberalism's assault on God's plan for marriage constitutes an impeachment of God. It undermines the holiness of God from which ensues the very laws intended to promote holiness in the conjugal state. Liberalism's spurious models for marriage negate God's grace and love in providing stringent rules for regulating and thus safeguarding the home. Moreover, they open the door to marital infidelity, hence the crippling of man's sexual nature. God hates divorce (Mal. 2:16). Tragically, the fallacious theories of liberalism encourage the very thing God hates. Indeed, the spirit of liberalism is an enemy of marriage as designed by God.

17

Liberalism and the Role of Women

The power of women in every area of life for either good or evil defies depiction. Efforts to characterize the powerful influence of women in the world fall far short of reality. The proverb, "the hand that rocks the cradle rules the world," is not an exaggeration. From the very beginning of time, though often unnamed and out of public sight, women have played a major role in the events that have shaped human history. There is nothing more lovely than a woman robed in the beauty of holiness. Conversely, there is no sight more repulsive than a woman devoted to evil.

Genesis 4:16 avers, "And Cain went out from the presence of the Lord." When Cain left God's presence, he commenced a line of profane people who, partaking of his nature, totally corrupted the course of humanity. In describing Cain's descendants, Genesis 4:17-24 points to their absolute secular and materialistic nature. Totally lacking spirituality, they were wholly committed to the affairs of the flesh. Lamech is illustrative of Cain's descendants. He violated God's pattern for the home, the basic unit of society, by taking two wives. Furthermore, he boasted of his violent nature.

Genesis 4:25 introduces the righteous lineage of Seth. When Seth's son, Enos, was born, in striking contrast to Cain and his descendants, inspiration affirms, "Then began men to call upon the name of the Lord" (Gen. 4:26). Seth's descendants came into God's presence for worship and fellowship.

Genesis 5 is a record of the righteous descendants of Seth.
Enoch and Noah serve to illustrate the kind of people who
came from the loins of Seth. Tragically,

> when men began to multiply on the face of the earth, and
> daughters were born unto them, that the sons of God saw the
> daughters of men that they were fair, and they took them wives
> of all which they chose (Gen. 6:1-2).

The unbroken flow of the context makes it clear that the *sons
of God* were the righteous descendants of Seth and the *daughters of men* were the unrighteous descendants of Cain. Consequently, the disastrous state of humanity related in Genesis
6:5, that made inevitable the judgment of God in the flood,
was the direct result of the overwhelming influence of the
women in Cain's lineage upon the men in the progeny of Seth.
With the exception of eight people, they devastated the righteous descendants of Seth. If this incident had no companions, it alone would be sufficient testimony regarding the
enormous power wielded by women.

Balaam coveted the wealth and honor offered by Balak,
king of Moab, as rewards for cursing Israel (Num. 22). Peter
said he "loved the wages of unrighteousness" (2 Pet. 2:15).
However, three attempts later, unable to "curse whom God
had not cursed" (Num. 23:8), "Balaam rose up and went and
returned to his place" (Num. 24:25). Lamentably, the story
does not end there. Balaam knew well the extraordinary influence that women could exert upon men. Therefore, he "taught
Balak to cast a stumbling block before the children of Israel,
to eat things sacrificed unto idols, and to commit fornication"
(Rev. 2:14). Balaam counseled Balak to have the women of
Moab to entice the men of Israel to come to their beds and
then to their idols, knowing that such conduct would call for
the judgment of God.

> The people began to commit whoredom with the daughters of
> Moab. And they called the people unto the sacrifices of their
> gods, and the people did eat and bowed down to their gods
> (Num. 25:1-2).

The result was calamitous. "And those that died in the plague were twenty and four thousand" (Num. 25:9).

Solomon was the wisest man the world has ever known except for Jesus Christ. His name is synonymous with wisdom. He is as "wise as Solomon" is a proverbial sentiment often heard on the lips of even non-religious people. As is characteristic of humanity, the stories of Solomon's wisdom, wealth, and greatness surely had been exaggerated many times by the time they reached the ears of the queen of Sheba. But still the text reads,

> And she said to the king, It was a true report that I heard in mine own land of thy acts and thy wisdom. Howbeit I believed not the words, until I came, and mine eyes had seen it; and behold, the half was not told me; thy wisdom and prosperity exceedeth the fame which I heard (1 Kings 10:6-7).

In addition, Solomon was a deeply spiritual man. His vigilance in implementing the exacting nature of God's pattern for the temple embracing the seven years of its construction and his prayer and subsequent statements at the dedication of the temple bear witness to Solomon's great love for God, concern for His truth, and spirit of humility (1 Kings 6-8). One would tend to view such a man as almost beyond the reach of the influence of women bent on evil. Sadly, however, "it came to pass, when Solomon was old, that his wives turned away his heart after other gods" (1 Kings 11:4). The words of Nehemiah 13:26 are noteworthy: "even him" did pagan women cause to sin.

Jereboam corrupted God's pattern of worship for the northern kingdom of Israel and positioned the nation on the road to ruin (1 Kings 12). Jereboam's action paved the way for the second great departure from God by the kingdom of Israel. Ahab took up where Jereboam left off and introduced the worship of Baal into the religious life of Israel (1 Kings 16:31-32). Inspiration asserts that "Ahab did more to provoke the Lord God of Israel to anger than all the kings of Israel that were before him" (1 Kings 16:33). What drove Ahab to such excess of iniquity? "But there was none like unto Ahab, which did sell himself to work wickedness in the sight of the Lord, whom Jezebel his wife stirred up" (1 Kings 21:25).

Josiah was the last righteous king to reign over Judah. In the thirteenth year of his reign, God called Jeremiah to commence his "repent or perish" theme to the nation. Jeremiah was forbidden to marry, attend funerals, or engage in occasions of festivity (Jer. 16:1-9). His very life was symbolic of the spiritual condition of the nation and the approaching judgment, barring swift national penitence. Four decades later, the prophet's worst fears became realities as the hammer of divine judgment shattered the nation of Judah and the people were carried into Babylonian captivity.

However, a remnant of the survivors migrated into Egypt. With the screams of death yet ringing in their ears and the smoldering ashes of Jerusalem yet lingering in their nostrils, they persisted in the very idolatry that had called for God's judgment upon the nation. Jeremiah raised his voice and made one final plea for a return to God (Jer. 44:1-14).

> Then all the men which knew that their wives had burned incense unto other gods, and all the women that stood by, a great multitude, even all the people that dwelt in the land of Egypt, in Pathros, answered Jeremiah saying, As for the word that thou hast spoken unto us in the name of the Lord, we will not hearken unto thee. But we will certainly do whatsoever thing goeth forth out of our own mouth, to burn incense unto the queen of heaven, and to pour out drink offerings unto her, as we have done, we and our fathers, our kings and our princes, in the cities of Judah, and in the streets of Jerusalem; for then had we plenty of victuals, and were well and saw no evil (Jer. 44:15-17).

The wives and mothers of Judah played a major role in the spiritual deterioration of the nation that culminated in the judgment of God.

Paul preached a powerful gospel sermon in Antioch of Pisidia (Acts 13). He began with the exodus from Egypt and closed with a quotation from Habakkuk 1:5 as an exhortation for his audience to submit to the gospel. Interest in the gospel was so great that the following sabbath day witnessed a major portion of the city, assembling to hear the Word of God.

> But the Jews stirred up the devout and honorable women, and the chief men of the city, and raised persecution against Paul and Barnabas, and expelled them out of their coasts (Acts 13:50).

There can be no doubt but that women were integrally involved in efforts to impede the spread of the gospel over the first-century world. Moreover, the church at Corinth was afflicted by women in rebellion against the principle of authority (1 Cor. 11:1-16) and women's acting inappropriately in the worship assembly (1 Cor. 14:34-35). Two women were disrupting the peace and unity of the church at Philippi (Phil. 4:2), and the single criticism of the church at Thyatira focused on a woman whose character was akin to the world of heathenism (Rev. 2:20-23). The power of women to disturb, harm, and destroy is indeed great.

In a world of indescribable debauchery, eight people found grace in the eyes of the Lord (Gen. 6). These eight people were all part of one family, and four of them were women. Hence, four righteous women played a critical role in God's preservation of the human race. Understandably, as head of the family, the biblical record concentrates on the faith of Noah. But who would argue with the assertion that the faith of Noah's wife was equally great? Noah was a "preacher of righteousness" (2 Pet. 2:5). For over a century, while constructing the ark, he preached to a world whose appetite for sin was unquenchable. If a single person was converted under Noah's preaching, he died prior to the flood. Who cannot point to some preacher who vacated the pulpit under far less discouraging circumstances? There can be no doubt but that Noah would have been the first to admit that his accomplishments by God's good grace were due in large measure to the continual help and encouragement of his devoted wife.

The period of the judges was a sad time in the history of Israel. Twice the divine record states, "In those days there was no king in Israel; every man did that which was right in his own eyes" (Judg. 17:6; 21:25). Israel needed great spiritual leaders. Samuel filled that need. Relative to his personal righteousness, Samuel was above reproach. When he placed himself before the people and invited any justified criticism, the people confirmed his record of spotless integrity (1 Sam. 12:1-5). Samuel exerted a tremendous influence for good on the nation of Israel.

However, there would never have been a Samuel had there not been a Hannah. Hannah had been barren for years. She was an object of ceaseless ridicule because of her infertile state (1 Sam. 1:6-7). Fervent prayer enjoyed its desired end, and Hannah was blessed with Samuel. Several years later, in fulfillment of her vow, Hannah returned Samuel to the Lord (1 Sam. 1:10-28). How difficult was it for Hannah to implement her vow? Only a parent can answer that question. Samuel was a mother's gift to the nation of Israel. What greater gift could she have given? Had she suffered a martyr's death, her influence for the cause of truth and righteousness would not have been as great as that exerted through the life of Samuel. Hannah made an immense contribution to the spiritual life of Israel through the unexcelled gift of her son.

Nabal was a man of great wealth but totally lacking in character. His own wife described him as a "man of Belial" (1 Sam. 25:25). As Nabal's servants watched over his flocks in the fields, David's men were a protective wall about them. David commissioned ten of his men to go to Nabal in hopes that he would extend a helping hand in his time of need. Nabal reviled David and sent his men away empty-handed. David ordered four hundred of his men to prepare for battle and stated his intentions of killing every male in Nabal's household and workforce. Having been informed of Nabal's conduct, Abigail his wife prepared provisions to fulfill David's need, reached David before he could consummate his objective, and reasoned with him regarding the ill-advised nature of his course. David expressed gratitude to God for His providential intervention, praised Abigail for her wise counsel, received the gifts from her hand, and returned to his place of abode.

Inspiration describes Abigail as a "woman of good understanding, and of a beautiful countenance" (1 Sam. 25:3). Many lives were saved, homes preserved, wives spared the loss of their husbands, and children their fathers because of the action of this godly, insightful, and wise woman. Also, David was averted from shedding innocent blood, an act of personal vengeance in a moment of unrestrained anger, therefore carrying the guilt of a temporary lapse of self-control to his grave. The times in the course of human history are innumerable in which devout and discerning women have saved men from themselves.

Ahab and Jezebel's influence on the northern kingdom of Israel was disastrous. Unfortunately, their influence was not limited to Israel. Their daughter, Athaliah, was married to Jehoram, king of Judah. When Jehoram ascended to the throne of the southern kingdom, the record affirms, "And he walked in the way of the kings of Israel, as did the house of Ahab; for the daughter of Ahab was his wife; and he did evil in the sight of the Lord" (2 Kings 8:18). The time had arrived for God's judgment to befall the house of Ahab. Jehu, one of the military officers of Israel, was designated to take the lead in the extermination of Ahab's descendants. God said, "For the whole house of Ahab shall perish" (2 Kings 9:8). Having slain Jehoram, king of Israel, he then ordered the death of Ahaziah, king of Judah, the grandson of Ahab and Jezebel. "So Jehu slew all that remained of the house of Ahab in Jezreel, and all his great men, and his priests, until he left him none remaining" (2 Kings 10:11).

"And when Athaliah the mother of Ahaziah saw that her son was dead, she arose and destroyed all the seed royal" (2 Kings 11:1). Athaliah's savagery included her own grandchildren. Had Athaliah succeeded in destroying David's descendants, there would have been no "Jesus Christ our Lord,

which was made of the seed of David according to the flesh"
(Rom. 1:3), hence no spiritual king on David's throne (Acts
2:29-30). As a result, God's plan to redeem the world by the
"seed of woman" (Gen. 3:15), the "seed of Abraham" (Gen. 12:3),
and the "seed of David" would have been thwarted by the
action of one evil woman.

> But Jehosheba, the daughter of king Joram, sister of Ahaziah,
> took Joash the son of Ahaziah and stole him from among the
> king's sons which were slain; and they hid him, even him and
> his nurse, in the bedchamber from Athaliah, so that he was
> not slain (2 Kings 11:2).

Jehosheba risked her own life in order to save the remaining
son of David's lineage. That risk embraced six long years
(2 Kings 11:3). Athaliah had the power of the throne of Judah
at her disposal, but that was no match for the power of the
throne of Heaven in the hand of godly Jehosheba. The scheme
of redemption was hanging on the life of one baby. God preserved that life and the ancestral line through which His Son
would come by use of a woman. There is immense power in
the influence of one godly woman walking with God.

> And all the king's servants, that were in the king's gate, bowed
> and reverenced Haman, for the king had so commanded con-
> cerning him. But Mordecai bowed not, nor did him reverence
> (Esther 3:2).

Mordecai's conduct provoked Haman to make plans for the
annihilation of the Jewish race (Esther 3:6). Execution of his
scheme would have abrogated God's blueprint for human
redemption through the "seed of Abraham" (Gen. 12:3; Gal.
3:16). However, Esther had indeed "come to the kingdom for
such a time as this" (Esther 4:14). With the "it has begun"
problem of sin of Genesis 3:6, the "it is finished" of John 19:30
was inevitable. The book of Esther is God's announcement to
the world of His intention to reach Calvary and of the futility
of the efforts of the Hamans of the world to frustrate that
purpose. Esther played an integral part in the continuation
of God's plan to redeem man from sin.

In the words of Hebrews 11:32, "Time would fail me to tell of" Sarah who through faith "received strength to conceive seed, and was delivered of a child when she was past age, because she judged him faithful who had promised" (Heb. 11:11); Deborah, who was a "mother in Israel" (Judg. 5:7); Jael, who slew the enemy of Israel (Judg. 5:24-27); the widow of Zarapheth, whose faith superceded that of the widows in Israel (Luke 4:25-26); the woman of Shunem who provided for the prophet of God (2 Kings 4:8-10); the little Jewish maid who initiated the cleansing and conversion of Naaman (2 Kings 5:2-4); Mary, "of whom was born Jesus, who is called Christ" (Matt. 1:16); Anna, who "departed not from the temple, but served God with fastings and prayers night and day" (Luke 2:37); the women who were last at the cross and first at the grave; Priscilla, who helped teach Apollos the way of God more perfectly (Acts 19:26); Phoebe, "a servant of the church which is at Cenchrea" (Rom. 16:1); and Persis, who "labored much in the Lord" (Rom. 16:12). From time's inception, godly women have made a monumental contribution to the cause of God, truth, and right.

However, as powerful as a woman's influence is in teaching, work, worship, and service, she is to operate within a submissive framework. "But I suffer not a woman to teach, nor to usurp authority over the man, but to be in silence" (1 Tim. 2:12). The term *nor (oude)* is explicative in nature. Women are commanded to teach (Titus 2:3-4). Priscilla assisted Aquila in teaching Apollos (Acts 18:26). Consequently, rather than issuing a blanket prohibition against teaching, Paul proceeds to explain the kind of teaching forbidden to a woman—that kind of teaching that would place her in a position of authority or dominion over a man.

It is apparent that just one thing is forbidden in this passage: "a woman exercising authority over a man." It is not teaching per se that is disallowed, but only that kind of teaching that would place her in a dominant position over a man. Paul could have enumerated a number of other activities, but his primary point would still have been that in regard to those things specified, as well as all others, a woman is not to employ her talents in a position of authority over man.

Far from a cultural matter, Paul undergirds this divine truth regarding woman's submissive role by reaching back to the beginning and pointing to the order of creation and Eve's deception by Satan (1 Tim. 2:13-14). Therefore, it has never been God's will for woman to occupy an authoritative position over man. First Timothy 2:12 is merely an extension of a law that God set in motion at the very beginning. Even before her transgression, Eve's role was submissive in nature. Eve was created as a helpmeet for Adam, not Adam for Eve (Gen. 2:18). Woman is the glory of the man; she is of man, and she was created for man (1 Cor. 11:7-9). Paul describes man as the image and glory of God and woman as the glory of man (1 Cor. 11:7).

Paul is not affirming that only the man bears the image of God, for God created both man and woman in His own image. However, there is a sense in which man reflects the image and glory of God, and the woman does not. Man reflects God's image as a ruler, as one in authority. This the woman does not and cannot do. In the beginning, God designed woman to fill a subordinate role to man, and any effort on her part to exert dominion over man is a usurpation of divinely bestowed authority; an act of rebellion.

Regarding positions of leadership, dominion, or authority, God has always selected men over women. In the beginning, God created man first and set him in dominion over woman. When God destroyed the world and began anew, He chose a man to fill the role of a leader. Throughout the Patriarchal Age, God picked men to fill the leadership role. The heads of the twelve tribes of Israel were all men. Following years of slavery, God chose the man Moses to deliver His people from Egypt. During the centuries between the death of Joshua and the reign of Saul, God selected various individuals to serve as deliverers and judges of Israel. Every choice was a man save

Deborah, a choice which arose out of necessity due to man's failure to fulfill his responsibility (Judg. 4:8).

When Israel rejected God's rule, God selected the man Saul as king, the first of thirty-eight, with Athaliah the usurper as the only exception. Though not personally selecting every king, God set in motion a system bringing men to the throne. As Israel and Judah would lapse into sin, God commissioned men as prophets to herald divine messages to His people. Women like Huldah (2 Kings 22), who did function as prophetesses, did so in a quiet and subordinate manner without violating God's will.

Following four hundred years of prophetic silence, God chose the man, John the Baptist, to serve as a forerunner for His Son. Christ chose twelve apostles, all men, to function in a relationship with Himself and the church enjoyed by no others. The seven special servants of Acts 6 were all men. Their work involved authority. Concerning their selection, the apostles said, "Whom we appoint over this business" (Acts 6:3). By divine direction, only men can serve as elders and deacons in the church. The Bible itself is the work of God by means of the pen of man. The principle enunciated in 1 Timothy 2:12 is testified to throughout the entirety of the biblical record.

The universe and all things therein were made according to design. The sun was fashioned to rule the day and the moon to govern the night. If man possessed the ability to tamper with the heavenly bodies as he has with every aspect of biblical teaching, he would have destroyed the earth and himself long ago. However, being forever removed from man's intrusive nature, the monarchs of earth's day and night perform their duties in perfect harmony with God's design. Though sharing similarities, man and woman are as different as the sun and moon. Externally and internally, the physical distinctions are vast and complex. Equally so are the psychological and emotional differences. They do not think alike.

They do not feel alike. Relative to the same matter, they are often poles apart in their thinking or feeling.

God designed the woman to serve Him and humanity in a subordinate role. Her very essence as fashioned by God befits her for this duty. By nature, woman is more delicate, sensitive, gentle, and emotional than man. These are not traits of weakness, but attributes of loveliness as devised by God and greatly appreciated by men whose senses are properly refined. A godly woman's employing the intricacies of her enchanting nature in harmony with God's design is a portrait of inexpressible beauty. In the home or in the church, there is nothing like a woman's touch, the sound of a woman's voice, or the fruit of a woman's toil. A thousand men with the similitude of Noah's righteousness, Abraham's faith, Solomon's wisdom, and Paul's courage cannot accomplish what one devoted woman of God can achieve. A woman is queen in her own world as planned by God. A man can no more function in a woman's sphere as her equal than a bird can fly without wings. One just as well ask the sun to do the moon's work.

However, God's blueprint for woman does not contain a room designated "authority over man." Therefore, when a woman enters that room, she does so at the peril of her nature and, if she becomes a permanent fixture, at the peril of her soul. God planned that room with man in mind. God designed that room to fit man and man to fit that room just as surely as He designed the water for fish and fish for water. Can a bird swim in the sea? Can a fish fly in the heavens? It would be as reasonable to expect nature to be interchangeable as to envision man's and woman's operating with equal effectiveness in each other's roles.

A woman's attempt to enter the sphere of dominion is a blatant intrusion into a forbidden realm. She has no right to be there. She has arrayed herself against God. She may claim the right of entrance by virtue of an eldership's invitation. If so, then both are in defiance of God. Elders who invite women to teach, pray, sing, and serve over men have robed themselves in the authoritative, legislative mantle of deity. They have invited women into an area wherein God has placed "Stay Out" signs from one end of the Bible to the other. Such men are in mental kinship with the Cains, Korahs, and Nadabs and Abihus of the world who, driven by self-will, hesitate not to brazenly intrude into an area void of, or expressly precluded, by divine authority.

However, such is the brash, pompous, irreverent spirit of liberalism. Liberalism delights in opening doors that God has closed. It is devoid of respect for the limitations that God has placed upon women. Only the self-exalting, audacious spirit of liberalism would dare replace God's "Off Limits" sign with its "Enter In" sign. Liberalism does not believe in limits. There are no boundaries in liberalism's world. A man under the influence of liberalism, whose conscience yet feels the tug of divine limitations, is not yet thoroughly converted; moreover, he is wholly inconsistent. His degree of liberalism allows the implementation of some unauthorized or even expressly forbidden practices, while refusing to allow that same liberty to others, whose conscience regarding limits has few to none. If a man allows himself the "no big deal" spirit toward any aspect of biblical teaching, he must concede that same right to all others relative to every biblically addressed subject or else be branded a hypocrite by the very philosophy he has embraced. It does not take a genius to discern the end to which this way of thinking leads.

What is 1 Timothy 2:12? It is a great summary statement of God's will for woman in her relationship to man and authority from time's beginning to time's end. It is a divine effort to preserve woman's nature. It is an expression of God's love for woman by providing her with a law that harmonizes with the very traits of her being as formed by His own hand. It is God's grace making provisions for woman's happiness, contentment, and sense of fulfillment. It is God's endeavoring to motivate woman to pursue a course consistent with the purpose for which He created her. It is a divine restraint to encourage woman to exercise her talents in a manner compatible with her very essence as designed by God. It is a divinely constructed wall of limitation to prevent woman from entering a realm that would prove destructive to her nature, role, and soul. It is a wall of protection and preservation, keeping woman enclosed in her own world: a world having no male peers; a world where great spiritual leaders are made; a world with unmatched hands of love and tenderness; a world where fears are calmed, wounds are healed, and hearts are encouraged; and a world where she can most effectively employ her talents in service to God and man as designed by hands divine.

Nestled among the many rich truths in Moses' final words to Israel are these: "And the Lord commanded us to do all these statutes, to fear the Lord our God, for our good always, that he might preserve us alive, as it is this day" (Deut. 6:24). The beautiful sentiment, "for our good always," is characteristic of every law that God has given to govern, direct, control, and restrain man's mind, will, emotions, and behavior. Whether directive or prohibitive, every divine law has God's love for man written all over it and is intended for man's good always.

Consequently, 1 Timothy 2:12 is woman's friend, not her enemy. It is for her good always. Its aim is not to limit or constrain just for the sake of limiting or constraining. God does not issue orders just to prove that He can. Divine law is not the potter's saying to the clay, "I made you, I'm stronger than you, and therefore, I can tell you what to do." Divine law is an expression of God's love and grace's moving in man's best interest. Liberalism has never understood this principle. That is the reason it plants swords in the hands of grace and law and positions them on the field of battle as though they were enemies.

Authority inheres in the eldership. Give some men a handful of authority and they will build a mountain of pride. God's prohibition regarding a novice in the eldership is a law of love aimed at preventing the new convert from being lifted up with pride, and thus falling into condemnation (1 Tim. 3:6). Men are often drawn to the eldership, not out of a desire to serve God and His sheep, but rather to crack the authoritative whip over the heads of the flock. Men of humility with genuine concern for souls have entered the eldership only to be conquered by the seductive power of pride. Pride lurks in realms of authority like a wild beast's seeking to devour its prey. A man designed by God to function in an authoritative capacity must struggle with pride and is often vanquished by it. How much more susceptible to defeat by this unsavory disposition is woman, who by nature through creation is lacking in traits essential to perform in the realm of dominion. As 1 Timothy 3:6 is to the new convert, 1 Timothy 2:12 is a divine law of love endeavoring to avert woman from being consumed by pride, hence falling into condemnation.

A woman intent on breaking the yoke of submission and ruling her own life has chartered a course of ruin. As Eve gazed upon the forbidden fruit, she pondered the words of Satan, "Ye shall be as gods" (Gen. 3:5). A forbidden role in the form of desire slowly began to settle in her heart. How much better to be her own god than helpmeet to a man—to be her own glory than the "glory of man" (1 Cor. 11:7); to be for herself rather than "for the man" (1 Cor. 11:9). This kind of thinking destroyed her innocence and commenced a global flood of evil that would embrace every generation until time's end. A woman who gazes with covetous eyes upon the throne of dominion is looking upon forbidden fruit. Should she neglect to bar her own path by penitence, she is headed down the same road paved by Eve. It is this very thing that 1 Timothy 2:12 is endeavoring to prevent. This divine principle of restraint is woman's ally, not her adversary.

Liberalism does not respect woman. If liberalism respected woman, it would respect the law of limitation that God has placed upon her. It would view that law as a shield to protect woman from the woes of attempting to operate in a sphere for which she is not designed. Instead, liberalism discards the shield and invites woman to join man as his equal in matters relating to authority. Moreover, liberalism does not believe that woman has sufficient work and responsibilities to fulfill, operating in her own world as ordained by God. Liberalism wants woman to assume man's role and tasks in addition to her own.

Liberalism erodes femininity. What words are adequate to describe the feminine qualities of the spiritual woman of God? When words generally used are brought to bear upon this subject, there seems to be something yet missing. Viewing himself as a work of God in his mother's womb, David said, "I will praise thee, for I am fearfully and wonderfully made; marvelous are thy works, and that my soul knoweth right well" (Ps. 139:14). Every man whose mind has been shaped by divine principles would agree that these sentiments take on even deeper meaning when applied to a godly woman. There is a wonder and depth to femininity to which words cannot descend for adequate characterization.

Effectiveness in the realm of dominion demands traits peculiar to masculinity. Only one void of reason or blinded by the spirit of liberalism would argue this point. When liberalism entices a woman to exchange her garment of submission for the robe of dominion, she embarks on a road of incremental erosion of her femininity. There is a gradual diminishing of softness, gentleness, and sense of decorum. There is a progressive adoption of more masculine traits. Prolonged presence in the world of dominion can alter a woman's entire demeanor.

Why should this be difficult to understand? This same principle is applicable to godly men who enter a work environment wholly foreign to spiritual values. The world hates the spiritual man and is his constant enemy (John 15:19). Therefore, any setting dominated by worldly people possesses the potential of impeding a man's spiritual priorities. However, some mediums are so hostile to Christianity as to render foolish one's entrance therein. Such an environment would erode a man's spiritual traits just as surely as an environment of dominion will adulterate a woman's femininity. By opening the door of dominion to woman, liberalism is in rebellion to an eternal principle of God and is tampering with the very nature of woman as designed by God.

Some women react negatively to the idea of submission due to false concepts regarding its nature. They equate submission with inferiority. They feel that a subordinate role is a form of semi-slavery and that it destroys a woman's personal identity. The fallacy of these impressions can be discerned by considering other subordinate roles such as employees to employer, citizen to civil authority, or members to elders in the church. Others cast a disapproving eye at the subservient role because they view headship as a position of honor instead of a role that involves great responsibility with severe consequences for failure.

God, Christ, man, woman: that is the divine order (1 Cor. 11:3). How far we have departed from this principle. The problems resulting from such departure are legion. In many instances, the spirit of liberalism has sought to reverse God's divine arrangement for man and woman. "From the beginning, it was not so."

18

Liberalism and Pride

Sin is an extremely nefarious thing. Its calamitous nature transcends human expression. At the apex of his comprehensive powers, man falls light years short of grasping the abhorrent essence of sin. Sin cannot dwell in the presence of God's holiness. Just one unforgiven transgression bars the gate to the heavenly realm. Sin reigns eternal in the unspeakable world of the damned.

Relative to consequences, some sins are worse than others. Pride is such a sin. Pride is a foundational sin. A world of iniquity has been constructed on the sin of pride. Pride possesses volcanic power. Evil rolls from its bosom down the hill of humanity destroying everything in its path. Thus, when inspiration recorded seven things that God hates, "a proud look" headed the list (Prov. 6:17).

The Moabites were descendants of Lot, the nephew of Abraham. Beginning with Balak's attempt to curse Israel (Num. 22), the enmity between Moab and Israel was deep and perpetual. Nestled among the mountains, with the desert's inhibiting the enemy to the east and the Dead Sea's serving as fortification to the west, Moab enjoyed a geographic shelter. Lying off the well-worn path of nations greedy for power, spoil, and expansion, Moab had lived in relative quiet all her national life.

Though no stranger to invasion and the exaction of tribute, with the exception of her defeat by the coalition of Judah, Israel, and Edom (2 Kings 3), Moab had never felt the heavy hand of destruction upon her cities nor tasted the bitter dregs of captivity. The national, social, and political life of Moab remained intact. Moab's basic problem was pride. Jeremiah declared, "We have heard the pride of Moab, (he is exceeding proud), his loftiness, and his arrogance, and his pride, and the haughtiness of his heart" (Jer. 48:29).

Moab's arrogant pride lay in her greatness as a nation—her god, treasures, military might, attainments, and position of power in the world. No nation can long stand with pride as its foundation, for "righteousness exalteth a nation, but sin is a reproach to any people" (Prov. 14:34). Jeremiah 48 gives a detailed description of God's judgment on Moab. Indeed, "pride goeth before destruction, and an haughty spirit before a fall" (Prov. 16:18).

Liberalism and pride are blood brothers. They breathe the same air. Liberalism is the conduit through which pride flows. Liberalism and pride are as inseparable as the sun and heat. Pride follows liberalism just as the night follows the day. Pride inheres in liberalism. It is an integral part of the very essence of the liberal spirit.

Christianity is a grace-taught (Titus 2:11-12), blood-sealed (Matt. 26:28), Spirit-instructed (2 Pet. 1:20-21), faith-driven (2 Cor. 5:7), love-compelled (John 14:15) religion. The self-willed spirit of liberalism disallows the restrictive teachings of grace, loathes the concept of law sealed by the blood of Christ, refuses the singular nature of the Spirit's instruction, rejects the walk of faith based solely on a "thus saith God," and nullifies love by demeaning law, the only means of love's expression. It takes a mountain of pride to raise a defiant fist in the face of every basic tenet of New Testament Christianity, but such is the spirit of liberalism.

Truth is singular. Liberalism is diverse. Truth is tight. Liberalism is loose. Truth is narrow. Liberalism is broad. Truth is objective. Liberalism is subjective. Truth condemns. Liberalism excuses. Truth limits. Liberalism allows. Truth draws lines. Liberalism erases lines. Truth thinks. Liberalism feels.

Truth points to one. Liberalism points to many. Truth affirms, "It's a very big deal." Liberalism avers, "It's no big deal." It takes a massive amount of arrogance to array one's self against truth, but such is the spirit of liberalism.

Political liberals are egotists. They regard themselves as inhabiting an intellectual sphere a notch above their conservative foes. They swagger about with a pompous air, boasting of insights not available to the conservative mind. Religious liberals are made in their image. They claim a height of spirituality to which the conservative mentality cannot climb. They speak of grace as if they discovered it; the principle of grace as though only they understand it; and the gospel of grace as if they are the only ones who preach it. It takes pride in mammoth form to thus view one's self, but such is the spirit of liberalism.

Over a century ago, the pure gospel of Jesus Christ was planted in the hearts of honest men and women in a southern city. They were taught that salvation was by grace through the obedience of faith because of Calvary. The church grew and prospered. All believed, taught, and practiced the same truth. Love and unity prevailed. A Christian school added its strong voice to the propagation of New Testament Christianity. Many gospel preachers have gone forth from that area to literally bless the world with the gospel that commenced in Jerusalem two millenniums ago. Countless souls have embraced eternity in a state of spiritual security because of the gospel of grace that has permeated that area for over a hundred years.

However, just five years ago, a young man with a penchant for liberalism arrived on the scene and initiated a frontal attack on the spiritual integrity of the church in that city. Moreover, he couched his assault in a striking example of unexcelled, self-trumpeting effrontery. In a series of sermons on Galatians, he depicted the church in that city as being in slavish bondage to law, ignorant of the amazing grace of God, and tightly bound by the chains of legalism.

He described legalists as people who do not understand the cross, who never quite comprehend what Christ did at Calvary, and who rely on law-keeping for salvation instead of the blood of Christ.[1] He declared legalists to be the "most proud people on the earth because they trust in what they do instead of what God did." He affirmed that the church in that city is composed of "thousands who quit on the path of legalism." He asserted that for many in the audience, the only sermons heard by them in the past on the subject of grace solely alleged that "we can fall from it."[2]

He then made this stunning statement: "Every week I spend my week picking up the pieces of people's lives that have been broken and destroyed by legalism."[3] One is left to wonder how the church in that area has survived in the past, much less flourished, without his presence. He paints a picture of "legalists who boil down the commandments of God to just a few they can keep, and preach these over and over while ignoring heart and motive matters."[4] He describes assemblies of legalists where prayers of thanksgiving for the plan of salvation are heard, but not a word of appreciation for "what Jesus did on the cross."[5]

He proceeded to describe at least some in the audience of the congregation where he preaches as having "discovered grace," clearly implying that such discovery was made under the sound of his preaching as opposed to that of other faithful preachers in the area. He even went so far as to inform the audience of the "significant role" that legalism may have played in their former spiritual life if they would allow such to "convict them of their need of grace and lead them to the Savior they need."[6]

---

1. Buddy Bell, Sermons: "I'd Rather Fight than Switch," Major League Grace," and "A Gospel That Isn't"; delivered at the Landmark Church of Christ, Montgomery, AL.
2. Bell, "Amazing Grace."
3. Bell, "I'd Rather Fight than Switch."
4. Bell, "Free at Last."
5. Bell, "Major League Grace."
6. Bell, "From Slavery to Sonship."

How tragic that in all the years some of those people worshiped in other congregations in that city, along with thousands of others, they had never learned such crucial truths as their need of grace and a Savior until this enlightened brother appeared on the scene. One wonders at whose feet all these thousands of people learned such a distorted concept of the blessed gospel of Christ. It takes pride of gargantuan proportions to speak in such a manner, but such is the spirit of liberalism. However, such pretentious speech should not be surprising when coming from the lips of one who would dare stand in the presence of the Almighty God, point to an unauthorized piece of machinery in a worship assembly and presumptuously declare, "It's no big deal." Liberalism and pride are inseparable companions.

Max Lucado is the preacher for the Oak Hills Church of Christ in San Antonio, Texas. He is a prolific writer. Among his writings is a booklet entitled, "He Did This Just for You." The greatest question of the ages is, "What must I do to be saved?" At the close of this booklet, brother Lucado responds to this momentous question with the answer that denominationalism has been giving for five centuries. He urges his readers to pray, "I am a sinner in need of grace. I believe that Jesus died for me on the cross. I accept your offer of salvation." He exhorts his readers to be baptized as a demonstration of their decision to follow Christ, read the Bible, and join a church. Brother Lucado quotes the words of Jesus in Mark 16:16 and the words of Ananias to Saul in Acts 22:16 and places them on the other side of salvation. He removes the water that Jesus placed in the new birth (John 3:5). He converts "the church" established by Christ and purchased by His blood into "a church" and leaves the impression that selecting a church is a right conferred by God upon each individual.

God's plan to save man from sin is divine love's acting in man's behalf. It is God, through love, endeavoring to draw man unto Himself. It is the great love of God reaching out to man and pleading with him to "come unto me" (Matt. 11:28).

God's loving plan to redeem man from sin involves baptism. Jesus said, "He that believeth and is baptized shall be saved; but he that believeth not shall be damned" (Mark 16:16). What must be God's attitude toward the man who would nullify man's ability to be embraced by the love of God by corrupting the very plan that enables the sinner to benefit from the provisions of God's love?

God's plan to rescue man from sin is divine grace at work. It is grace's striving to turn darkness into light. It is grace's attempting to elevate man from the valley of sin to the mountain of holiness. It is grace's "teaching" (Titus 2:12) man how to participate in its provisions in the cross. This marvelous plan of grace includes baptism. An inspired apostle affirmed that baptism is "for the remission of sins" (Acts 2:38). How must God view the man who would negate man's ability to be clasped in the arms of grace by perverting the very plan that grace has provided to allow the sinner to appropriate its provisions in the cross?

God's plan to save man by love and grace points to the cross. It was God's plan from eternity to save man from sin by the blood of His Son. Every drop of animal blood shed for sacrificial purposes pointed to the blood of God's perfect Lamb on Calvary. The cross is the pivotal point of all human history. The past, the present, and the future have as their center the cross of Jesus Christ. Apart from the cross there is no joy in birth, no purpose in life, and no hope in death. Severed from the cross, nothing matters. Connected to the cross, everything matters. Acts 2 grows out of the cross, not the cross out of Acts 2. Without the cross, there is no Acts 2, no gospel, no church, no redemption, and no hope.

It is the blood of Christ that remits sins (Matt. 26:28). It is the blood that justifies (Rom. 5:9). It is the blood that produces forgiveness (Eph. 1:7). It is the blood that brings man near to God (Eph. 1:13). It is the blood that makes peace between God and man (Col. 1:20). It is the blood that yields redemption (Heb. 9:12). It is the blood that sanctifies (Heb. 13:12). It is the blood that effects continual cleansing from sin (1 John 1:7). It is the blood that washes away sin (Rev. 1:5).

What is baptism? It is man's responding in the "obedience of faith" (Rom. 16:26), to God's love and grace. It is man's respecting the "teaching" (Titus 2:12) of grace. It is man's esteeming the plan that God has given to grant him access to His Son's blood. It is man's affirming, "I cannot save myself. I am a spiritual pauper. I have no solution for my sin. I am void of spiritual strength. Apart from the grace of God and the blood of Christ, I am hopeless, helpless, and lost for time and eternity. I am reaching for mercy. My trust is in Calvary." Baptism is God's means of enabling man to claim the riches of His grace in the forgiveness of his sins through the power in the blood of His Son. What must God think of the man who would dare to be so presumptuous as to remove from His divine plan the very act that allows man to be clothed with Christ and the cleansing power of His blood?

God's plan to procure man's redemption involves faith. Faith comes from hearing the Word of God (Rom. 10:17). Every step in the walk of faith (2 Cor. 5:7) is a step based on a "thus saith God." Salvation is by grace "through faith" (Eph. 2:8). The faith that saves is the faith that submits to the will of God (Matt. 7:21). From revelation's sunrise to revelation's sunset, saving faith screams, "I am not alone" (James 2:24).

What is baptism? It is faith's obeying God. It is faith's acting in harmony with its very nature. It is faith's manifesting trembling reverence for the Word of God. It is faith's completing its mission in compliance with the final condition of the gospel of grace, therefore permitting man to enjoy the provision of grace, tied exclusively to the blood of Christ. How must God regard the man who extracts the power from faith to reach the blood of Jesus, causing him to die in his sin, without God, without Christ, and without hope?

God's plan to redeem man from sin embraces the church. What is the church? It is the product of God's eternal purpose (Eph. 3:1-11). It is the fulfillment of the promise of Christ

(Matt. 16:18). It is the supreme object of the love of Christ (Eph. 5:25). It is God's house (1 Tim. 3:15). It is God's temple (Eph. 2:19-22). It is the body of Christ (Eph. 1:22-23). It is the sphere of reconciliation to God (Eph. 2:16). It is the result of the one gospel (Acts 2). It is the saved (Eph. 5:23). There is only one (Eph. 4:4), and it alone was purchased by the blood of Christ (Acts 20:28). How must God consider the man who would attempt to rob His Son of the exclusive church for which He died, negate its divine nature, and reduce it to the level of a denomination?

Brother Lucado has corrupted the gospel of Jesus Christ. He has perverted the grace of God. He has nullified the nature of biblical faith. He has constructed a barrier between the sinner and the cross of God's Son. He has dared to extract from the gospel the very act of faith that enables man to reach the blood of Christ. He has joined denominationalism, the enemy of God, in defaming the one body of Christ. It takes an enormous, indescribable degree of pride for a mere man to tamper with the will of the Almighty God. Relative to God's plan of salvation and the church for which His Son died, brother Lucado, by his own words, has postured himself at the foot of the cross, gazed upon the dying Christ, and arrogantly affirmed, "It's no big deal." Such is the scandalous spirit of liberalism. Liberalism and pride are inseparable companions.

19

Liberalism and Its Fruit

Liberalism is diabolical. It originated in the mind of the chief adversary of man just as surely as truth finds its origin in the mind of God. Liberalism is one of the most formidable weapons in Satan's arsenal to the subversion of truth. Jesus said, "Wherefore by their fruits ye shall know them" (Matt. 7:20). The fruit of liberalism bears witness to its fiendish nature.

Liberalism divides. Liberalism creates a division between man and God. The spirit of liberalism separated Adam and Eve from the perfection and innocence of Eden. If Eve had not allowed the "no big deal" spirit of liberalism to surmount her "very big deal" attitude toward God's prohibition regarding the tree of the knowledge of good and evil, she and Adam would never have lost their purity and been severed from the Tree of Life.

For approximately half a century, Isaiah preached to the dying nation of Judah. The nation had wrapped itself in the filthy garments of sin. Every national pore oozed with iniquity (Isa. 1:5-6). Like Sodom, Judah wore her sin as a symbol of pride (Isa. 3:9). Truth lay dead in the street (Isa. 59:14). Like those of Noah's day, "their thoughts are thoughts of iniquity" (Isa. 59:7). They refused God's counsel so they could "add sin to sin" (Isa. 30:1). They called "evil good and good evil" (Isa. 5:20). Therefore, the prophet affirmed, "Your iniquities have separated between you and your God, and your sins have hid his face from you, that he will not hear" (Isa. 59:2).

Judah would never have descended into such depths of human depravity had she not developed an insouciant attitude toward the Word of God. During the normal course of its useful life, an automobile will not deteriorate into a non-usable state as long as it undergoes regular maintenance. Even so, the spiritual mind cannot wane in its attitude toward the Word of God from a "trembling reverence" status to a "no big deal" status as long as it experiences consistent maintenance. However, apart from such diligence, the spirit of liberalism will work its devious, erosive power on the mind until one acquires the disposition that "will not hear the law of the Lord" (Isa. 30:9).

The church is presently reeling under the divisive power of liberalism. Liberalism does not ascend to the podium and exclaim, "I have come to divide and conquer." Liberalism dons the cloak of a coward. Liberalism is a dissembler. Liberalism is a "wolf in sheep's clothing" (Matt. 7:15). It "creeps in unawares" (Jude 4). It works house-to-house until it amasses sufficient numbers to raise the flag of victory. The faithful remnant are often left with no alternative but to leave the work to which they have devoted the better part of a lifetime, lest they be numbered among those who, refusing to abide "in the doctrine of Christ, hath not God" (2 John 9). At the apex of its evil work, the X-ray of liberalism is now plain for all to see. Its detestable picture is reminiscent of the loathsome sight that Ezekiel beheld when he finally dug through the wall of the temple (Ezek. 8:7-12).

Liberalism deceives. Herein lies much of its power. It sounds so good to those who have neglected to have their spiritual "senses exercised to discern both good and evil" (Heb. 5:14). Liberalism deludes man into confusing emotionalism with spirituality. Hands extended heavenward with a strained, teary countenance, goose flesh, and feelings of mental lightness are not evidences of spirituality. A warm, fuzzy feeling, physical exuberance in the assembly, and conversations laced with "praise God" and similar expressions are not proofs of spirituality. A soft, sweet voice, a saintly look, and a Bible on the dashboard of one's car do not certify spirituality. Charisma, a pleasant disposition, and involvement in religious activity do not confirm the presence of spirituality. Dimmed lights, hand holding, swaying, hugs, and spine-tingling sensations in an emotionally charged assembly are not signs of spirituality.

Spirituality grows out of faith, and faith is based on the Word of God (Rom. 10:17). Spirituality is a manifestation of one's attitude toward God and His Word. One's attitude toward the Word of God is one's attitude toward God. Spirituality reveres the Bible. One can no more sever spirituality from a trembling reverence for every jot and tittle of the law of God than he can cleave blue from the sky. Spirituality exclaims: "I have respect unto all thy commandments" (Ps. 119:6); "Teach me thy statutes" (Ps. 119:12); "I will delight myself in thy statutes" (Ps. 119:16); "Make me to go in the path of thy commandments; for therein do I delight" (Ps. 119:35); "So shall I keep thy law continually for ever and ever" (Ps. 119:44); "And I will delight myself in thy commandments, which I have loved" (Ps. 119:47); "The law of thy mouth is better unto me than thousands of gold and silver" (Ps. 119:72); "O how I love thy law; it is my meditation all the day" (Ps. 119:97); "How sweet are thy words unto my taste; yea, sweeter than honey to my mouth"(Ps. 119:103); and, "I love thy commandments above gold; yea above fine gold" (Ps. 119:127).

Spirituality is man's discarding self-will and submitting to God's will. It is faith's responding to the source of faith (Rom. 10:17) in the "obedience of faith" (Rom. 16:26). It is love's obeying God (John 14:15). Spirituality is "faith working by love" (Gal. 5:6), responding to the "teaching" of grace by "denying ungodliness and worldly lusts," and living "soberly, righteously, and godly in this present world" (Titus 2:11-12). Spirituality is faith's and love's exercising diligence to grow and mature spiritual virtues so as not to be "barren nor unfruitful in the knowledge of our Lord Jesus Christ" (2 Peter

1:5-8). Spirituality is faith's and love's refraining from the "works of the flesh" (Gal. 5:19-21) while engaging in the "fruit of the spirit" (Gal. 5:22-23).

Spirituality is the practice of pure and undefiled religion in caring for widows and orphans and living godly in this evil world (James 1:27). It is restoring the fallen (Gal. 6:1); working to "keep the unity of the spirit in the bond of peace" (Eph. 4:3); being "tenderhearted, forgiving one another" (Eph. 4:32); abounding "yet more and more in knowledge and in all judgment" (Phil. 1:9); "in everything giving thanks" (1 Thess. 5:18); seeking "first the kingdom of God and his righteousness" (Matt. 6:33); and loving God supremely in addition to one's neighbor as one's self (Matt. 22:37-39).

Spirituality is: "Thus did Noah, according to all that God commanded him, so did he" (Gen. 6:22); "Thus did Moses, according to all that the Lord commanded him, so did he" (Exod. 40:16); "Then Zerubbabel the son of Shealtiel, and Joshua the son of Josedech the high priest, with all the remnant of the people, obeyed the voice of the Lord their God, and the words of Haggai the prophet, as the Lord their God had sent him, and the people did fear before the Lord" (Hag. 1:12); "And immediately there fell from his eyes as it had been scales; and he received sight forthwith, and arose and was baptized" (Acts 9:18). Void of argument, debate, human reasoning, and expressions of self-will, spirituality is love's compelling faith to obey God.

Spirituality is Aaron's submissive silence in the presence of his slain sons (Lev. 10:6-7); Moses and Aaron's incarceration of the man who violated the Sabbath until they received instructions from on High (Num. 15:32-36); Samuel's, "Speak, for thy servant heareth" (1 Sam. 3:10); David's, "We sought him not after the due order" (1 Chron. 15:13); Micaiah's, "What the Lord saith unto me, that will I speak" (1 Kings 22:14); Job's, I "repent in dust and ashes" (Job 42:6); Peter's bitter weeping (Matt. 26:75); and the publican's, "God be merciful to me a sinner" (Luke 18:13). Spirituality is man in reverent fear of God; man in veneration of the Word of God; man's acknowledgement of his sinful state in the sight of God; and man's pleading for mercy as a gift from God.

Liberalism's spirituality is fleshly, emotional, shallow, and fleeting. Biblical spirituality is mental, spiritual, profound, and constant. Liberalism's spirituality has a ho-hum attitude toward any aspect of divine law inconsistent with its own view of truth. Biblical spirituality possesses a deep, inflexible reverence for every letter in every word in every verse in every chapter in every book of God's revelation to man; for the "judgment, mercy, and faith" matters as well as the "mint, anise, and cummin" matters (Matt. 23:23). Liberalism's spirituality is raucous, showy, and theatrical. Biblical spirituality is quiet, unpretentious, and personal. Liberalism's spirituality applauds the speaker. Biblical spirituality pays homage to God. Liberalism's spirituality is self-centered. Biblical spirituality is God-centered.

Liberalism deceives man into viewing humanly devised family life centers as an authorized, divinely acceptable work of the church. What does a two-million-dollar material structure complete with a gymnasium, walking track, theater, popcorn machine, pool tables, and various other toys have to do with evangelism, benevolence, and spiritual edification? In connection with its amusement center, the sign of a particular congregation issued an invitation to sign up for basketball and cheerleading. That is light years away and in some book other than the Bible as contrasted with, "Join us for worship and Bible study." In a weekly publication placed in various business establishments throughout the city, this same congregation has a prominently displayed advertisement which reads in part,

> Upward Cheerleading. As an Upward Cheerleader you will enjoy an Upward Cheerleading shirt, pom-poms, spirit decals, parent's handbook, the Upward Bible, end-of-the-year awards, individual award after each game, and one-hour practice and game each week. Cost per cheerleader is fifty-five dollars.

The co-sponsor of this advertisement is a local denominational church. The Upward Bible contains testimonials from professional basketball players.

The spiritual mind stands aghast at such palpable foolishness. There is not a reasonable man in the church who would argue for such puerility's being associated with the church in Jerusalem, Antioch, Philippi, or Thessalonica. Laodicea? Perhaps. By such conduct, this congregation has demonstrated its inability to discern the nature, mission, and work of the church for which Jesus died. This congregation is joined by many others of kindred spirit throughout the brotherhood.

Suppose spiritually minded elders are characterized by deep love for God, the truth, the church, and the souls of dying men. Acutely aware of their stewardship accountability for proper use of His money, they have at their disposal two million dollars. They can either construct a physical edifice full of amenities to appease the flesh, which provides a place for those under their oversight to relax and recreate, or they can send ten missionary families to some receptive mission field and support them fifty thousand dollars each for four years with the potential of saving hundreds, perhaps thousands, of souls destined for eternity. Is there any doubt whatsoever as to which decision they would make?

There is a family life center in God's plan for man. It is called the home, and it is God's center for family life. Each room in God's blueprint is designed for man's happiness and well-being. There is the "instruction" room. Children receive instruction from various sources and, upon the basis thereof, they build a life. God's formula for child-rearing is threefold: Love God with all your being, receive His Word into your heart, and teach it incessantly to your children (Deut. 6:4-9). Children are admonished to "hear the instructions of thy father, and forsake not the law of thy mother" (Prov. 1:8). There is no substitute for parental instruction.

There is the "example" room. The best of instruction can be quickly nullified by a bad example. Children must have parental visual aid to accompany their teaching. Jehoshaphat "walked in all the ways of Asa his father, he turned not aside from it, doing that which was right in the sight of the Lord" (1 Kings 22:43). Ahaziah "did evil in the sight of the Lord, and walked in the way of his father, and in the way of his mother" (1 Kings 22:52). The difference in Jehoshaphat and Ahaziah was the difference in the example of their parents.

There is the "entertainment" room. God's blueprint has the entertainment room in the home, not the church. Zechariah pictures the return of God to Jerusalem and the restoration of the city with the delightful scene of children's "playing in the streets" (Zech. 8:5). There is a time to play. Families need to spend some fun-time together. Instead of "go play," there is a time when parents need to say, "Let's play." Innocent fun and merriment is the responsibility of the home, God's family life center—not the church.

Consequently, a humanly devised family life center as an adjunct to the church is an empty counterfeit for the real thing. Family life centers are monuments to the flesh. They are indicative of modern society's propensity for materialism, pleasure, and self-indulgence. They are shrines to the "me" generation. They constitute a monumental misuse of God's money laid aside for spiritual purposes. It is frightening to reflect upon elders' having to account to God on the day of judgment for such flagrant abuse of His money. "But all the silver and gold and vessels of brass and iron are consecrated unto the Lord; they shall come into the treasury of the Lord" (Josh. 4:19). Not one penny of the spoil of Jericho was to be taken by Israel and used for common purposes. If Achan and his family suffered death for Achan's misuse of a handful of items consecrated to God, what must be God's attitude toward elders who would take massive amounts of financial gifts consecrated by God's will for spiritual uses and build entertainment centers for fleshly gratification? Only a philosophy as patently deceptive as liberalism could convince men who once understood the spiritual nature, mission, and work of the church of the legitimacy of such obvious profane use of financial gifts intended for evangelism, benevolence, and spiritual edification to the glory of God.

Liberalism deceives man into viewing "children's church" as a practice acceptable to God. The Bible is silent on children's church. Inherent in the title is its own condemnation. The same philosophy would allow teenagers' church, senior citizens' church, singles' church, young marrieds' church, divorcees' church, blue-collars' church, and professionals' church. The Lord established His church (Matt. 16:18). However, the world has never accepted it, and some in the church are eager to revise it.

There is no divine authority for children's church. The absence of a "thus saith the Lord" says that God doesn't want it, like it, or approve of it. A thousand reasonings within the human mind cannot alter God's pattern for the church. Man's thoughts are not God's thoughts (Isa. 55:8). What man likes, feels, and thinks are not the criteria for determining things acceptable with God.

Children's church is a blatant intrusion upon God's legislative prerogative. By such action, man has tampered with God's design for the worship of the church. He has disrupted the unity of the assembly. Children's church is not an expression of faith, for faith is based on what God says (Rom. 10:17), and there is no word from God authorizing this practice. Grace "teaches" (Titus 2:11-12). Children's church is not a response to the teaching of grace, for there is no word from grace granting permission for this practice. The blood of Christ has ratified the New Testament (Matt. 26:28). Children's church is not a demonstration of reverence for the ratifying power of the blood of Christ because there is no confirmation of this practice in the New Testament.

The rupture of the family is a national tragedy. On almost every level parents have turned over the responsibility for their children to someone else. One of the many blessings of the assembly is in its promotion of family unity. A family united in a worship assembly of the church is a portrait of loveliness. Children's church destroys this bastion of family oneness.

There are lessons for children to learn in the worship assembly as designed by God. Observing adults sitting quietly in an assembly in reverential awe of God, engaging in divinely ordained acts of worship, can have a profound influence on a child. When a parent leaves the assembly with a child, he should learn quickly that it is for the purpose of discipline, not play. It is not unusual for a small child to amaze an adult by what he has gleaned from a worship assembly of the church.

On one occasion a two-year-old child was playing in a pew during the Sunday morning worship hour, seemingly oblivious to the sermon's being preached. During the course of the lesson, a few brief references were made regarding the yoke that Jeremiah wore, symbolizing the yoke of Babylon on the neck of Judah (Jer. 28). Several days later, having received no input from the parents concerning the lesson, the child approached the preacher and said, "Tell me about Jeremiah's yoke."

The church has a weekly appointment to meet with God and one another in "one place" (1 Cor. 11:20; 14:23). Children's church is an effort to fulfill man's desire, not God's will. There are some elders who are concerned about truth, but have implemented this practice due to insufficient study and reflection. There are others who have been so deceived by liberalism as to render them incapable of discerning its true nature.

Liberalism darkens. Christianity is a taught religion. God foretold the nature of His will under Christ when He said, "I will put my law in their inward parts, and write it in their hearts" (Jer. 31:33). God writes His will on the heart of man through preaching, teaching, and study. The last words of Christ on earth mandated the preaching of His will to the world (Mark 16:15). Only God can draw men to His Son (John

6:44). That drawing power is exercised through teaching. "It is written in the prophets, and they shall be all taught of God. Every man therefore that hath heard, and hath learned of the Father, cometh unto me" (John 6:45).

Emanating from God, that which is taught is truth. Pilate raised the question, "What is truth?" (John 18:38). Jesus answered that question one chapter earlier when He affirmed, "Sanctify them through thy truth; thy word is truth" (John 17:17). Truth enlightens. The psalmist averred, "The entrance of thy words giveth light" (Ps. 119:105). The good news from Christ is a light that shines (2 Cor. 4:4).

A mind severed from divine truth is an indescribably appalling thing. When a man refuses or neglects to allow the illuminating power of God's truth to continually shine in his heart, hence molding and shaping his thoughts, the fountain source of all actions (Prov. 4:23; Matt. 15:18-19), the results are always tragic. Cain closed his mind to the light of truth and subsequently, reddened the earth with his brother's blood (Gen. 4:1-8). The antediluvian world discarded the light of God's truth and transformed the world into a cesspool of sin (Gen. 6:5). The first generation of Abraham's descendants to exit Egypt rejected the light of God's will and were buried in the wilderness.

An unnamed man dismissed God's instructions for observing the Sabbath day and died under a hail of stones (Num. 15:32-36). Korah, Dathan, and Abiram spurned God's authority in Moses and the priesthood in Aaron and perished in the heart of the earth (Num. 16). The period of the judges was a ceaseless cycle of Israel under subjugation to foreign nations because they succumbed to their own will instead of walking in the light of God's truth (Judg. 21:25). David's temporary departure from the light of God's way led to the dark world of adultery and murder (2 Sam. 11).

In the closing years of his reign, Asa left the lighted path of truth he had so faithfully walked, and died in the grip of a great disease (2 Chron. 16:12). Walking in the light of truth brought prosperity to righteous Uzziah (2 Chron. 26:5).

> But when he was strong, his heart was lifted up to his destruction, for he transgressed against the Lord his God and went into the temple of the Lord to burn incense upon the altar of incense (2 Chron. 26:16).

Smitten by God, he died a leper (2 Chron. 26:21). The Pharisees substituted the murky world of tradition for the clear light of truth, thus sealing their own doom (Mark 7:1-13). The Roman world rejected the light of God's word and "their foolish heart was darkened" (Rom. 1:21). A state of almost incomprehensible perversity is demanded for the God of all love, mercy, and longsuffering to be left with no alternative but to say, "I have given up on you." However, these divine sentiments are affirmed three times in Romans 1:22-32. When time comes to its inevitable end, having repudiated the light of God's truth, the masses of the world will hear those mournful words, "Depart from me ye cursed into everlasting fire, prepared for the devil and his angels" (Matt. 25:41).

Liberalism wraps the mind of man in a veil of darkness. The spirit of liberalism abrogates the enlightening power of truth and brings on the night. Inherent in each of the foregone examples is the "no big deal" spirit of liberalism regarding the truth of God. Sin resulting from fleshly weakness succeeded immediately by penitence and prayer is one thing, but willful, planned, and continuous sin can only ensue when one possesses the indifferent spirit of liberalism toward the Word of God.

Liberalism desecrates. Intrinsic in one's love for God is an ineffable, venerate spirit for everything associated with God; every syllable of the Word of God. It was this very spirit that motivated Enoch to "walk with God" (Gen. 5:22); Noah to cautiously follow the pattern from God in constructing the ark (Gen. 6:22); and Bezaleel and Aholiab to exercise exceeding diligence in following the meticulous blueprint for the tabernacle and the apparel of the priest (Exod. 35-39). It was this very spirit that motivated Moses to comply with the will of God and take the blood of the ram of consecration and "put it upon the tip of Aaron's right ear and upon the thumb of his right hand, and upon the great toe of his right foot" (Lev. 8:23).

It was this profound sense of veneration for God and His will that provoked the faithful in Israel to refrain from eating the meat of the peace offering on the third day (Lev. 19:5-8); planting two kinds of crops in the same field or wearing a garment made of wool and linen (Lev. 19:19); eating the fruit of newly planted trees in Canaan until the fifth year (Lev. 19:23-25); covering the ark of the covenant with badger's skins of any color than blue (Num. 4:5-6); using fruit trees in bulwarks in besieging a city (Deut. 20:19-20); taking the mother in addition to the young from a bird's nest (Deut. 22:6-7); and yoking an ox and a donkey to the same plow (Deut. 22:10).

It was this very spirit that impelled Jehoshaphat to say to Ahab, "Is there not here a prophet of the Lord besides that we might inquire of him?" (1 Kings 22:7); that motivated Obadiah to risk his life in saving a hundred prophets of God from Jezebel's wrath (1 Kings 18:13); Jehosheba to save Joash from Athaliah (2 Kings 11:2); and that incited young Josiah to initiate spiritual reforms in the dying years of Judah prior to the Babylonian captivity (2 Chron. 34).

It was this very spirit that urged Paul to say, "That ye all speak the same thing, and that there by no divisions among you, but that ye be perfectly joined together in the same mind and in the same judgment" (1 Cor. 1:10); to warn against preaching "any other gospel" (Gal. 1:8), or any "other doctrine" and to withdraw from those who did (1 Tim. 6:3-5); to hold forth the church as the one body of Christ (Eph. 4:4; 1:22-23), the object of God's love (Eph. 5:25), the only sphere of reconciliation (Eph. 2:16); and that which Jesus saves (Eph. 5:23); and to present God's exclusive pattern for the worship of the church (1 Cor. 11-16), reinforced with "If any man think himself to be a prophet or spiritual, let him acknowledge that the things that I write unto you are the commandments of the Lord" (1 Cor. 14:37).

Liberalism extracts the sacredness from spiritual things. A disposition of heart that would open the door of fellowship to religious groups unknown to the hallowed halls of divine truth, deny the exclusiveness of New Testament Christianity, characterize the intrusion into God's holy presence with an unauthorized act of worship as "no big deal," and assert that the church for which Jesus shed His blood must change or die is profane. A disposition of heart that would hold up the church that belongs to Christ before an assembly of sectarians as an object of scorn, reduce the profound nature of spirit-and-truth worship to shallow theatrics and emotionalism, and categorize doctrinal matters as merely optional is irreverent.

Referring to the Holy Spirit as a "guy," to Jesus Christ as "J. C.," and commencing one's prayer to the majestic God with "Dear Daddy" is evidence of liberalism's desecration of sacred things. A youth minister from a congregation drunk on the spirit of liberalism appeared before an assembly of high school students at a Christian school. Slovenly dressed, he began his remarks with derisive references to the school's dress code. At that moment his cell phone rang. He lifted the phone and said, "Hello, God, I'll get back to you." Such is the shameless, disparaging irreverence of liberalism. In November of 1992, Andre Resner, a professor at Abilene Christian University, wrote an article for *Wineskins*, edited by Rubel Shelly and Mike Cope, entitled "Christmas at Matthew's House." He initiated his article with a crass description of Judah's adultery with Tamar (Gen. 38). He then proceeded to suggest that what transpired between Boaz and Ruth at the threshing floor (Ruth 3:8-14) was far from innocent. Having referred to David and Bathsheba's adultery, he brazenly culminated his blasphemous piece by depicting Mary, the mother of Jesus, as "another sexually questionable woman." Such are the unspeakable depths of the coarse, vulgar, irreverent desecration of spiritual things to which liberalism can descend.

Liberalism dominates. Jesus said, "Whosoever committeth sin is the servant of sin" (John 8:34). Sin demands subservience. Sin wants to reign (Rom. 6:12). Sin is not satisfied with anything short of total dominance. This trait is innate to liberalism. Liberalism enslaves the mind. Liberalism is determined to wield the scepter over man's mental activities. Liberalism is jealous. It is territorial. It allows no room for conservative thinking. Liberalism will not crack its mental door to a single conservative thought. Conservative contemplation is liberalism's worst nightmare.

When one enthrones the spirit of liberalism in his heart, he is no longer free. As is characteristic of communism, liberalism does not permit man to think for himself. Independent thinking is liberalism's enemy. Liberalism does not share its space. Liberalism shouts, "It's my way or no way!" It imprisons the mind. At the height of its power, its walls are impenetrable. Generally speaking, one just as well attempt to bore through concrete with a toothpick as to drill through the mental wall of liberalism.

The dominating power of liberalism renders one incapable of giving ear to those of a converse spirit. It is not possible to tell one something who already knows everything. Liberalism has no questions, because it already knows the answers. Liberalism demands an audience, not a discussion; an assembly, not a debate; spectators, not participants; a lecture, not dialogue. There is no equal time in liberalism's world. Liberalism's feelings of superiority brand those of contrary convictions as unworthy of its attention. It views with eyes of pity those who would be so presumptuous as to assume a position counter to its own.

The demon-possessed man of Gadarea was controlled by Legion (Mark 5:9). He lacked the ability to speak for himself. It was the unclean spirit who confessed the deity of Christ (Mark 5:7); who answered the question of Jesus concerning his name (Mark 5:9); and who pleaded with Jesus to be allowed to remain in the country (Mark 5:10). When Jesus broke Legion's dominion, the man was found "clothed, and in his right mind" (Mark 5:15). Liberalism is demonic. It possesses the mind. It enters to retard, injure, wreck, and ruin. Questions posed to a man dominated by liberalism fall on mentally deaf ears. The ability to answer requires autonomous study and thought, conduct prohibited in liberalism's domain. Occasionally, the power of truth will shatter the repressive might of liberalism. The result is spiritual freedom and the restoration of one's right mind. Liberalism destroys.

> Let no man say when he is tempted, I am tempted of God, for God cannot be tempted with evil, neither tempteth he any man. But every man is tempted, when he is drawn away of his own lust and enticed. Then when lust hath conceived, it bringeth forth sin, and sin, when it is finished, bringeth forth death (James 1:13-15).

When sin can draw a man to the close of his life and inscribe "the end," the result is always death. Such is the nature of liberalism. Unchecked, the spirit of liberalism will carry a soul ever downward to its inevitable destruction.

Once liberalism pierces the mental door and commences its erosive work on man's trembling reverence for the absolute authority of every "thus saith God," there is no end to its destructive work. There are no warning signs or stop signs on the road of liberalism. The biblical road is replete with such signs, but liberalism has removed every one of them. A man traveling on the unhindered road of liberalism who says to himself, "This far, but no further," is self-deceived. Liberalism's appetite for something new, different, exciting, and emotionally titillating is insatiable. The search for experiences to placate the flesh is unending.

Only the most supreme form of arrogance would reserve for itself alone the right to apply the "no big deal" spirit of liberalism to some biblically addressed matter. If one man has the right to attach this spirit to a selected aspect of biblical teaching, every man has that right. The end result is every man's doing that which is "right in his own eyes" (Judg. 21:25), the elimination of any need of the Bible, the destruction of New Testament Christianity, and eternal perdition for every soul that bears the fruit of liberalism.

20

Liberalism and Exclusiveness

Webster's Dictionary defines *exclusive* to mean, "excluding all others; shutting out other considerations, happenings, etc." The term implies one of a kind. With regard to that which is exclusive, there are no rivals, there is no competition, there is no comparison. It is unique. It is distinctive. It stands alone. Such is the religion of Christianity. It is incomparable, unequaled, and unrivaled. If one had access to all the annals of human history, he would search in vain for a religion like Christianity. Christianity is the foundation of the home and the hope of the world.

Suppose one could proceed back in time to the very beginning and begin a slow, selective march through the succeeding centuries. He selects the Solomons of every age and assembles the greatest minds the world has ever known. He combines all of their knowledge, wisdom, and genius and formulates the most perfect religion of which the human mind is capable. Contrasted with Christianity, this humanly devised religion would be like comparing a minute to the ceaseless ages of eternity, a dew drop to the mighty oceans of the world, and the light of a candle to the brilliance of the sun at noonday.

Where Christianity is unknown, the world is enmeshed in atheism, idolatry, superstition, and mysticism. Islam sprang from the womb of violence and marked its place in the world with a sword. Hinduism worships at the shrine of the Indian social structure. Jainism bows at the altar of asceticism. Taoism worships in the sanctuary of nature. Shintoism pays homage in the temple of patriotism. Catholicism bows at the feet of a pope, and denominationalism lies prostrate before a perverted Bible.

The marvelous beauty, simplicity, and oneness of New Testament Christianity transcends human expression. It produces faith, purifies the mind, and secures the soul. It sheds light, ends fear, and provides hope. It cancels the power of sin and death. Its divine nature is instantly discernible. Christianity is an exclusive religion.

Christianity embraces an exclusive God. Of Himself, God declared, "I am the Lord and there is none else" (Isa. 45:18). The scribe was right when he said, "There is one God, and there is none other but he" (Mark 12:32). He is eternal. He is sovereign over all the universe. He is all-powerful, all-knowing, and all-wise. He is so holy that He "cannot look on iniquity" (Hab. 1:13). He is omnipresent. He is loving, patient, kind, and merciful. He is perfect in all His ways.

Christianity embraces an exclusive church. It was God's intention from eternity to go beyond the patriarchs, Judaism, Jerusalem, and the temple and unite all nations, races, and peoples in one church by means of the cross of Christ and man's obedience to the gospel of Christ (Eph. 3:1-11). The prophets pointed to the church (Mic. 4:1-2; Dan. 2:44). Jesus promised to build that church (Matt. 16:18). The gospel produced that church (Acts 2). Every seed brings forth after its kind. The one gospel of Christ gave birth to the one church of Christ. The church and the gospel that begat it are as incompatible with Catholicism, denominationalism, Oriental mysticism, and cultism as is sin with righteousness. The church of Christ is distinctive. It is unique. It is one of a kind.

Christianity embraces an exclusive revelation. Islam has its Koran. The Latter Day Saints have the Book of Mormon. Jehovah's Witnesses have the Watchtower. Catholicism has the pope, church fathers, and the catechism. Denominationalism has its manual, prayer book, and discipline, but Christianity has the Bible. "Forever, O Lord, thy word is settled in heaven" (Ps. 119:89). When the Bible says it, that settles it. It is the only authority in all religious matters. God has spoken, and that word as set forth in the Bible constitutes God's exclusive revelation for all men for all time.

Christianity embraces an exclusive Savior. Man's problem is sin. Sin is a universal malady. "For all have sinned, and come short of the glory of God" (Rom. 3:23). Man cannot save himself. A lifetime of good works cannot construct even one plank on a bridge back to God (Titus 3:5). Jesus Christ is God's only remedy for sin. All of the power to remove sin is in the blood that He shed on Calvary. "For this is my blood of the New Testament which is shed for many for the remission of sins" (Matt. 26:28). The blood of Christ is God's exclusive cure for sin.

Christianity embraces an exclusive plan of salvation. Man wants to be saved, but on his own terms. He struggles with the concepts of grace and mercy due to their conflict with his pride. Informing man that apart from such expressions of deity, he is helpless and hopeless strikes at the very heart of his pompous spirit. He had rather pound his chest like the Pharisee than bend his knee like the publican.

God's plan to save man is a grace-faith system (Eph. 2:8). Salvation originates with grace (Titus 2:11). It culminates with faith (Rom. 5:1). Repentance (Luke 13:3), confession of Jesus as God's Son (Matt. 10:32), and baptism (Acts 22:16) constitute the obedience of faith (Rom. 16:26) responding to God's grace, looking to the cross for forgiveness. Because of Calvary, God saves when man obeys. Christianity has exclusive rights to God's plan of human redemption.

Christianity embraces an exclusive pattern of worship. Acceptable worship must conform to God's pattern (John 4:24). It involves the right object, the right act, and the right motive. Regardless of one's sincerity, worship based on human will and desire is utterly futile (Matt. 15:9). Determined to have his own way, Cain offered his sacrifice on the altar of self-will, and God rejected his worship (Gen. 4:5). Nadab and Abihu perverted the worship of God by the use of unauthorized fire and were destroyed by the very element they had misused (Lev. 10:1-2). Jeroboam completely revamped God's blueprint for Israel's worship, therefore laying the foundation for the nation's destruction (1 Kings 14:16). Driven by Cain's self-will, false religions and erring brethren walk in the sins of Jereboam, offering up Nadab and Abihu's strange worship. Conversely, the exclusive church of Christ enters into God's presence by that "new and living way" (Heb. 10:20), offering spirit-and-truth worship according to God's exclusive pattern.

Christianity embraces an exclusive manner of life. Man has lost sight of the repulsive nature of sin. Man laughs at sin as though it were comedic. However, only fools mock sin (Prov. 14:9). "Were they ashamed when they had committed abomination? Nay, they were not at all ashamed, neither could they blush" (Jer. 8:12). The blushing cheek has been replaced by the arrogant brow.

Sin is an ugly, corrupting, defiling act of insanity. It ruins everything it touches. However, the gospel has life-changing power. It produces holiness of life, "without which no man shall see the Lord" (Heb. 12:14). It follows, then, that no man can obey the gospel and continue to mimic the world, drink at the fountain of sin, or be allied with false religions. Relative to anything other than God's will and way, the clarion call of scripture is "come out from among them and be ye separate" (2 Cor. 6:17). Indeed, Christianity is an exclusive religion.

The spirit of liberalism detests the spirit of exclusiveness. Liberalism and exclusiveness are as incompatible as light and darkness. Exclusiveness is very restrictive, and liberalism views restrictions with intense disdain. Divine exclusiveness confines music in worship to singing. Liberalism abhors that limitation, points to unauthorized playing and shouts, "It's no big deal."

Biblical exclusivity is grace's teaching (Titus 2:11-12), faith's walking (2 Cor. 5:7), and love's obeying (John 14:15).

Liberalism negates this triune truth. Exclusiveness is narrow, taut, and singular. Liberalism is broad, loose, and diverse. Exclusiveness walks cautiously with fear and trembling reverence into the presence of God singing, "Have Thine Own Way, Lord." Liberalism strolls causally into God's presence exclaiming, "I'll have my own way."

The spirit of exclusiveness has quavering reverence for the silence of God's voice. It exercises the highest degree of vigilance, careful not to veer from its divinely marked and brightly illuminated path into that dark, forbidden world of divine silence. The spirit of liberalism views that same world as a playground for its own self-will. The grace of God does not cover that world. The blood of Christ has not sanctified that world for man's use. Faith cannot operate in that world, for it is void of a "thus saith God." However, such weighty considerations are of no concern to liberalism. It surmounts the barrier of exclusiveness, marches haughtily into that forbidden land, and proceeds to build monuments to self-appeasement.

Several months ago, in opposition to a crusade led by Billy Graham's son and joined by churches of Christ in Lubbock, Texas, the Southside congregation placed an article in the local paper setting forth fundamental truths of the gospel. An elder in one of the congregations supporting the crusade expressed his sadness over the "attitude of exclusivity" that was manifested in the article. Such is the spirit of liberalism. Had he so desired, this erring brother could not have utilized a term that more perfectly describes the very nature of New Testament Christianity than *exclusivity*.

Billy Graham has finally reached the far country's pigpen of liberalism. He is on record affirming divine acceptability of any person who is sincere in his religious beliefs, even though he does not believe in Jesus Christ. Jesus said, "If ye believe not that I am he, ye shall die in your sins" (John 8:24). However, emulating Satan before Eve and manifesting the invective "no big deal" spirit of liberalism, Billy Graham presumptuously exclaims, "Ye shall *not* die in your sins."

Jesus described Himself as the door through which man must enter in order to be saved (John 10:7-9) and affirmed, "No man cometh to the Father but by me" (John 14:6). However, by his own words, Billy Graham has labeled Jesus as a false teacher and opened his own door to salvation for any person sincere in his religious beliefs. Thus, he has rejected Jesus Christ as the exclusive Savior of the world. Billy Graham is a million miles from "abiding in the doctrine of Christ" (2 John 9). And yet, once-faithful brethren have drawn him to their bosoms and are shouting his praises to a lost world. Such is the pernicious spirit of liberalism.

The church that Jesus promised to build (Matt. 16:18), did build (Acts 2), and for which He died (Eph. 5:25) is in the throes of apostasy. In many congregations, the sweet sound of pure gospel truth has vacated the pulpit. The edifying, instructive, faith-building, incessant tone of a "thus saith God" has been superseded by philosophy, human-interest stories, jokes, personal experiences, theatrical performances, and social prattle. After-dinner speeches have displaced gospel preaching, youth ministers have replaced parents, a board of directors rule instead of shepherds, and family life centers with their fun and frolic have supplanted the mission of the church.

In many congregations preachers say, "Let's talk" rather than, "God said." The best voices jockey for positions as soloists or praise team participants, and the sound of the mechanical instrument can be heard in the hearts of the members. There are congregations that have classrooms where Andy Griffith substitutes for the Bible; where each member shares what he thinks or feels about a scripture instead of allowing scripture to speak for itself; and where donuts, coffee, and a social hour have replaced deep study of biblical truth. There are congregations where Bible-centered preaching is viewed as archaic and out-of-date, where female voices can be heard over men in the assembly, and where fellowship is extended to sects unknown to the Bible and destined to be uprooted and destroyed. Tragically, there are entire communities where the solid sound of exclusive, distinctive New Testament Christianity has been silenced and all because of noxious, malignant liberalism.

However, in spite of the immense problems fostered by this devilish spirit, the "seven thousand in Israel, all the knees which have not bowed unto Baal" (1 Kings 19:18) is a minute number in contrast to those in spiritual Israel who have not bowed the knee to the Baal of liberalism. Unlike the adherents of liberalism, they possess a trembling reverence for every Word of God. They had rather their tongues be severed from their roots than to enunciate a "no big deal" spirit relative to any aspect of biblical teaching. They stand with Samuel declaring, "Speak, for thy servant heareth" (1 Sam. 3:10).

There are elders, deacons, preachers, teachers, missionaries, and members of the blessed body of Christ all over the world who tread the old path with a resolute spirit of delight. They esteem the authority of the Bible. They love God and the truth above their own lives. They are concerned with what God wants, not what they want. Their desire is to please God, not appease self. They adore the exclusive church of Christ, the object of God's love and affection. May God add to their number until the "earth shall be full of the knowledge of the Lord, as the waters cover the sea" (Isa. 11:9).

IN FOCUS

MAN RAY

PHOTOGRAPHS

from

THE J. PAUL GETTY MUSEUM

The J. Paul Getty Museum

Los Angeles

In Focus
Photographs from the J. Paul Getty Museum
Weston Naef, *General Editor*

© 1998 The J. Paul Getty Museum
1200 Getty Center Drive
Suite 1000
Los Angeles, California 90049-1687

Christopher Hudson, *Publisher*
Mark Greenberg, *Managing Editor*

Library of Congress
Cataloging-in-Publication Data

Ray, Man, 1890–1976.
    In focus : photographs from the J. Paul Getty
Museum / Man Ray.
        p.   cm. — (In focus)
    ISBN 0-89236-511-0
    1. Portrait photography. 2. Photography,
Artistic. 3. Ray, Man, 1890–1976. 4. J. Paul Getty
Museum—Photograph collections. 5. Photograph
collections—California—Los Angeles. I. J. Paul
Getty Museum. II. Title. III. Series: In focus
(J. Paul Getty Museum)
TR680.R358   1998
779'.092—dc21   98-2908
                                            CIP

Contents

Foreword

Man Ray, the American expatriate who spent most of his adult life in Paris, returned to the United States in 1940 and lived for ten years in Los Angeles. It was not a satisfying time for him, for he felt he wasn't getting the serious attention he deserved. Fifty years later, Man Ray is recognized as one of the most important artists of the twentieth century, and Los Angeles is where his achievements as a photographer can best be appreciated. In 1984 the Getty Museum's purchase of the collection of Arnold Crane brought to California 173 of Man Ray's pictures, an array unrivaled anywhere else in America. More have been added since. From these Katherine Ware has chosen examples for this book that show how brilliant, nimble, and, at times, perverse this artist could be. I am grateful to her for providing texts for the plates and for coordinating the project.

Man Ray's life and work were discussed at length at a colloquium held at the Getty Museum in Malibu on June 21, 1996. The transcript of this conversation, skillfully condensed by moderator David Featherstone, reflects his informed comments as well as those of participants Jo Ann Callis, Merry Foresta, Weston Naef, Francis Naumann, Dickran Tashjian, and Katherine Ware. I thank them for their insightful perspectives on this enigmatic artist.

Thanks are also extended to Museum staff members who contributed their talents to this volume, including Carol Cini, Julian Cox, Michael Easley, William H. Fisher, Michael Hargraves, Marc Harnly, Stacey Hong, Ivy Okamura, Rebecca Vera-Martinez, Elaine Vogel, and, as always, Weston Naef, the general series editor. Helpful information about the artist and his work were generously shared by Emmanuelle de l'Ecotais, Wendy Grossman, Stefanie Spray Jandl, Amelia Jones, Leslie Kendall, Laura Muir, Christian Passeri, Sandra Rosenbaum, and Naomi Sawelson-Gorse.

Deborah Gribbon,
Associate Director and Chief Curator

4

Introduction

The inventive art of Man Ray (American, 1890–1976) requires imagination of those who view it. "The experiment lies with the spectator in his willingness to accept what his eye conveys to him. The success of the experiment is in proportion to the desire to discover and enjoy," he wrote in the catalogue for a 1945 exhibition at the Julien Levy Gallery in New York. Man Ray delighted in astounding viewers by juxtaposing familiar elements in incongruous ways, his intent nothing less than the transcendence of normal thought patterns. His ideas were not constrained by the boundaries of any particular medium—throughout his long career he made photographs, paintings, assemblages, drawings, sculptures, and films. Much work has already been done to establish the interrelatedness of his art in these various forms; this volume will examine the nature of his photographic achievements.

As a young artist in New York in the teens, Man Ray initially took up photography in order to record his other creations. He was aware, however, of the medium's potential for artistic expression through the example of Alfred Stieglitz, whose gallery at 291 Fifth Avenue he often visited. Abandoning native soil for the adventure of Paris in 1921, Man Ray relied on the camera as a way to support himself, establishing a portrait studio whose profits allowed him the freedom to pursue painting unconstrained by any concern for its marketability. His strictly commercial portraiture can be uninspired, but when he was engaged with his subject, the results are magnificent. His pictures of friends and acquaintances in Paris—a catalog of creative luminaries of the 1920s and 1930s—demonstrate a skillful economy of means and stand among his best work.

These portraits were made with an eight-by-ten-inch view camera (see pl. 32), the negatives later cropped and enlarged in the darkroom. Any graininess that resulted did not trouble Man Ray, who considered it as integral to a photograph as a brush stroke is to a painting. He had little patience for those who inquired about the nature of his photographic equipment or exposure times, finding such questions as absurd as asking a novelist what sort of typewriter he or she used. Not surprisingly, Man Ray was ill suited to teach photography to others, but his darkroom assistants—including Berenice Abbott (pl. 4), Lee Miller, Bill Brandt, and Jacques-André Boiffard—learned much by observation and are recognized today for their own pictures.

At the same time he was making portraits, Man Ray was exploring the medium's other creative applications. In 1922 he began making a series of cameraless photographs he called Rayographs. The process itself can be traced to the inception of photography in the 1830s, when William Henry Fox Talbot and others exposed plant and fabric specimens laid on chemically treated paper to light, producing a silhouette of the objects. The other technique closely associated with Man Ray is the Sabattier effect, more commonly known as solarization. Named for the man who discovered it in 1862, the effect involves exposing a photographic print to light during the development process to create an unpredictable reversal of tones in some areas. Solarization was used by Man Ray to give an otherworldly quality to certain subjects and as a method of realizing a psychological portrait of a sitter alongside the physical likeness.

Another important aspect of Man Ray's photographic oeuvre is his fashion work, which reached its apex in the late 1930s. Paris was the center of the fashion world at the time; Man Ray's imaginative approach to his assignments enhanced the glamour of designers' garments in periodicals such as *Harper's Bazaar* and *Vogue.* Long before the advent of today's "aspirational advertising" trend, he knew that creating an aura of excitement was more important than showing every detail of a particular item. These are the pictures for which he perhaps became best known, and because of this lopsided view of his career, he began to disassociate

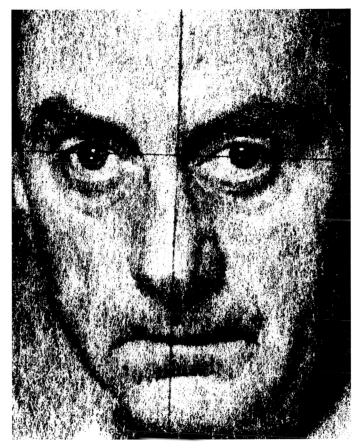

Man Ray. *Self-Portrait, Hollywood,*
1963 photoengraving from a 1947 negative, 19.9 × 15.7 cm. 84.XM.1000.76.

himself from photography upon returning to the United States in 1940.

Any discussion of Man Ray's work requires references to Dadaism and Surrealism, two cultural movements with which he was closely associated. The Dadaists staged rebellious, chaotic performances and embraced chance elements and randomness in their work as a reaction against the "sensible" society that had permitted the horrors of World War I. Dadaism was not a style, but an attitude that infused the poetry, music, and art of its sympathizers. The group lost its drive in the early 1920s, just after Man Ray's arrival in Paris, but many of its members aligned themselves with the French writer André Breton, who over the course of several years began to formulate an organized, if sometimes contradictory, philosophy that incorporated some elements of Dadaism but also embraced his growing fascination with the dream therapy of the Viennese psychoanalyst Sigmund Freud. Breton's *Manifesto of Surrealism* officially launched the new movement in 1924. Man Ray not only documented the members, works, and activities of the Dadaists and Surrealists with his camera, he actively explored their ideas through photography, experimenting with the aforementioned Rayographs and solarizations as well as with color film and movies, double exposures and distortions.

The prints reproduced in this volume are drawn from the Getty Museum's holdings of three hundred photographs by Man Ray. Most of these were purchased directly from the artist in the mid-1960s by the collector Arnold Crane, who sold them to the Museum in 1984. The collection also includes a bound copy of Man Ray's 1922 portfolio *Les champs délicieux*, inscribed by the Dadaist Tristan Tzara and later by Man Ray to Crane; a copy of the 1929 volume *1929*; a copy of the 1947 album *Mr. and Mrs. Woodman*; what is believed to be a unique copy of a 1958 album of eight images from the Unconcerned Photographs series; and a copy of the 1966 album *Résurrection des mannequins*. Most prints are signed and dated by Man Ray and were made around the time he created the negatives, making the Museum's gathering the largest accumulation of vintage prints by the artist in the United States. The collection is strongest in its representation of portraits made in Paris in the 1920s and 1930s and in prints from the artist's California period in the 1940s, with a sparser selection from his early years in New York and later years in Paris.

For Man Ray, photography was ultimately just one tool of many in the service of his ideas, but he demonstrated a remarkable facility for manipulating the medium in the creation of art. During his seven decades as an artist he never seemed to waver from the philosophy that his work was, as he wrote in the 1945 Julien Levy catalogue, "designed to amuse, bewilder, annoy, or to inspire reflection, but not to arouse admiration for any technical excellence usually sought for in works of art. The streets are full of admirable craftsmen, but so few practical dreamers."

Katherine Ware, *Assistant Curator, Department of Photographs*

Plates

PLATE I

Self-Portrait

1916

Gelatin silver print
9.5 × 7 cm
86.XM.626.22

Representative of Man Ray's earliest photographs, this picture was taken to document *Self-Portrait,* an assemblage displayed at his second one-man show at the Daniel Gallery in New York in 1916. Visitors to the exhibition were reportedly disappointed by the inoperative doorbell. The artist delighted in such contradictions; the inviting but ultimately impenetrable doorway is a fitting self-portrait. The object is sympathetic in spirit to work being done concurrently by the Dadaists, the European absurdist artists with whom Man Ray was soon to make contact.

Man Ray's initial interest in photography was prompted by his desire for high-quality reproductions of his own artworks. In his autobiography, *Self Portrait* (1963), he recalls acquiring his first camera some-

time before his initial show at the Daniel Gallery in 1915 and teaching himself how to use it. Man Ray believed that an artist was best suited to interpreting his own work with the use of a camera; his photographs of compositions in other media form a kind of parallel oeuvre. In some cases the photograph is the only remaining record of a piece, as is the case with this assemblage, now lost.

PLATE 2

Woman Smoking
a Cigarette

1920

Gelatin silver print
8.5 × 6.8 cm
84.XM.1000.43

In the spring of 1920 two of Man Ray's photographs (*Homme* and *Femme*) were exhibited in Paris at the *Salon Dada: Exposition Internationale,* the first known display of his work in this medium. Originally submitted for use in a journal, the pictures were co-opted for the show by Tristan Tzara (pl. 23). Man Ray's credentials as Dada's representative in America were further established in 1921 with the publication of the sole issue of the journal *New York Dada,* which he edited with Marcel Duchamp (pls. 14–15).

In *Woman Smoking a Cigarette* Man Ray moves beyond photography as documentation to employ it as a means of creative expression. This tiny print was carefully mounted, signed, and dated by the artist, indicating that he considered it a completed work of art. The image is daring both in its composition and content. The subject is pictured from an unusual vantage point, with the crown of her head at the center of the plate. Made at a time of social and legal conflict about equality for women—the same year the suffragettes won the right to vote in the United States— the photograph flouts convention by showing a woman smoking, her head thrown back in wild abandon.

The desire to foster and promote progressive art led Man Ray, Duchamp, and Katherine Dreier to found the Société Anonyme in 1920. Nine years before the Museum of Modern Art opened in New York, the Société organized exhibitions of works by contemporary masters, amassing a significant collection that was later donated to Yale University.

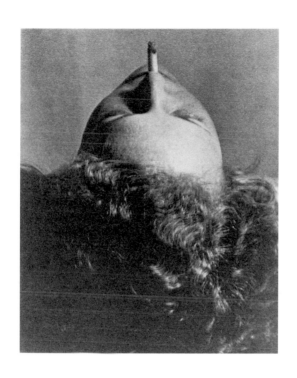

PLATE 3

L'inquiétude
1920

Gelatin silver print
9.3 × 12 cm
86.XM.626.7

Early in his career as a photographer, Man Ray challenged the notion that photography was a limited medium for artistic expression due to its reliance on recording the observable world. Here he explores the medium's potential, photographing a cloud of smoke surrounding a sculpture in his studio. By manipulating his camera, he blurs the subject beyond recognition and creates a sense of velocity and disequilibrium. One of Man Ray's guiding principles was to do the things that one is not supposed to do, and here he uses the camera to make a picture of something intangible: an emotion. Unknown to the viewer is the fact that *L'inquiétude* (Anxiety) is the title of the clockwork assemblage in the photograph, making this a craftily antidocumentary document of the three-dimensional piece.

The picture shows a kinship with Vortographs—images created by the American photographer Alvin Langdon Coburn with the aid of a kaleidoscopic mirror apparatus. Considered the first intentionally abstract photographs, the Vortographs were made in London beginning in 1917. Coburn, whose figurative work would have been familiar to Man Ray from the pages of Alfred Stieglitz's journal *Camera Work*, became interested in the photograph as an image composed of shapes and tones without respect to the subject being depicted, undoubtedly an appealing idea to an antiaesthetician such as Man Ray.

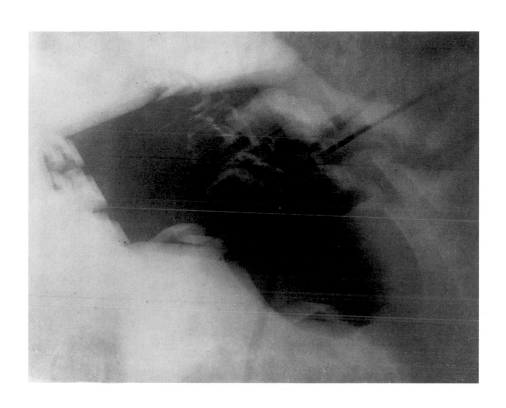

PLATE 4

Berenice Abbott

1921 negative,
printed later

Gelatin silver print
19.8 × 15.9 cm
84.XM.230.3

Berenice Abbott moved to New York from Springfield, Ohio, in 1918 to study journalism at Columbia University but soon decided to pursue her interest in sculpture. She lived in a boardinghouse in Greenwich Village that was occupied by writers and artists and through her circle of friends came to know Man Ray and Duchamp, with whom she sometimes socialized.

This photograph of Abbott is one of Man Ray's early camera portraits, and its bold simplicity anticipates the style that would later bring him fame in Paris. Abbott's bobbed hair and frank, determined gaze mark her as one of a breed of urban women whose lives no longer centered on housekeeping, although there are vestiges of a pale, dreamy Ohio girl as well. Her disembodied head and hands appear to float against the plain background, reminiscent of the treatment of the subject in *Woman Smoking a Cigarette* (pl. 2).

Abbott relocated to Paris in the spring of 1921 and worked as Man Ray's darkroom assistant from 1923 to 1926. She took up the camera at his encouragement and became a well-respected photographer best known for her 1930s architectural studies of New York.

PLATE 5

Eiffel Tower

1922

Gelatin silver print
28.3 × 22.8 cm
84.XM.1000.45

Paris was the capital of the art world in the 1920s; Americans in search of culture inevitably made a pilgrimage there. Feeling stifled in New York, Man Ray decided to go to France. At Stieglitz's suggestion, he secured the patronage of Ohio businessman and art collector Ferdinand Howald to finance his travels. With the aid of this funding, Man Ray arrived in Paris in July 1921. He was met by Duchamp, who immediately introduced him to the Dadaists. In December, Man Ray was given a one-man show of work he had brought from New York at Librairie Six. The poet Philippe Soupault, whose wife ran the bookstore, wrote upon the occasion: "Light resembles Man Ray's painting as a hat does a swallow as a coffee cup does a lacemaker as easy as falling off a log."

This photograph, one of at least three views Man Ray made of the Eiffel Tower, seems to express the exuberance and liberation of an American in Paris. The structure, completed in 1889 as part of the celebration of the hundredth anniversary of the French Revolution, was a symbol of modernity. Man Ray's picture is unexpected in its dynamic portrayal of the static monument, with two legs of the tower poised as if to spring forward. The unfocused quality of the image was part calculation and part chance, suggesting an application of Dadaist principles to photography. By taking pictorial liberties with the French icon and prominently signing the finished work "Man Ray—Paris," the artist proudly proclaims his arrival on the scene.

PLATE 6

Jean Cocteau
1922

Gelatin silver print
11.9 × 9.8 cm
84.XM.839.3

Although welcomed by the Paris art community and relatively successful in exhibiting his work, Man Ray was frustrated by lack of sales. In early 1922 he made the decision to establish himself as a professional photographer as a way to support himself. One of his strategies was to photograph paintings and sculptures by other artists and afterward to request a portrait sitting, the results of which often charmed his subjects and resulted in the sale of additional prints. The making of these portraits was also a way to get acquainted with art world celebrities, many of whom became friends and helped Man Ray meet society figures who commissioned pictures.

Jean Cocteau, an artist known for his personal style and ubiquity as much as for his artistic talents, met Man Ray in late 1921 and became one of his first portrait subjects in Paris. This photograph, made at the beginning of the following year, was taken in the drawing room of the house where Cocteau lived with his mother. His own best creation, Cocteau centers his head within a picture frame, his earnest face echoed by the sculpture behind him.

Well dressed and photogenic, socially connected and friendly with a variety of artists, Cocteau provided Man Ray with a model of what life in Paris could be like. Although sometimes spurned as a dilettante, Cocteau refused to restrict his creative impulses to any one medium and remained independent of any particular school or movement. In the course of his career he produced ballets, drama, drawings, fiction, films, and operatic librettos.

PLATE 7

Alice B. Toklas
and Gertrude Stein

1922

Gelatin silver print
16.8 × 21.8 cm
84.XM.1000.67

In 1903 the American-born Gertrude Stein moved to Paris and took up residence with her brother Leo. The two, passionate collectors of the art of their time, were early supporters of such painters as Paul Cézanne, Henri Matisse, and Pablo Picasso. In 1905 their studio became an important gathering place for artists and writers, a tradition Gertrude continued with her partner, Alice B. Toklas, after Leo moved to Italy in 1913.

According to Stein's 1933 book *The Autobiography of Alice B. Toklas,* Man Ray met the two women through mutual friends and asked if he could photograph them. At the time this picture was made, Stein had not yet achieved literary success, but she was a celebrity in the art world who had been immortalized in a painting by Picasso

in 1906. The opportunity to photograph her was granted as a privilege, lending Man Ray prestige and giving him a salable commodity. Accordingly, in this view he posed the legend and her muse at home in their celebrated salon—revealed by the camera to be a rather traditional interior presided over by Stein's collection of Cubist paintings—then carefully labeled the mount with their names. Stein made a portrait of Man Ray in her own medium: "Sometime Man Ray sometime. Sometime Man Ray sometime. Sometime Man Ray sometime. Sometime sometime" (1924 unpublished manuscript). She granted him exclusive rights to photograph her until 1930, when he had gained sufficient stature to present her with a bill for his services, effectively ending their cordial relations.

PLATE 8

The Marquise Casati

1922

Gelatin silver print
15.3 × 10.4 cm
84.XM.1000.136

As a young artist in New York, Man Ray had aspired to emulate the American painter John Singer Sargent, best known for his dramatic, large-scale society portraits. Although he pursued portraiture in another medium, Man Ray was able to write to his patron, Ferdinand Howald, in May 1922 that "my new role of 'photographer' has made it possible to go everywhere and be much talked of." One of his early commissions was from the Marquise Casati, an eccentric Italian aristocrat who was an important patron of the Ballets Russes and the Futurists during the teens.

Casati's audacious hair and makeup were part of the fantastical world she constructed to give license to her taste for extravagant clothing, interior design, costume balls, and pets. She commissioned a portrait sitting in her salon, surrounded by her favorite objets d'art. In his autobiography Man Ray reports that his lighting equipment blew the fuses in her suite, requiring him to use ordinary illumination and to request longer poses. While he was dissatisfied with the results, Casati was delighted and declared that her essence had been captured by an accidental multiple exposure in which she seemed to have several sets of eyes (see p. 119).

In the portrait pictured here, Casati stares through the panes of a showcase that contains an exotic artificial plant. She enacts a performance for the camera, appearing as a kind of gypsy sorceress with her lacy shawl and crystal ball (in which Man Ray's reflection can be seen). She is as much a curiosity as the items on display.

PLATE 9

James Joyce

1922 negative,
printed later

Gelatin silver print
25 × 20.3 cm
84.XM.1000.75

James Joyce was sent to Man Ray's studio in 1922 by Sylvia Beach, proprietor of the Paris bookshop and literary gathering place Shakespeare and Company, for publicity shots to use in conjunction with her publication of his already controversial novel *Ulysses*. The Dublin-born author, a resident of Paris since 1920, had been unable to find an English or American publisher for his monumental work due to passages that were considered obscene. Along with Gertrude Stein and the Dada poets, Joyce rejected traditional narrative structure in favor of a style that more closely approximated the human thought process. A parallel course was underway in the visual arts; Man Ray's Rayographs (pls. 10–12, for example) can be seen as a related abandonment of legibility in favor of the primacy and mystery of objects themselves.

The Getty Museum's collection includes a more conventional view of Joyce from the same portrait session, but this plate is interesting for its candid quality. While much could be supposed about his anguished pose, in truth he was simply reacting to the bright studio lights, having recently undergone eye surgery. Beach sent many of her British and American authors to Man Ray to have their portraits made; the resulting photographs graced the walls of her store.

PLATE 10

Untitled Rayograph

1922

Gelatin silver print
21.8 × 17.1 cm
84.XM.840.2

PLATE 11

Untitled Rayograph

1922

Gelatin silver print
21.8 × 17 cm
84.XM.840.9

PLATE 12

Untitled Rayograph

1922

Gelatin silver print
22.4 × 17.5 cm
84.XM.840.8

In April 1922 Man Ray wrote to Ferdinand Howald, "I have freed myself from the sticky medium of paint and am working directly with light itself," confirming that for the artist photography had become far more than a way to make a living. A darkroom mishap while developing pictures for fashion designer Paul Poiret reportedly led Man Ray to his experiments with Rayographs (cameraless photographs). The process, called photogenic drawing in the nineteenth century, involves placing an object on photographic paper, which is then exposed to a light source.

This work seized the imagination of Tristan Tzara, who worked with Man Ray to produce a portfolio of twelve images that was published in December 1922 under the title *Les champs délicieux* (The delicious fields). In his preface for the portfolio Tzara writes, "When all that one calls art was covered with rheumatism, the photographer lit the millions of lights of his lamp, and the sensitive paper absorbed by degrees black." The portfolio title is a reference to *Les champs magnétiques* (The magnetic fields), a 1920 collection of writings by André Breton and Philippe Soupault composed from purportedly random thought fragments recorded by the two authors. Similarly, the Rayographs refuted photographic objectivity by creating images that, while traced by light from actual three-dimensional objects, depicted an internal landscape rather than an external one.

With this technique Man Ray subverted his role as a photographer by making photographic images without a camera. Since they were made without a negative, however, Rayographs were—like paintings—one of a kind. In order to create the portfolio, three of whose pictures are shown here, Man Ray had to rephotograph the Rayographs so he could make multiple prints.

PLATE 13

Untitled Rayograph
(Kiki and Filmstrips)

1922

Gelatin silver print
23.8 × 17.7 cm
84.XM.1000.173

At about the same time he was establishing himself as a photographer in Paris, Man Ray met Kiki (Alice Prin), the most celebrated woman in Montparnasse, the city's bohemian quarter. Kiki was a country girl who became a nightclub star in the 1920s by singing risqué songs with an innocent demeanor. Although she had worked as a model for many painters, she was reluctant to pose for the camera, considering the photographic image too clinical. Man Ray convinced her of his prowess as both an artist and a man, and she soon became a frequent subject of his work as well as his lover.

While continuing to practice portraiture for financial reasons, Man Ray also worked freely with photography in pursuit of his own expressive aims. Here he achieves a wonderful sense of mobility and dimension with a downpour of filmstrips cascading from the top of the picture as if dropped by someone above. In the lower left corner is a glass negative of Kiki that appears to shatter as it hits the bottom of the composition. In the year of his discovery of the Rayograph technique, Man Ray hereby symbolically discards these traditional methods of picture making.

PLATE 14

Rrose Sélavy

1923

Gelatin silver print
22 × 17.6 cm
84.XM.1000.80

Marcel Duchamp arrived in New York for the first time in the summer of 1915, already notorious for his painting *Nude Descending a Staircase* (1912). The Cubist-inspired work, displayed at the 1913 Armory Show, was attacked by American critics resistant to the new European styles presented there. Man Ray was galvanized by the exhibition and wrote that it took him months to digest what he had seen. As he relates in his autobiography, one day Duchamp appeared at his door, accompanied by the collector Walter Arensberg. Despite a language barrier, the two artists quickly recognized one another as kindred spirits, and a lifelong friendship was inaugurated. Duchamp's rejection of the artist's role as tastemaker and his embrace of unusual media and mechanical drawing

were just the inspiration Man Ray had been seeking.

The two collaborated on a variety of projects, including the creation of a female alter ego for Duchamp, Rrose Sélavy (*Eros c'est la vie,* or "Eros is life"). Credited with authorship of several of Duchamp's works of art, she appeared in a number of pictures by Man Ray and loaned her byline to an essay in a 1934 book of his photographs.

PLATE 15

**Duchamp with
"Water Mill
within Glider,
in Neighboring
Metals"**
1923

Gelatin silver print
8.5 × 15.1 cm
86.XM.626.4

Made as a study for Duchamp's masterpiece, *The Bride Stripped Bare by Her Bach-
elors, Even* (*The Large Glass*, 1915–23),
the glass painting *Water Mill within Glider,
in Neighboring Metals* (1913–15) is here
photographed in a collaboration between
Man Ray and Duchamp. Lying on a table,
Duchamp is posed as an integral part
of the composition. An inscription on the
back of the picture indicates that he cut
the image of the painting out of the larger
photographic print. A full-frame version in
the Getty Museum's collection shows
the table on which the glass rests as well
as other portions of the studio. By trimming
away the visual clutter of the background,
Duchamp heightened the impression that
he and the work were one.

Water Mill within Glider was purchased
by the couturier Jacques Doucet on the
advice of André Breton. This photograph
was made after Duchamp framed the piece
for delivery to its buyer. When hung, the
straight edge of the glass would have been
vertical instead of horizontal.

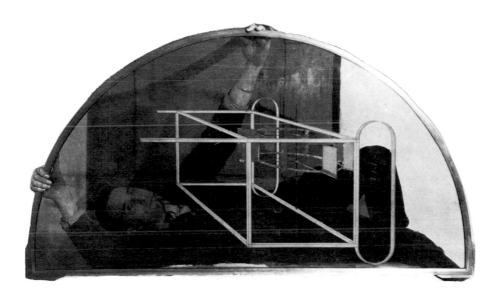

PLATE 16

**Untitled Rayograph
(Gun with
Alphabet Squares)**
1924

Gelatin silver print
29.5 × 23.5 cm
84.XM.1000.171

In the autumn of 1924 André Breton published the first manifesto of Surrealism, out-
lining the tenets of a movement that had
been gaining momentum over the course of
several years. Surrealism shared many
essential features and members with its
predecessor, Dadaism, but was codified into
an organized philosophy under Breton's
direction. In 1922 he had defined the term
(coined by the French poet Guillaume Apol-
linaire) as "a certain psychic automatism
that corresponds rather closely to the state
of dreaming." In his lengthy treatise Breton
encouraged writers to directly record
dreams and thoughts unedited by the rational mind.

Although visual artists involved with
the group (including Man Ray) were only
mentioned in a footnote to Breton's book, a
number of them had already applied this
free-associative technique to their work
and were soon reproducing their images in
Surrealist journals. Rayographs were sympathetic in spirit to Surrealist aims, using
objects from the known world to create
ambiguous dreamscapes. In this example,
alphabet stencils are scattered like bullets
shot from the revolver glowing luminously
against the inky backdrop. The letters defy
rational interpretation, refusing to assemble
themselves into recognizable words.

PLATE 17

Violon d'Ingres

1924

Gelatin silver print
29.6 × 23 cm
86.XM.626.10

Man Ray was an admirer of the paintings of Jean-Auguste-Dominique Ingres and, inspired by the master's languorous nudes, made a series of photographs of Kiki in a turban. Ingres was considered an important precursor by the French avant-garde; two of his drawings were included in the 1913 Armory Show in New York, and his work appeared in Francis Picabia's 1919 publication *Anthologie Dada*.

What was originally a classical nude has been altered here by painting the f-holes of a violin onto a print and then rephotographing the work. As a finishing touch, Man Ray adds the title *Violon d'Ingres*, a French idiom that means "hobby." Although not as irreverent as Duchamp's mustachioed Mona Lisa (*L.H.O.O.Q.*, 1918), this piece implies Man Ray's mastery of the history of French painting as well as his ability to "improve" on it.

Violon d'Ingres maintains a tension between objectification and appreciation of the female form. The transformation of Kiki's body into a musical instrument with the crude addition of a few brush strokes is humorous, but her armless form is also disturbing. The title seems to suggest that while playing the violin was Ingres's hobby, playing Kiki was a pastime of Man Ray's. The photograph was embraced by the Surrealists and published in their journal *Littérature* in 1924. The painted original photograph from which this print was made remained in André Breton's personal collection until his death.

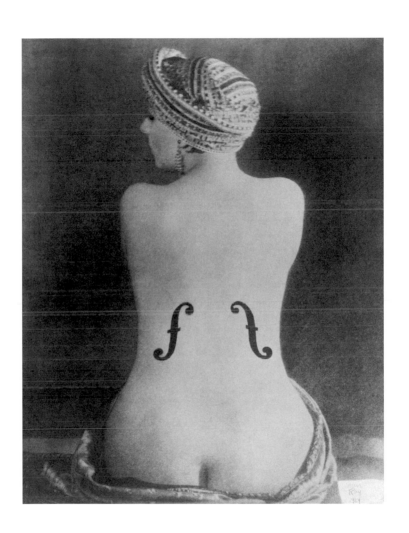

PLATE 18

Still Life
1924

Gelatin silver print
17.8 × 12.7 cm
84.XM.1000.106

This picture was made using the *cliché verre* (glass negative) process, which involves scratching a design into a layer of emulsion or pigment on glass, then using the plate as a negative to make photographic prints. Man Ray first worked with the technique in 1917 and returned to it on at least two later occasions, publishing the results in such journals as *Aventure* and *Der Sturm*. This still life, probably sketched from an existing arrangement in the artist's studio, includes pipes, glass vases, vials, and a photograph—the 1922 multiple exposure of the Marquise Casati (p. 119), recognizable by her numerous sets of eyes.

Man Ray's renewed interest in drawing may have been stimulated by the Surrealists' advocacy of "automatic writing," a stream of consciousness technique of recording mental states. He enjoyed challenging the boundaries of the media in which he worked; here he subverts the uniqueness of the drawing process by making it a reproducible medium while subverting photography by creating an image drawn by hand. The intended purpose of the piece is not clear, but a notation in the lower left corner indicates that an edition of five prints was planned.

4-5

PLATE 19

**Untitled Rayograph
(Net and Shavings)**

1924

Gelatin silver print
39.9 × 29.8 cm
84.XM.1000.161

While still in New York, Man Ray had explored methods of art production—such as painting with an airbrush—that challenged the idea of the painstakingly handcrafted masterpiece. In Paris, he concentrated on creating pictures with another machine, the camera. The Rayographs carried even further this refutation of the artist's role in image making by allowing the objects arranged on paper to be "drawn" by the action of light rather than by a human hand.

In this large print Man Ray uses net, wire, and wood shavings to create an animated abstract composition that defies direct interpretation. The spiral motif seen at the top of the picture often appears in the Rayographs as well as in Man Ray's paintings and assemblages. In a 1924 *Little* *Review* article on Dada, Georges Ribemont-Dessaignes writes, "Man Ray is a subtle chemist of mysteries who sleeps with the metrical fairies of spirals and steel wool. He invents a new world and photographs it to prove that it exists."

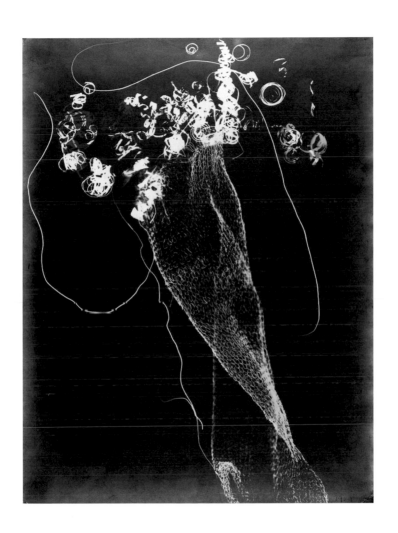

PLATE 20

Sinclair Lewis

1925

Gelatin silver print
23.2 × 17.2 cm
84.XM.1000.87

Sinclair Lewis was at the peak of his career when this photograph was taken during a visit to Paris. He had achieved sudden fame with the novels *Main Street* (1920) and *Babbitt* (1922), which lampooned middle-class Americans and condemned their embrace of consumerism at the price of individualism. This portrait was made to publicize his novel *Arrowsmith* (1925), which chronicled the life of a medical doctor torn between materialism and idealism. The book was awarded the Pulitzer Prize in 1926, but Lewis declined the honor; in 1930 he became the first American to be honored with the Nobel Prize in literature, which he accepted. Lewis harbored an affection for the American way of life he satirized in his writings but, like Man Ray, was impatient with the provincialism and commercialism of his native country.

Slumped against a wall, clutching his coat at the neck, Lewis is posed with a large wooden screw (from a winepress) that Man Ray reputedly found in an antique shop and kept in the studio of the sculptor Constantin Brancusi. Seen in profile, the author appears frail, distracted, and lost in reverie.

PLATE 21

**Barbette Applying
Makeup**

1926

Gelatin silver print
22 × 16.3 cm
84.XM.839.1

Barbette was the stage name of a vaude- ville performer of tremendous international popularity in the 1920s and 1930s. Born Vander Clyde in Round Rock, Texas, in 1904, he was fascinated with the circus as a boy. His first job was with Austin's "world-famous aerial queens," the Alfaretta Sisters, one of whom had recently died. Acting as a replacement required him to dress as a woman, something he viewed as part of theatrical tradition dating back to Shake-speare. Barbette traveled to England and then to Paris in 1923, where his act took the art world by storm. Making his entrance in elaborate feathered gowns, he walked the tightrope and performed trapeze stunts to the music of Richard Wagner and Nikolai Rimsky-Korsakov. At the end of the show he removed his wig to reveal his true gender.

In contemporary reviews of Barbette's act it is clear that his performances were appreciated for their delicacy and refinement and not as burlesque entertainment. "He walked tightrope high above the audiences without falling—above incongruity, death, bad taste, indecency, imagination," Jean Cocteau wrote in 1926. As Barbette told Francis Steegmuller in 1966, "I wanted an act that would be a thing of beauty—of course it would have to be a strange beauty."

This portrait captures the somewhat retiring man in a quiet moment as he trans-forms himself with stage makeup at a lacy dressing table. His face is reflected in two mirrors, a composition that parallels his double life. Barbette later returned to the United States, where he trained young acro-bats and trapezists, dying in Austin in 1973.

PLATE 22

Noire et blanche

1926

Gelatin silver print
11.3 × 7.9 cm
86.XM.626.14

In this photograph of Kiki posing with an African ceremonial mask, Man Ray creates a commercially viable masterpiece that also embodies Surrealist principles. The picture invites the viewer to contrast the two elongated faces: one white, the other black; one living, the other inanimate; one modern, the other traditional. The title is probably a playful reference to both the black-and-white photographic process and the positive/negative quality of the faces. A variant of this image, with Kiki's somnolent head resting on a table, was reproduced in the May 1926 issue of Paris *Vogue*.

Masks are often used in ceremonies to signal a heightening of consciousness, a condition in which the human wearer is receptive to a supernatural spirit and where ordinary behavior and appearances are suspended. The Surrealists considered this state the source of creative activity. Man Ray was attuned to this idea and to the long-standing interest among members of the French avant-garde in art produced outside mainstream Western culture. The Surrealists, in particular, collected masks and other crafts made by indigenous peoples in Africa, the Americas, and Oceania as well as images made by children and psychiatric patients. By incorporating the mask in this picture, Man Ray alludes to all of these concepts in the context of what is essentially an elegantly constructed fashion photograph.

PLATE 23

Tristan Tzara

1928 negative,
printed later

Gelatin silver print
25.2 × 18.7 cm
84.XM.1000.89

Born Sami Rosenstock in a small town
in Romania, Tzara went to Zurich in 1916
to study mathematics but instead became
one of the founders of the Dada movement.
The Dadaists expressed their antimilitarism
and disgust for the placidity of the bour-
geoisie by staging outrageous events and
embracing chance elements and nonsense
in their work. Tzara's recipe for creating
a Dada poem, for example, called for clip-
ping words from a newspaper article and
jumbling them in a hat, then pasting them
down in the order in which they were
drawn. "Every man must shout," he wrote
in his 1918 *Dada Manifesto*. "There is
great destructive, negative work to be done.
To sweep, to clean."

Tzara moved to Paris in 1919, where
he continued his writing and involvement
in Dada happenings. His vitality and orga-
nizing abilities held the factious group
together into the early 1920s, long enough
to welcome Man Ray into the ranks.
Man Ray's presence revitalized the Dadaists
for a brief time before they disbanded, many
to declare allegiance with the Surrealist
movement. In this unguarded portrait, Tzara,
a short, energetic man invariably photographed with his monocle, is shown not as
a revolutionary nihilist but as a man whose
friendship with Man Ray transcended
their involvement in any particular group.

PLATE 24

**Untitled Rayograph
(Sequins)**

1930

Gelatin silver print
28.4 × 22.6 cm
84.XM.1000.62

With Rayographs, Man Ray was able to create pictures as imaginative as anything a
painter might fantasize. In 1923 the French
poet Robert Desnos wrote in *Le journal,*
"From this simple process he has proceeded
to create landscapes foreign to our planet . . .
[and] here the miracle lets itself be captured
without resistance, and something else
besides leaves its anguishing mark on the
revelatory paper."

This image presents a constellation of
sequins scattered across a circle of light, a
reminder of the simplicity of the photogram
process. It was probably made with little
preconception of the final result, a situation
in which materials at hand were employed
spontaneously. The work forces the viewer
to draw upon his or her own experiences
and imagination in order to make sense of
it, to invent the new reality of a crater-pocked
orb or a pocketful of tears.

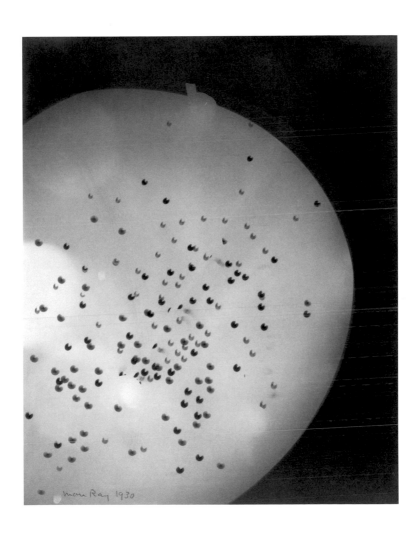

PLATE 25

Larmes

1930–32

Gelatin silver print
22.8 × 29.7 cm
84.XM.230.2

Judging from its inclusion in other of his prints (see, for example, pl. 34), Man Ray must have considered *Larmes* (Tears) one of his most successful pieces. Indeed, this simple composition of a woman's face dotted with glass beads has so pervaded public consciousness that it has become an icon for Man Ray's photographic work. A cropped version of the image with a single eye was chosen by Man Ray to be the first plate in the 1934 publication *Photographs by Man Ray 1920 Paris 1934*. The picture is a metaphor for the artificiality of art making, a scene that is staged for the camera, a device renowned for its truthfulness. Like a silent-screen star, the woman plaintively gazes upward to indicate her distress. However, the large, glistening teardrops are melodramatic, an exaggerated sign of sad-ness that makes a mockery of the senti-ment, suggesting a connection with Man Ray's abandonment by his lover Lee Miller in 1932.

To the Surrealists, the eye was an important symbol of inner vision, a concept central to their philosophy. For Man Ray, it seems to have had a more personal iden-tification as well, appearing in his assem-blages, films, and photographs.

PLATE 26

Calla Lilies

1930

Gelatin silver print
(solarized)
34.4 × 27 cm
86.XM.626.17

This floral arrangement is dramatized by the use of the Sabattier effect (solarization). The method, which involves partially developing a photograph, then briefly exposing it to light before continuing normal processing, is difficult to control but usually results in a dark outline around an area of partially reversed tonality. "The technique enabled me to get away from photography, to get away from banality . . . , and here was a chance to produce a photograph that would not look like a photograph," Man Ray told an interviewer in 1964. Claiming to have accidentally come across the procedure in collaboration with his assistant and lover, Lee Miller, he used it extensively in the 1930s.

Man Ray made a series of photographs of calla lilies in 1930, one of which was reproduced in *Photographs by Man Ray 1920 Paris 1934*. The solarized blooms did not find favor with the august critic Lewis Mumford, who reviewed the book for the *New Yorker*. "A photographer who can deal intelligently with the human face should not waste his time photographing calla lilies so they will look like a drawing by a second-rate academician," Mumford wrote. In a densely worded rebuttal sent to the magazine, Man Ray elaborately corrected what he perceived as Mumford's misperceptions and questioned the author's ability to even distinguish second-rate academic drawing. Mumford's praise for the artist's Rayographs was apparently edited out of his review, weighting the article more toward criticism than was intended. Man Ray's response never appeared in the *New Yorker*, which had no letters column at the time. His attack on Mumford's review, however, is testament to the artist's profound disappointment in the tepid reception his volume received in his native land.

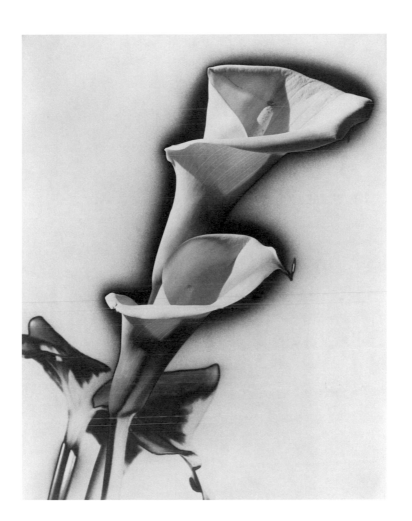

PLATE 27

La prière

1930 negative,
printed later

Gelatin silver print
23.9 × 18.2 cm
84.XM.1000.52

Even before the advent of the Surrealist movement, much of Man Ray's work was motivated by a desire to create a momentary shock in the viewer that would arrest rational thought processes and stimulate fresh ways of seeing. This piece, with its awkward juxtaposition of hands, feet, and buttocks, is also meant to shock in a more conventional sense. The artist had photographed the nude female form from the back on other occasions, but in benign, classical poses. The truncated presentation of the woman shown here and the hint of subjugation implied by her posture remove this picture from that category of nudes.

The Surrealists lionized the French writer known as the Marquis de Sade as a model of liberation from society's norms. He promoted the pleasures of sexual cruelty, a theme that recurs throughout Surrealist work in relation to the female body. Man Ray, an admirer of Sade, painted an "imaginary portrait" of the author in 1938 and made several photographs in homage to him, including a 1933 picture of a woman's buttocks enclosed in the shape of a cross. In *La prière* (The prayer), the figure's pose more directly evokes Sade's predilection for sodomy; the title recalls his strong anticlerical stance. It is illustrative to compare *Violon d'Ingres* (pl. 17) with this print, the former reflecting the spontaneous, disjunctive humor of the Dadaists, the latter revealing a more Surrealist exploration into the primal forces of desire.

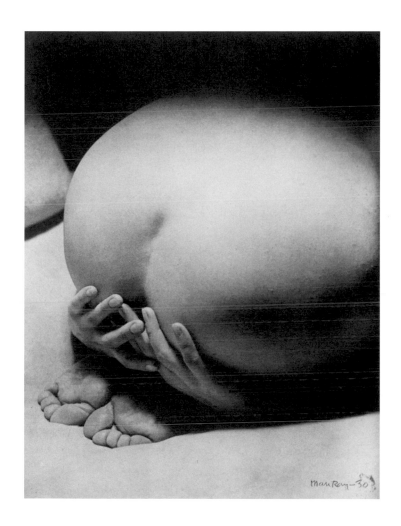

PLATE 28

Cuisine

1931

Photogravure
19.7 × 26.1 cm
84.XM.1000.5

PLATE 29

Le souffle

1931

Photogravure
26 × 20.2 cm
84.XM.1000.102

PLATE 30

Le monde

1931

Photogravure
26 × 20.5 cm
84.XM.1000.104

In 1931 the Paris electric company CPDE commissioned Man Ray to produce a series of images promoting the personal uses of electricity. The resulting portfolio, *Électricité,* included ten Rayographs reproduced as gravures. It was released in an edition of five hundred for distribution to top executives and special customers.

The series is a vibrant visual evocation of the company's commitment to increase domestic use of electricity by middle- and lower-income customers, a challenge compounded at the time by the lack of electrical outlets in many urban dwellings. Man Ray was uniquely qualified to convey this corporate message, for not only was he famous and fashionable in Paris, he was also an American and a photographer, which automatically associated him with the positive values of modernity and technology.

The portfolio begins with a literal view of electricity—a single light bulb surrounded by a Milky Way of particles. The photograph suggests both the dawning of a new age and the unseen forces that make it possible. In subsequent pictures the uses of electricity in each room of the house are presented, as in *Cuisine.* The whimsicality of many of the prints lends a friendliness to the mysterious power CPDE was marketing. In *Le souffle* (The breeze), for example, the stir of air is hinted at by the rotating fan blades (caused by moving the fan during the Rayograph's exposure) and the web of rippling lines. *Le monde* (The world), a picture of the moon above an electrical cord, posits that even celestial bodies are dependent on CPDE for their illumination.

The *Électricité* project is an example of the successful joining of commercial and artistic motives. The use of Rayographs must have seemed fitting to Man Ray, since the images were created by exposing objects on photographic paper to an electrical light source in his darkroom.

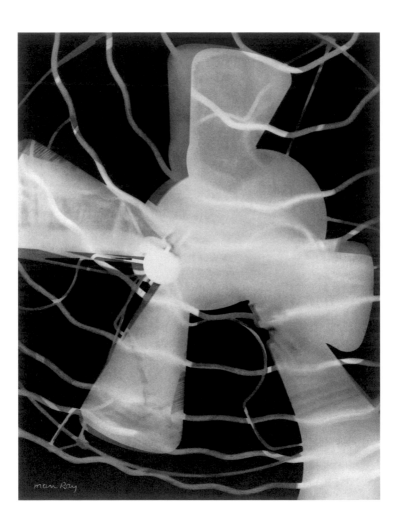

PLATE 31

Interior

1932

Gelatin silver print

29.9 × 22.4 cm

84.XM.1000.126

According to André Breton's original conception, the central principle of Surrealism was the expression of an inner vision through words that were placed according to the dictates of the subconscious mind. In the realm of images, photography was uniquely situated to perform this function by focusing on ordinary objects and rendering them extraordinary by decontextualizing them in some way. In the case of this picture, Man Ray employs multiple negatives of a nude torso and a photographer's lamp to create a dreamscape. Shadows and reflections make the subject of the work ambiguous; the light bulb in the center could be a doorknob or a crystal ball. The piece is particularly successful in creating on paper an illusion of three-dimensionality.

Man Ray wanted to distract viewers from the literal interpretation of his photographs and guide them toward a more subjective understanding. "After all, photography is not restricted to the mere role of a copyist. It is a marvellous explorer of aspects that our retina will never register," he said in *Paris soir* in 1926. This picture is another example of how he bent the medium's limits to accommodate his vision.

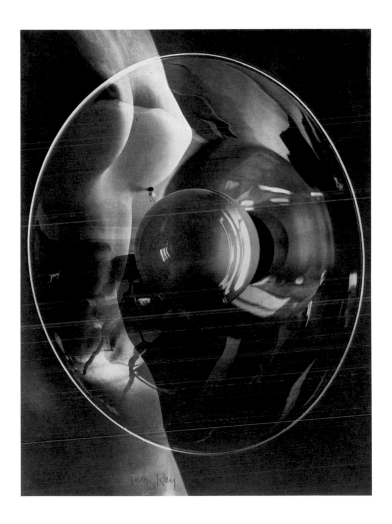

PLATE 32

Self-Portrait
with Camera

1932

Gelatin silver print
(solarized)
29.2 × 22.8 cm
84.XM.1000.14

Throughout his life Man Ray orchestrated and executed numerous self-portraits in a variety of media (see also pls. 1, 34). This example appears in *Photographs by Man Ray 1920 Paris 1934*. The volume was intended as a triumphal presentation to an American audience of the full range of his work in France over more than a decade. As validation of his stature, the book included essays, a poem, and even a portrait of the expatriate by Picasso.

In the picture Man Ray shows himself in profile, intently adjusting the focal range on his view camera as if for a portrait session. The camera is directed at the audience, on whom his attention was indeed concentrated at the time. The touch of his hand on the focusing ring serves as a reminder of the human artistry required to

make photographs, a departure from his more accidental approach to creating work in other media. The portrait is solarized, directly associating this signature process with its practitioner.

One of a number of different croppings of this picture appears in the 1934 *Échiquier Surréaliste* (Surrealist chessboard), a photomontage by Man Ray containing twenty portraits of the movement's leading lights. Among those featured are André Breton, Tristan Tzara, and Joan Miró (in a variant of pl. 37).

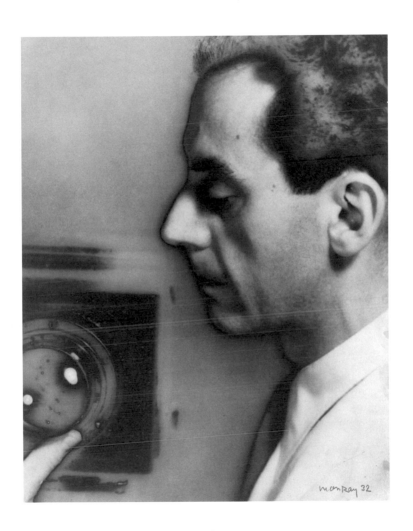

PLATE 33

Male Figure Study

1933

Gelatin silver print
(solarized)
34.4 × 27 cm
84.XM.839.4

Although female nudes are plentiful in his oeuvre, Man Ray made very few male figure studies. For that reason and because of the subject's resemblance to the photographer (see pl. 32), this image has sometimes been thought of as a self-portrait. However, another picture taken at the same photo session reveals that the model was not Man Ray.

The purpose for this work is uncertain; the absence of clothing seems to rule it out as a fashion photograph. The image carries a magnificent erotic charge. The man's exaggerated pose displays his torso in a sinuous S curve interrupted only by a swath of fabric covering his groin. Shadows and solarization further emphasize the contours of the torso and suggest the radiation of body heat. It is a highly tactile picture, from the way the lighting highlights the model's body hair to the slight impression on the skin left by his undergarment, rolled down to reveal the curve of his hip. It was not until 1939 that the electromagnetic field surrounding living organisms was first photographed, but here, using solarization, Man Ray was able to imply such a force.

PLATE 34

Still Life

1933

Three-color
carbon transfer print
30.7 × 23.9 cm
84.XM.1000.6

Man Ray made only a small number of color prints in the 1930s. This stylish still life, used in the December 1933 issue of the Surrealist journal *Minotaure*, was made using the carbro process (the name derived from carbon and bromide), a laborious method that required three separate negatives to achieve a finished work. It seems surprising that an artist so intrigued by new techniques would not seize on the possibilities of color photography, but Man Ray expressed dissatisfaction with the results of color processing. He returned to color materials later in his life, when he felt the chemistry had improved, creating an extensive body of photographs of his second wife, Juliet.

This still life may have been made as a trial cover for *Photographs by Man Ray 1920 Paris 1934*. The composition centers on a bust of the artist, which was constructed from a plaster life mask (see p. 144). The bust is surrounded by a constellation of circular objects and hands—common motifs in Man Ray's work. In the background is *Larmes* (pl. 25), the woman's eyes looking upward in counterpoint to the downcast gaze of the sculpture. The picture seems slightly didactic, intended to indoctrinate the audience into the mystery and significance of the photographer and his creations. The final cover for the book, also in color, incorporates the same elements with the addition of a female model.

PLATE 35

Augustabernard
Gown

1936 gelatin silver print
from a 1934 negative
28.8 × 22.7 cm
84.XM.1000.53

Commissions from the French couturier Paul Poiret in the early 1920s in Paris led Man Ray to additional fashion work. By the 1930s the artist's stylish pictures were in great demand. Popular magazines published his copious commercial assignments as well as his other images and were the source of his most consistently favorable reviews. Ironically, such periodicals as *Harper's Bazaar, Vanity Fair,* and *Vogue* were so successful in publicizing Man Ray's photographs that when he returned to the United States in 1940, he found that he was known only for his work with the camera.

This picture, originally published in the October 1934 issue of *Harper's Bazaar,* reveals Man Ray's prowess in combining the eye of the artist with the requirements of commercial work. The elegance of the evening gown by the French designer Augustabernard is graphically telegraphed to the viewer by the exaggerated, sinuous line, broken only by the dramatic flare at the hem. The model's face is in shadow, giving her an air of mystery that extends to the dress. Her anonymity and the absence of background detail other than the edge of the dressing mirror in which she is reflected ensure the viewer's complete concentration on the designer's creation.

Born in 1886, Augustabernard combined her first and last names in order to distinguish her house of couture, open in Paris from 1923 to 1935, from those with similar names. The designer, who died in 1946, was famous for the long lines and slim silhouettes of her dresses.

Man Ray 36

PLATE 36

Pablo Picasso

1934

Gelatin silver print
25.2 × 20 cm
84.XM.1000.77

Man Ray became acquainted with Picasso in the early 1920s in Paris and made a number of portraits of him over the years, including one that appeared in the July 1922 issue of *Vanity Fair*. It wasn't until the mid-1930s, however, that their friendship seems to have blossomed, perhaps in relation to Picasso's involvement with Surrealism. The Spaniard was one of André Breton's favorite painters and was mentioned in the first Surrealist manifesto as being "by far the most pure" practitioner of the principles with which the movement aligned itself. Despite its analytical basis, Picasso's Cubist style of painting in the early 1900s was considered an important precursor to Dadaism and Surrealism in its break from traditional modes of representation. Reciprocally, Picasso became interested in Surrealism's reliance on nonrational sources for visual imagery, including dreams and the subconscious mind, and allowed his work to be exhibited under its aegis.

Picasso had moved to Paris in 1904 and by the 1930s was already recognized as a master of twentieth-century art. In this monumental, almost sculptural portrait, Man Ray presents the artist as a working man whose gargantuan hands attest to his manual labors. Picasso was a practitioner of photography himself; Man Ray wrote an introduction to a selection of Picasso's work in this medium that was published in a 1937 issue of *Cahiers d'art*.

PLATE 37

Joan Miró

1936 gelatin silver print
from a circa 1934 negative
23 × 17.6 cm
84.XM.1000.146

Joan Miró, a painter from Barcelona, became dissatisfied with the increasing insularity and nationalism of Catalonia's literary and artistic vanguard and so moved to Paris in 1919. Not long after his arrival he sought out his countryman Pablo Picasso (pl. 36), whose work he admired for attempting to penetrate beyond the surface of things. Another important association was with his next-door neighbor André Masson, an artist who was instrumental in formulating Surrealism. The movement's nascent philosophy resonated with Miró's desire to express the essence of his subjects rather than simply their appearance, and in 1923–24 he rapidly developed a vocabulary of colorful, gestural biomorphic forms, prompting André Breton to hail him as one of the movement's most important artists.

Miró undoubtedly met Man Ray through mutual friends. This portrait lends a mysterious Jekyll-and-Hyde air to the unassuming painter, with half of his face appearing normal and the other half distorted by shadow. A rope loops behind his head, introducing an element of Surrealist menace and ambiguity into the picture and suggesting the mobile quality of line in Miró's own art.

PLATE 38

Mathematical
Object
1934

Gelatin silver print
30 × 23.3 cm
84.XM.1000.59

According to Man Ray, it was the artist Max Ernst who brought to his attention a group of three-dimensional models at the Institut Henri Poincaré in Paris. The forms, made of metal, wire, plaster, and wood and meant to illustrate algebraic equations, were so visually intriguing that Man Ray decided to photograph them. A dozen of the resulting pictures were published in a 1936 issue of the journal *Cahiers d'art* that was devoted to the Surrealist object. Man Ray and André Breton proposed substituting evocative titles for the models' original analytical labels in order to transform the photographs from rational images into irrational ones.

Man Ray took this group of pictures with him when he moved to Los Angeles in 1940, where they inspired the Shakespearean Equations, a series of twenty oil paintings. These canvases were shown at the Copley Gallery in Beverly Hills in 1948, each bearing the title of a different play by Shakespeare. This particular photograph was the basis for the painting *Measure for Measure*, named after the bard's dark comedy of 1604. Although the forms in the prints were the impetus for the series, Man Ray freely combined elements from the various models in composing the paintings. "The formulas accompanying them meant nothing to me, but the forms themselves were as varied and authentic as any in nature. The fact that they were man-made was of added importance to me," Man Ray wrote in his autobiography about the objects.

PLATE 39

Banana Plant

1935

Gelatin silver print
23.9 × 17.3 cm
84.XM.1000.49

The inspiration for this picture was undoubtedly the odd shape and texture of the gnarled banana plant. The image is somewhat unusual in having been taken outdoors; Man Ray was almost exclusively a studio photographer. By reducing some of the natural highlights and making this a dark print, he obscures some of the legibility and three-dimensionality of the image, creating a sense of dislocation. The surface quality of the object is reminiscent of a Surrealist painting technique called decalcomania, which involves pressing wet paint between two surfaces to achieve an unpredictable and highly textured effect.

The co-opting of found objects into the realm of art had been a practice of Man Ray's since his New York years, catalyzed by his association with Duchamp, who had exhibited readymades—common items, such as a snow shovel and a urinal—as artworks. These pieces challenged notions about worthy subject matter for art and the importance of the technical virtuosity of the artist. For Man Ray, photography was a way to create an instant replica of his found objects. He often claimed that a good copy was as good as the original to him.

PLATE 40

Monument
to Niépce

1937

Gelatin silver print
19.2 × 24.6 cm
84.XM.230.4

This print is Man Ray's homage to the French photographic pioneer Joseph Nicéphore Niépce. Niépce was born in 1765 in Gras, near Chalon-sur-Saône, and with his brother Claude was responsible for a number of inventions. In 1822 Niépce began his experiments with fixing images on glass plates, in 1826 he made the first known photograph on metal, and in 1829 he began collaborating with Louis-Jacques-Mandé Daguerre. After Niépce's death in 1833, Daguerre continued to advance this work, which resulted in the announcement of the process that bears his name—daguerre-otypy—in 1839. This rather imposing monument to Niépce was erected in 1933 near his hometown to correct the omissions of history.

Niépce's contributions to the develop-ment of photography have often gone unacknowledged, but there seems to have been a strong awareness of it among the Surrealist circle. In describing Man Ray in 1926, Robert Desnos wrote in *Paris soir*, "He has upset all established opinions in the now centenary discovery of Niépce." The scientist is also mentioned in *Surrealism*, the catalogue for an exhibition at the Julien Levy Gallery in 1936. The lavishness of this local remembrance of Niépce may have been heartening to Man Ray, who by this time had created a significant body of photographic work. He had already linked himself with early practitioners of the medium in his revival of the photogram and his use of the Sabattier effect; recording this monument connected his work with that of photography's founder.

PLATE 41

A Day and Night

July 1941

Gelatin silver print
24.5 × 19.6 cm
84.XM.1000.91

After having lived abroad for nearly two decades, Man Ray moved back to the United States in the summer of 1940. He was reluctant to leave Europe, but Nazi troops had occupied Paris. Recounting his return to America in his autobiography, Man Ray wrote: "I was overcome with a feeling of intense depression. Leaving twenty years of progressive effort behind me, I felt it was a return to the days of my early struggles, when I had left the country under a cloud of misunderstanding and distrust." After a short stay with family in New Jersey, he crossed the continent by car in the company of a traveling salesman, ending his journey in Los Angeles in October. With its thriving film industry, temperate climate, and swelling population of expatriate artists, writers, and musicians, Hollywood seemed like a good place to wait out the war.

Although Man Ray continued to make photographs until the end of his life, beginning in the 1940s his writings reflect an impatience with being associated primarily with that art form. This mixed-media work includes a photograph of the Los Angeles Coliseum (the rows of seats are visible through the archway), which the artist has used as the background for a pen-and-ink sketch. Drawn directly on the print, this study was later developed into the painting *L'homme infini* (The infinite man) of 1942. An inscription in the lower left corner of the image declares Man Ray's presence in Hollywood.

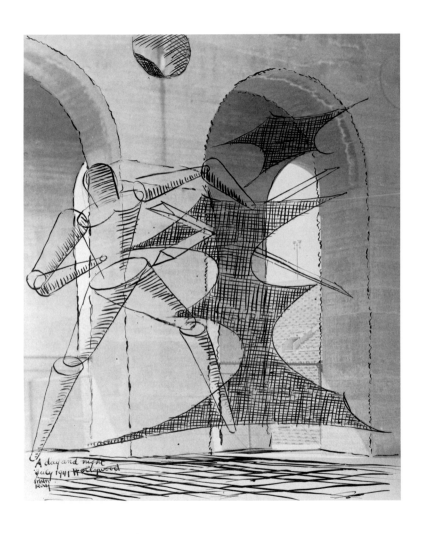

PLATE 42

Henry Miller
and Margaret Neiman

1942

Gelatin silver print
25.2 × 20 cm
84.XM.1000.133

Man Ray and the novelist Henry Miller were born a year apart, and both grew up in Brooklyn. The two were practically neighbors in Paris in the 1930s, but it wasn't until they both moved to California in the 1940s that they met and formed a close friendship. Like Man Ray, Miller had abandoned Europe only under duress and found himself at odds with his native land. After being rejected for a Guggenheim grant, he secured an advance to write a book chronicling his travels across America (published as *The Air-Conditioned Nightmare* in 1945) and left New York at about the time Man Ray was settling in Los Angeles. Arriving there months later, Miller took up residence with Margaret and Gilbert Neiman, an artist and writer who had befriended Man Ray.

Miller, author of the controversial novels *Tropic of Cancer* (1934) and *Tropic of Capricorn* (1939), joined their outings and parties, which sometimes included music, dancing, and impromptu entertainment. Man Ray recorded some of these occasions with his camera, photographing a visit to the Angel's Flight funicular as well as his friends cavorting in masks he had made. This image, a variant of another picture in the Getty Museum's collection, was taken outside Man Ray's Vine Street studio. Stripped to the waist, a masked Margaret Neiman hovers behind Miller, whose calm demeanor and full wardrobe provide an almost humorous contrast to his animated muse. In printing the negative, Man Ray rippled the photographic paper to distort the top of the composition.

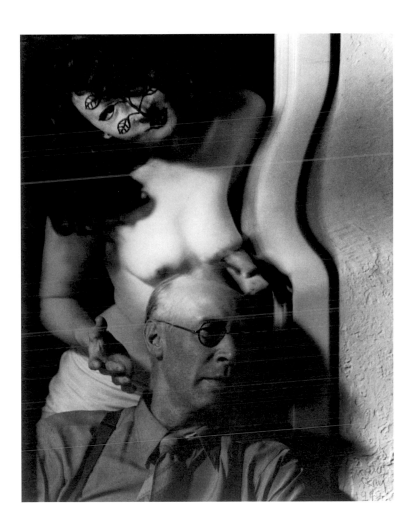

PLATE 43

Dead Leaf

1942

Gelatin silver print
24.1 × 19.9 cm
84.XM.1000.55

Remarkable for its starkness, this photograph of a brittle castor bean leaf recalls the banana plant (pl. 39) in its pure appreciation of form. The picture appeared with four others by Man Ray in the October 1943 issue of *Minicam Photography.* In his caption for the image, Man Ray writes with uncharacteristic poignancy of knowing that "the dying leaf would be completely gone tomorrow." It is tempting to interpret the work in terms of the artist's growing discontent in Los Angeles. "Aside from the weather, the atmosphere here is suffocating," he wrote to his sister Elsie in 1941.

Throughout the 1940s Man Ray's compositions were exhibited at major California cultural centers, including the M. H. de Young Memorial Museum in San Francisco, the Santa Barbara Museum of Art, the Pasadena Art Institute, and the Los Angeles Museum of History, Science, and Art. The mounting of these shows was something of a challenge since the artist had only a limited selection of pieces on hand in America and had to borrow pictures from friends and family to put on display. Despite these efforts, he was often dismissed as a novelty by reviewers and found few California collectors willing to acquire his creations. Once a celebrated member of the Paris vanguard, he was now incognito in a city that valued film stars more than artists. On top of this loss of identity, Man Ray also feared the loss of the body of work he had left behind in France. In letters to family and friends throughout the decade he writes of his mounting despair over the fate of his artworks, his comrades, and the whole way of life he had known.

PLATE 44

Ruth, Roses, and Revolvers

1942–44

Gelatin silver print
24.9 × 19.8 cm
84.XM.1000.113

Although Man Ray initially entertained the idea of working in the Hollywood motion picture industry, he quickly realized that he would have to relinquish the Chaplinesque creative control he had enjoyed in France. Unwilling to face the complications of collaboration, he rejected offers to serve as a cameraman, believing that a film's potential as art could only be realized in the hands of an auteur. However, a piece of short fiction he published under the title "Ruth, Roses, and Revolvers" in the December 1944 issue of the journal *View* was used as the basis for a cinematic scenario in the movie *Dreams That Money Can Buy* (1948), by the German filmmaker and former Dadaist Hans Richter.

This photograph appeared in conjunction with the original story, which refers to a withered rose stuck in dog excrement. The *vanitas* melancholy of the blowsy, plucked rose, with its scattered petals, is underscored by the pistol on the table, which contributes to the film noir atmosphere. On closer inspection, however, the pistol turns out to be merely a toy, adding a ridiculous and melodramatic air to the scene.

PLATE 45

Juliet with Vines

1943

Gelatin silver print
34.5 × 26.8 cm
84.XM.1000.54

In his first few days in Los Angeles, Man Ray had found a studio, purchased a car (see p. 129), and met his future wife, Juliet Browner, a thirty-year-old dancer who had come to California looking for work in the movies. Juliet had lived in the Greenwich Village section of New York, where she was associated with the Abstract Expressionist painter Willem de Kooning, and knew of Man Ray's work.

In this picture it seems that Man Ray has captured Pan in mid-frolic in the forest. The model is Juliet, whose "faun-like features and slanted eyes" he described in his autobiography. She devoted herself to her role as Man Ray's muse; over the course of their thirty-six years together he photographed her hundreds of times. The theatrical style of this image is a departure from Man Ray's figurative work of the 1920s and 1930s, which is generally quite stark. Although many of the pictures of Juliet are formal studies in which the eye is drawn to the beauty of her shape and features, others from the Los Angeles period introduce a narrative aspect, perhaps due to the influence of Hollywood. Juliet, with a background in modeling and modern dance, may also have inspired this fresh approach to photography, which often included the use of props and scenery.

The dramatic lighting seen in this image is also a heightened element in Man Ray's work during his decade in California. The print was made with a filter that created a textured effect. Man Ray often spoke of his desire to make photographs that didn't appear to be photographs—this technical experimentation may have been one way in which he addressed that concern.

PLATE 46

Juliet with Headdress

Circa 1945

Gelatin silver print
16.4 × 11.8 cm
84.XM.1000.69

This photograph captures the beauty of the
woman with whom Man Ray fell in love
and who became an important subject for
him. Juliet presents an elegant profile,
swathed in a scarf crowned with a Brazilian
headdress of straw and shells. A typed caption on the back of the picture suggests that
it may have been intended for publication,
possibly as a fashion image.

In this composition, as in *Noire et
blanche* (pl. 22), Man Ray poses his model
with an ethnographic object, contrasting
tribal aesthetics with the Western art tradition. However, while the mask cradled by a
bare-breasted Kiki unleashes a range of
assumptions of the time regarding African
social and sexual mores, the hat on Juliet's
head remains relatively neutral, functioning primarily as a prop to lend the portrait
an unspecified but exotic queenliness.

PLATE 47

Juliet in a
Blonde Wig

1951

Gelatin silver print
14.3 × 10.5 cm
86.XM.626.26

After six years together in Los Angeles, Man Ray and Juliet married in 1946 in a double wedding ceremony with Max Ernst and Dorothea Tanning (see p. 142). The following year the Man Rays ventured back to Paris to recover his belongings, but it wasn't until 1951 that they decided to relocate there, taking a studio near the Luxembourg Gardens.

Of all Man Ray's models and muses, Juliet was the most enduring and perhaps the most pliable. This theatrical scenario suggests some of the contortions required of her in the line of duty. Uncharacteristically, in this image one senses her tension, her face expressing the rigors of modeling or her impatience with the session. Unlike most of Man Ray's photographs of his wife, which emphasize her beauty, this picture

of her is intentionally unflattering and has a degrading quality to it that harks back to the Surrealist treatment of the female figure. Playing the role of a floozy, Juliet wears a tawdry blonde wig and is crouched over in a stagy pose that simultaneously recalls the bathers of Degas and calendar pinups in which the model appears startled to be captured frolicking in the nude. After the return to Paris, Juliet became Man Ray's primary photographic subject; he continued to take pictures of her nearly up to the time of his death.

Man Ray. *Self-Portrait with Beret*, 1946.
Gelatin silver print, 33.8 × 26.4 cm. 84.XM.1000.139.

A Labyrinth of Media:
The Photographs of Man Ray

David Featherstone: Man Ray is perhaps one of the most widely recognized names in twentieth-century art, primarily due to his association with the Dadaists and Surrealists in Paris in the 1920s and 1930s. While he produced artwork in a variety of media during his long and prolific career, in this discussion we are going to concentrate on his photography. As a point of departure, it might be useful to establish something of his early biography.

Katherine Ware: Man Ray was born as Emmanuel Radnitsky in Philadelphia on August 27, 1890, the eldest child. His family moved to Brooklyn in 1897. After graduating from high school, he was an apprentice to an engraver and then worked as a commercial draftsman and graphic designer in New York.

In 1910 he enrolled in courses at the National Academy of Design; in 1911 he took anatomy classes at the Art Students League. It was at about this time that his family decided to change its last name from Radnitsky to Ray. People think that Man Ray created his unusual, artistic name, but in fact, since Man was a nickname for Emmanuel, Man Ray was not an entirely invented name.

DF: Today, Man Ray is often alphabetized under *M* rather than *R*. Is this just an anomaly of history or did he actually think of himself as Man Ray?

Francis Naumann: Whenever he wrote to people, he would ask them to refer to him as Man Ray, not Mr. Ray.

KW: I know his second wife, Juliet, took the name Man Ray, but libraries tend to file his books under *R*. I didn't realize he had embarked on a campaign of it.

Merry Foresta: Oh, he did. In his autobiography he makes a point of saying that the French understood it and always called him Man Ray, but in America they had a lot of trouble. I think he was referring as well to the fact that Americans also had trouble with an artist like him.

DF: Do you have any feeling for what his personal motivation was in wanting to establish this singular name?

MF: I believe he was Manny Ray as a student around New York, but at a later point he may have found Man Ray much more marketable and serviceable for a futuristic kind of identity.

Dickran Tashjian: It's also very macho, an assertion of his maleness. Physically he was a small guy.

MF: At what point did he realize that Man and *main*—"hand" in French—are pronounced the same? Was it when he met Duchamp? Or before that, when he was living with his French-speaking first wife?

KW: Let's come back to that. To return to Man Ray's early chronology, in 1912 he began attending classes at the Ferrer Center in New York, where one of his teachers was the painter George Bellows. He was actively visiting galleries in New York, including Alfred Stieglitz's 291, and was designing covers for some political journals. In 1913 he moved to an artists' colony in Ridgefield, New Jersey, where he roomed with the painter Samuel Halpert and the writer Alfred Kreymborg. He also met Adon Lacroix there, the Belgian poet who became his wife in 1914.

Weston Naef: There are a few other dates I think are important to mention. In 1910 he was a plein air painter, more like a Hudson River school artist than the one we think of today. In 1912 he began signing his work as Man Ray. Nineteen thirteen was the year of Alfred Stieglitz's first retrospective survey. Man Ray saw it and was deeply impressed. We might consider this as his first confrontation with photography as a possible art form. And, on February 17, 1913, the red-letter day in the history of American avant-garde art, the Armory Show opened.

DF: That show influenced him greatly and directly led to his move to the artists' colony in New Jersey.

KW: During his years there Man Ray was very active as a painter. He had his first one-man exhibition of paintings and drawings in 1915 at the newly opened Daniel Gallery in New York.

FN: And at the end of 1915, after that show, he moved back to New York.

DF: The first photograph we're going to look at—*Self-Portrait* (pl. 1)—dates from 1916, after he returned to New York. This is a picture of an assemblage, a painting with an inoperative doorbell placed at the bottom and two bells attached at the top.

KW: This is an interesting image, considering what Merry brought up about the hand and his name, because there is a handprint right in the middle. But first we should talk about why Man Ray took up photography.

FN: I don't see any reason to challenge the scenario he presents in his autobiography. He says he wanted to make reproductions of his paintings, so he acquired a camera and a set of filters and just followed the instructions. I don't think Man Ray approached photography as an art form. It was something he wanted for the purpose of publicity. If he had photographs available, he knew he could provide them to different people in the press and give his work even greater exposure. It's important to note that he prepared for this even before he had his first one-man show.

Jo Ann Callis: It's truly remarkable that, having started from that point, Man Ray quickly leaped ahead. I think he almost instantaneously realized that he could create a parallel body of work with this other medium—photography.

Notice how carefully he has cropped the photograph, right to the edge. This is another piece, almost like the original but subtly different. I think he begins to consider what the camera is capable of as a transforming medium.

WN: I would like to introduce the idea that, with this picture, he is not creating a second body of work, but actually a substitute. The original no longer needed to exist, because the photograph was a higher power of realization.

FN: I honestly don't believe Man Ray thought this photograph had artistic content. He really was recording his painting for documentary purposes alone, and of course the painting still existed at the time. Even though you may find artistic content in it, I think he needed to actually sign it before he realized it could be a finished artistic object. To my knowledge, that happens for the first time in 1918 with the egg-beater and light reflector photographs, *Homme* and *Femme*.

WN: Let's talk for a moment about the creative decisions beyond the construction of the object that was photographed. Man Ray persistently photographed his own works of art, and he did it in a very unusual way for someone who was a professional photographer of art. At a time when electric photofloods were in common use—and Man Ray used them for other purposes—he photographed his own work outdoors in broad daylight. That's important for this particular image, because where he places the painting in relation to the sun creates a shadow. An important creative decision concerning this picture, which does not exist in the original work, is the shadow, which is added by the process of photography and which he knew could be eliminated. He could have changed the orientation or chosen a day when it was cloudy, without this direct light.

MF: I think that proves the point that this was a purely documentary photograph. He was trying to render the multimedia piece as a three-dimensional object.

WN: The most delicate way to do that would have been to create a subtle shadow for a bas-relief effect. I am arguing that he positioned the object so that the shadow on the bells becomes a major compositional element in the photograph. When the picture was used for its intended purposes, presumably for reproduction, the reproduction would look very different from the original painting. It is the shadows on those particular elements that move this into the realm of something very special.

MF: The shadows—especially the ones on the bells—subtly change the nature of the work by making it more facelike. The bells become eyes that are looking in a certain way; the button becomes more of a mouth that might be open.

WN: We know from years later, when Man Ray was working with Brancusi, that the sculptor said that "only he himself would know how to photograph" his sculptures. For me, this is photographing a work of art from the perspective the photographer-artist imagines it to be seen, and those shadows add that element.

MF: And we know that shadows become a very important theme for Man Ray; he uses them throughout all the rest of his work.

JC: When you make objects and photograph them to be art photographs, it's different than when you just document them, but when you document them, you still have to consider the impact of the shadow.

MF: It took a certain amount of courage for an American artist to make this kind of assemblage at the time.

JC: And to make it a self-portrait.

MF: I am curious about how that powerful hand in the center actually functions. It's a double self-portrait in the sense that it's a face and a hand.

DT: *Main.* The hand. Man Ray.

MF: It's a gesture painting, the primal touch of the artist. It's extraordinary.

KW: There's also a defacing element—putting his paint-covered hand in the middle of the picture.

FN: For reasons I've never understood, this is never described for what it is, a doorway. Around the outer periphery he's even drawn the molding of the door. And what else do you have at a doorway but a doorbell? You press a button, but you can't get through because the bell is not working. Not only is it not working, his hand is right there to stop you from entering.

KW: Are those french curves that he would have used in his drafting work?

FN: Yes, but he sets them up like clef signs or sound holes.

KW: And the doorbell becomes a note on the scale that you don't hear because the button isn't working.

DF: I'd like to go back to what Merry said about the courage that Man Ray was showing. It occurs to me that, for Man Ray, perhaps the Armory Show came along at just the right time. If he had been born five years earlier, he might have been set enough in an artistic direction that he would have rejected what he saw. If he had been born five years later, he would have been eighteen years old and not mature enough to respond to it.

MF: In the painting world there was a huge, conservative backlash to the Armory Show. I think American artists stalled and retrenched.

FN: Man Ray said that it took him six months to recover from seeing the exhibition. The first portrait that he painted afterward was of Alfred Stieglitz; it seems significant that he immortalized Stieglitz in what is basically a Cubist picture.

DF: Would the Armory Show have been his first exposure to Marcel Duchamp?

FN: Yes, probably. He would have first heard the name there and seen *Nude Descending a Staircase*. They met in 1915 in Ridgefield. Man Ray recalls in his autobiography that they couldn't carry on a conversation because of a language barrier, so they played tennis instead.

MF: I think Man Ray, more than many young American artists at the time, was placed very well to engage in a kind of European intellectual exchange. He was comfortable with the political discussions at the Ferrer Center and had been living with a woman who was European. There were aspects to his life that allowed him to interact with artists like Duchamp and then with the Dadaists and Surrealists in Paris in the twenties.

DF: Man Ray is very closely identified with Paris in the public mind. What actually led to his going there?

FN: Man Ray was greatly attracted to French-speaking people, even before his marriage to Adon Lacroix. He longed to go to Paris. He entered into a correspondence with Tristan Tzara as early as 1920 and openly proclaimed that since Dada could not live in New York, he was anxious to get to Paris.

MF: Man Ray's photographs went to Paris even before he did. He sent the pictures that Francis referred to earlier to Francis Picabia to be published in a magazine, but then Tzara asked to use them in his big Dada show in 1920. This is important, because when Man Ray got to Paris in 1921, he was a known entity, at least within the Dada circle.

KW: And photography was a way to distinguish himself.

MF: In his autobiography he states that he arrived in France on Bastille Day, July 14. In fact, his boat docked several days later. I think he wanted to join his personal revolution with that of France. In Paris he was welcomed by Duchamp and quickly became established with the Dadaists.

WN: Established and accepted?

MF: Yes. It's an extraordinary thing, because American artists throughout the late teens and the twenties continually complained that they could not make inroads in Paris. The only people Americans sat with in the cafés were other Americans; Gertrude Stein would not talk to any of the Americans. Man Ray knew everybody very quickly, however. The Dada group was fabulously interested in the United States—cartoons and silent films and jazz and skyscrapers—and here comes Man Ray straight from New York to tell them what's what.

WN: He was a messenger coming from a place without a tradition of hundreds of years of art consciousness, unlike Europe. Modernism in America was born from the improbable parentage of popular culture mixed with machine age residue.

JC: And the Dadaists knew they could use him—they needed him.

MF: Right, for all the reasons that he had been useful in New York. He took portraits, created marketing for them, and made a record of the group via the camera.

DT: It's also important that he came on the recommendation of Duchamp, who held a special position within the Dada bunch, not only because he was the older brother but also because he had maintained his independence. Man Ray maintained the same kind of independence throughout his stay in Paris. He was sought after by various factions and groups but was never an official member.

DF: This next photograph, which Man Ray made two years after he arrived in Paris, depicts Duchamp with his glass painting *Water Mill within Glider, in Neighboring Metals* (pl. 15). The print has been trimmed to the shape of the piece.

MF: I think the occasion for taking this picture was the framing of the glass. This becomes both a documentation of the work and a portrait of the artist as a work of art.

DF: If you think of how the picture was made, it quickly becomes an act of performance art.

WN: Man Ray and Duchamp together were facing the problem of how to photograph a piece that's difficult to photograph since it has to be held upright. Here, Duchamp inadvertently becomes part of the picture.

JC: I don't think it's inadvertent. If you look at how Duchamp has his leg drawn up, it just fills that curve. Duchamp in his black suit makes it possible to read this picture; he is providing a background. Man Ray has asked him to draw his leg up to fill in the curve, and his sleeve is pulled back so that it doesn't interfere with the open part of the picture.

FN: So it's by no means a documentation; it's actually the opposite of the *Self-Portrait* (pl. 1).

DT: It's clearly a performance piece, I think. You have to pose like that, and it's an awkward pose. What's interesting to me is that the painting is transparent. One could ask, "If it's transparent, where is the artist in this work?" And suddenly, here is the artist, which suggests something about his self-identification with the work.

MF: This is not just an anomaly. Man Ray and Duchamp had collaborated in this kind of studio artwork portrait in New York as well.

FN: You have to ask yourself if Man Ray is just an innocent documentarian taking pictures. Obviously not, for Duchamp is allowing him the liberty to experiment. I'm sure that this is the result of a collaboration.

WN: Man Ray's name is on the front of many of the Man Ray-Duchamp pieces. An important demarcation point is when he gets the license from Duchamp to be almost an equal collaborator. I read this picture as a double portrait.

JC: Duchamp must have realized that the glass was not going to last and that this photograph was going to be the record of it. We talk about the camera documenting what's in front of it, but if what's in front of it is an abstract thing, then you produce an abstract work. Of course, Man Ray takes great liberties; he puts them in shadow and orchestrates the whole thing.

DF: How did they get from playing tennis together because they couldn't communicate in a common language to this picture of a close relationship?

FN: Man Ray learned a little bit of French through his marriage to Adon Lacroix, and Duchamp learned English well enough to be interviewed in the language.

KW: They were both involved in New York in establishing the Société Anonyme and publishing *New York Dada*. For a while they lived next to each other in Paris.

MF: When this photograph was made, they were working together, but there was competition as well. Man Ray was trying to be a famous artist; in a way, he wanted to be Duchamp. He wanted to have the kind of cachet, the European mystique that no American could ever really match. Man Ray wanted to be in Paris what Duchamp was in New York, and for a while I think he succeeded at that.

DF: Another area of photography Man Ray explored was the photogram, which he developed into a special technique he branded the Rayograph. This 1922 example (pl. 10) was included in a portfolio he produced called *Les champs délicieux*, which had a preface by Tristan Tzara.

KW: Around the time this image was made, a number of artists were experimenting with putting objects on light-sensitive paper and making pictures of them. László Moholy-Nagy called his pictures photograms; Christian Schad used the name Schadographs. We don't have any firm evidence that they had seen each other's work, but Tzara would have seen Schad's images in Zurich.

DF: The effect of a photogram is something that every photographer stumbles across at some point.

JC: Yes, and in every beginning photo class you teach about light-sensitive materials that way.

DT: It's a very tactile process. Notice in this image how Man Ray has included the hand again, like in the *Self-Portrait*. I've always been impressed by his ability to manipulate things; he seems to have these wonderful, adroit hands. Here you see the hands in the process itself.

KW: They also animate things. The gyroscope might seem immobile, but the hands start it spinning.

MF: There are a lot of wonderful reversals going on here. If indeed what he's emphasizing is the handwork that is necessary to make a Rayograph, then he is very directly addressing the old idea that a photograph can't be art because it's made by a machine. Here the handwork is literally making the image.

There are two thoughts about Man Ray's development of the Rayograph process. One is that he discovered it by accident, that if you put things down on the paper and turn on the light, you get this kind of image. It was a very exciting Dada discovery. The other is that he was actually working within a Dada system, trying to subvert both painting and photography at the same time. These are paintings with light, made without a brush or canvas; photographs made without a camera.

FN: In his autobiography, every time he says that something happened by accident, it's always one that happened in his favor. If something is invented by accident, like the Rayograph, then it has even more meaning if you happen to be the intelligent person who understands its ramifications. He's such a genius that he even creates by accident!

DT: If you think of a straight photograph as being a precise recording of something that gets reproduced exactly by virtue of camera exposure and a contact print, here is the logical extension of that; you put the objects down on the paper itself.

JC: And each print is unique. If you're a painter, to be able to make a unique image would be really important, but for a lot of photographers, that's not the case. My guess is that for Man Ray it was very important to be unique, but we also know he would photograph the Rayographs and then print multiple copies of them. I think the rarity of the Rayographs would have increased their respect in the painting world.

DT: I don't think he calculated that when he first began the process, but he probably did very soon afterward. He had that kind of mind; he was a very cerebral, self-conscious artist, and he would have seen the implications of this once he had "discovered" the process.

MF: Accident or not, it's a very elemental process that Tzara obviously picked up on as a Dadaist idea, but for Man Ray, the Rayograph fit into a line of thinking that he had begun with the airbrush paintings in New York. It was the aerographs that he took to Paris, and that's what made up most of his first show there.

KW: I'm amazed at Man Ray's decision in 1922 to prepare the limited edition album of Rayographs—*Les champs délicieux*—for sale, that he thought there was a market for these. Tzara may have been the one pushing to release it, but it seems that they were both excited by the work and wanted people to see it,

FN: I don't know how many were sold, but he must have felt that there was an audience.

MF: He tried desperately to get Gertrude Stein to buy one, and she would not. By that time, Gertrude and Leo's position as gatekeepers to the avant-garde in Paris was somewhat past, and she had become very anti-American.

WN: Man Ray knew something about the politics of art, and he clearly expected that Stein would be able to do something for his career. He was still fighting with the question as to whether he was a painter or a photographer, and many aspects of his career were contingent upon that self-definition.

DT: In the notes to his 1944 retrospective in Pasadena he comments that when he went to Paris he was terrified of being an alien in a foreign country without any visible means of support, so he frantically went to work as a photographer. It was economic necessity, real or imagined, that propelled him to turn himself into a photographer.

WN: At this point there was a division in his own mind. He had done a very major thing, leaving New York for Paris without an agreement with the Daniel Gallery that he would send some pictures back for sale. It seems to me that he would have wanted to maintain a presence in New York, because that was the only certainty.

But what does he do when he arrives in Paris? He begins hanging out with poets. He becomes fascinated with words and actions and gestures and, even worse, falls deeply in love with photography and, worse still, invents the Rayograph and falls more deeply in love with that.

MF: Man Ray was very busy with the Dadaists. He had lots to do, and I think he was beginning to be aware that he was not going to be able to do all things for all people. But he was still encouraged by the fact that everything he did seemed to be marvelous to this group, even though Dada was nearly over by the time he got there. He was the last brief resuscitation of it, and when he first began to make the Rayographs, I think he was still in that surge of all these things.

DF: In his early years in Paris, how actively was he actually painting?

MF: I think he had somewhat abandoned it. He was very caught up in the idea that he was painting with light and that he could also make films.

FN: Man Ray did see the Rayograph as a liberation from painting. He must have expressed this to Duchamp, because Duchamp wrote back to him, "I am very happy to see that you have finally given up the sticky medium of paint." I noticed in the Tzara-inscribed copy of *Les champs délicieux* in the Getty Museum's collection that Man Ray wrote to Arnold Crane in 1968, "The Rayograph is the first step in the liberation from photography." He defines *liberation* as "doing what one is not supposed to do." What's interesting is that, at first, he sees the Rayograph as a liberation from painting, then as a liberation from the camera.

MF: At this point I think he truly believed that the art world was going to change and accommodate all of these new forms.

DT: There was a utopian streak in the man.

FN: In New York, he was trying to resolve the formalist problem of rendering a three-dimensional world on a two-dimensional surface. Then in Paris, he found a medium that resolved all of these concerns, putting three-dimensional objects on a two-dimensional surface. He insisted in nearly every interview that the Rayograph was not a photogram in the traditional sense. He did something that a photogram didn't; he introduced depth into the images.

WN: Since the Rayographs are such an important part of his life, it might be useful to quote a statement about them. In 1963, on the occasion of an exhibition of Rayographs at a gallery in Stuttgart, Man Ray wrote: "Like the undisturbed ashes of an object consumed by flames these images are oxidized residues fixed by light and chemical elements of an experience, an adventure, not an experiment. They are the result of curiosity, inspiration, and these words do not pretend to convey any information." That's an interesting statement about what he intended to do. He says they are not documents in any way; they contain no information. He essentially tells us that they are visual poems, and their concreteness is what becomes so important to him.

DF: The next photograph we are going to discuss is the portrait of Picasso (pl. 36). Dickran described Man Ray as being anxious about how he was going to make a living in Paris—it seems that portraiture was what he found.

WN: Man Ray had demonstrated skill as a portraitist in painting well before arriving in Paris. He had a talent for capturing likenesses with his drawing. I recollect that he admired John Singer Sargent enormously. One of his very first artistic commissions was a portrait of a family friend, and he tried to do a Sargentesque, full-size portrait of her.

MF: I think a great part of that was becoming a society portraitist like Sargent was. What the camera and being a portraitist allowed him to do was gain entry to places that he would never have been able to go otherwise. He would never have been close to Gertrude Stein or known Picasso as well or become part of that elite group of aristocrats, moneyed Americans, and well-known artists that he very quickly joined in Paris in the twenties.

FN: But his entrée to Stein and Picasso was because he had received commissions to photograph their artworks—Stein's art collection and Picasso's work.

MF: He says in his autobiography that after photographing people's artworks, if he had an extra plate, he would ask if he could do their portrait. He would bring the pictures back, and people would see how good they were. What struck me was how much the portrait work came to be not only an ongoing source of income for him but also a kind of albatross, because he was stuck making people's portraits. I think it became a problem in that he was invited as a guest, but he was the person with the camera. Yes, he had entrée, but he was there working.

DT: By the early nineteenth century, portraiture was considered inferior to history and landscape painting. It seems that this was transposed to photography as well.

MF: In Man Ray's archive in Paris, when it still existed within his studio, if you looked through boxes of negatives, there were portraits of people you had never heard of, the most boring pictures imaginable. A portrait like this of Picasso certainly distinguishes itself as one of the quality pictures. You have Picasso, but you have the Man Ray signature on the bottom. It's like he's adding himself once again into this combination; they are connected.

JC: How would we react to this portrait if the subject were a plumber? On the merit of the image itself, on an aesthetic level, how important is it that this is Picasso? In Man Ray's portraits, how important is it that these are famous people?

DT: If this were not Picasso, but just a plumber, I think one would say that there is an amazing presence here. There are so many pictures in the Man Ray estate that are portraits like any other photographer would make. But when the sitter was a famous person, Man Ray must have said, "Look, I've got to put something in here that will partly capture what I know this person to be." The other people he didn't know at all, so what could he even do? But for Joan Miró, or for Picasso, he had to put something in the picture that would tell you it was more than just a standard portrait photograph.

JC: It has that quintessential Picasso gaze—it's really riveting. Look at the size of his hands! They're gargantuan! He's holding his face, and the line of his hair is continued down through his hands. You really get the feeling of touching the face.

WN: It's also worth noting, I think, that there is a continuous thread that runs through Man Ray's life of the conflict between what he *wanted* to do and what he *had* to do. It seems that he blossomed when he was in front of the people he photographed by choice rather than those who hired him to make their pictures. During these early years, he found his way into the presence of Henri Matisse, Georges Braque, Max Ernst, André Derain, Constantin Brancusi, Le Corbusier,

Sinclair Lewis, Ezra Pound, all celebrities, and he usually photographed them at his own expense.

MF: There is a wonderful series of correspondence that in fact was part of the breach between Man Ray and Gertrude Stein, arguing over why she hadn't paid him. She thought he should give her the pictures for free because she was Gertrude Stein and she was lending herself to him. He thought, "You're Gertrude Stein. You can afford to pay me. Give the artist some money."

DT: William Carlos Williams was astonished, and I think offended, at the price he had to pay for the portraits Man Ray took of him in Paris. He didn't want them!

KW: So there were actually two kinds of portraits in the twenties and thirties. There were those Man Ray made because they paid the bills and allowed him entrée into a certain group of people, and those he took out of a personal interest or connection to the subject. He understood the trade-off that this got him, because he talked about how some people had to pay a lot and some not at all. He was supporting himself with this work, but sometimes getting paid was also part of establishing his credibility as an artist worthy of remuneration.

MF: That's right. It was the twenties, before the crash; there was a lot of money, and people were coming in to be photographed. By the time this portrait of Picasso was made, in 1934, Man Ray had money in his pocket. He had established himself, and Picasso certainly was established. And in a year they would be vacationing together in the south of France. They were buddies, and they were equal in the sense that Man Ray was known around Paris. He was part of this set now, as opposed to the wacky group of Dadaists where he started in the early twenties.

WN: When Man Ray arrived in Paris, he surrounded himself mainly with writers, poets, and people who were literary, who had no product to see. Picasso is a man of the eyes, one who has realized for the eyes what these other people thought about. It must have been a tremendous boost to Man Ray's self-confidence to find that somebody as important as Picasso respected his work.

DF: Let's move on to this 1924 image, *Violon d'Ingres* (pl. 17), which shows Kiki—Man Ray's lover for a number of years in the twenties—with the f-holes of a stringed instrument superimposed on her back.

WN: This famous picture is so well known through postcards and other reproductions that it is etched in our consciousness.

MF: Before we historians jump into this, I'd be interested in having Jo Ann speak first. I'd like to hear what an artist has to say about it.

JC: I think this shows Man Ray's interest in the female form as an object or as something of reverence. Here he makes Kiki into a violin, an object of beauty and grace. Man Ray's reference is to Ingres's hobby, which was playing the violin. What is interesting here is the volume of her form and the tactility of her skin, the softness of that and the harder edge of the black f-holes. They sit up on the surface, but at the same time they also seem to be on her back. It goes back and forth; it's visually curious. I don't know how they were made. You could expose the picture from a negative and then lay a mask over it and burn in the black. That would be one of the easiest ways to create this.

FN: The original of this image is in the Pompidou Center in Paris, in the André Breton collection. Those sound holes are painted in gouache onto the surface of the picture. The print there is inscribed to Breton; Man Ray probably rephotographed it before it was inscribed. There are many that are signed in the same way that this version is, in the lower right-hand corner. The largest print of this is in a private collection in New York. It's probably thirty-six inches high, and the f-holes were done differently, actually just as Jo Ann described.

WN: So there are three ways this image was created: the first as a photograph with painting on it; a second state, which is that photographed—what we are looking at here; and a third state, which would probably be a later state, the very large version created by enlarging a copy of a copy.

MF: In the Man Ray studio there is a box of Kiki negatives, and about ten are clearly the same studio setting as this one. They were obviously trying out the pose to get the right one, because she's in different positions.

FN: That's why I think this photograph was not contrived. He was just taking pictures of her in a Turkish costume and saw this form and said, "Wow, that looks like a violin," and it came together. The title was an afterthought.

KW: I think this walks an interesting line between the classicism of the nude and the more contemporary act of adding the marks on her back, the appreciation of the female form versus the objectification of it. I like that it holds these contradictions. There is humor, but it's also an homage.

DF: It recalls the first photograph we looked at today (pl. 1), where the clef forms were part of a self-portrait. Here he's taken similar forms and imposed them on her.

FN: I wonder how much he knew about general history, because in seventeenth-century Dutch paintings an idle viola da gamba was considered a sexual invitation for a man to straddle his legs around it.

KW: What do you think would have been Man Ray's attraction to a nineteenth-century painter like Ingres, when he was so forward-looking in other respects?

MF: I think he had a great reverence for particular painters of the past—as the Surrealists did. They argued that certain ideas were already in place and therefore chose people who were proto-Surrealists and brought them forward.

FN: He had a great deal of respect for classical artists.

MF: Man Ray was also very interested in anatomical studies. The drawing class he took at the National Academy of Design was in anatomy. There are drawings from that period that he kept for many years, and they are typical model studies. There is a whole series of Kiki drawings that are classical anatomical studies. In a way, he always played with this idea of drawing the nude over and over again.

WN: And the photograph is another kind of drawing.

MF: It's a drawing in that way—the practice, the pose of the model. He constantly used it in that way as well as in more inventive ways like this.

FN: I'm always fascinated by how black and stark he made the shapes. He did not make any attempt to have you read this image as though the clefs were actually on her back, like tattoos.

WN: I think what I find so intriguing about this picture is that it's both playful and serious at the same time. It's a picture about a profound subject—the human form—and also about a major painting from the history of art—Ingres's *Turkish Bath*—yet somehow it's not a caricature of either womanhood or the painting it's derived from. It resides in this very delicate place that used to be called "the witty"—something that is still deserving of serious consideration without reaching caricature.

KW: Humor is so important in Man Ray's work. His titles often gave things a whimsical twist. Sometimes it can seem a little flippant, but we know that he was serious about what he was doing.

DF: This next portrait, of the Marquise Casati (pl. 8), exhibits some of that playful humor.

KW: The Marquise Casati was a famous, eccentric aristocrat who, according to Man Ray, appeared at the hotel where he was staying and asked him to do a portrait of her in her salon. She wanted to be surrounded by her objects, the things she loved. He wasn't pleased with the results, but she wanted to see the pictures anyway. One of the photographs from that sitting is the well-known portrait with the multiple eyes (p. 119). This image (pl. 8) is possibly from the same session. She's wearing a lacy shawl, and her hair is all awry, which is something that Man Ray describes in writing about the initial sitting.

MF: Casati came out of the tradition of the turn-of-the-century, moneyed, Proustian lower aristocracy, where everyone dabbled in the arts in a slightly eccentric manner. She was the last of that breed, in a way. She was also a very well-heeled client; she hung around the avant-garde and paid a lot of people's bills.

DF: This photograph is dated 1922, and there are others of her dated up to 1930. Did she have that long a relationship with Man Ray?

MF: Yes. Not just with Man Ray, but with the Dada circle and then with the Surrealists. At the same time, she also helped support the fashion industry. People like her bought the clothes that kept fashion going; they had the style that was part of the American attraction to Paris at the time.

DT: I like the way this photograph is an artifice unto itself, because it is the internal framing that sets up the picture. It's clearly very carefully posed, but at the

Man Ray. *The Marquise Casati*, 1922.
Gelatin silver print, 21.4 × 16.5 cm.
Philadelphia Museum of Art: Gift of Carl Van Vechten, '49-86-4.

same time she is set up as part of the artificial plant that's inside the glass case.

JC: Do you realize that Man Ray is in this picture, too? You can see him reflected in the ball, taking the picture. She's holding him in the crystal ball and telling his fortune, conjuring him up as though he is some kind of apparition.

WN: Look at her eyes—she's made up like a raccoon. That's probably the way she went around every day. It may be worth comparing this to the Picasso portrait (pl. 36), which is twelve years later, to give us an idea of how much Man Ray's sense of portraiture changed in the intervening years.

JC: In a way, this is not a portrait, but a setup. It's a still life with a person in it.

KW: There is also the difference between a portrait-for-hire and one done for a friend. The portrait of Picasso is very much Man Ray and Picasso mano a mano; this picture has to do with fashion and the avant-garde scene in Paris.

JC: She's just another object here. The picture is interesting to look at because her eyes are so compelling, but it seems contrived. It's dramatic but in no way natural.

DT: I think it is artifice, a kind of performance event, like the Duchamp photograph (pl. 15).

WN: *Violon d'Ingres* (pl. 17), when you think about it, is also a bit contrived.

MF: Wouldn't you say that it is a figure study more than a portrait of Kiki?

WN: Yes, but as a figure study it's still contrived by adding the sound holes so deliberately. It's the same thing as putting the figure of Casati behind the glass. It's a very deliberate, forceful artistic decision around which everything else revolves.

JC: But it seems like *Violon d'Ingres* was more about what you can do by combining a drawing element with the photograph. This portrait of Casati may be aesthetically pleasing, but it's not as compelling as that of Picasso, which really grabs you. She's within the frame, which makes it nice; she's holding the ball, and he's in the ball.

FN: He might have brought that sphere with him, because there is some evidence that he owned it. It shows up in other images. But I can't imagine taking a two-pound crystal ball to a photo session unless you think beforehand that you will need it.

WN: I'd like to go back to the fashion issue that Merry raised. I have always liked this picture because it's partway between a portrait of a person and a photograph of fancy clothes. When I first looked at it years ago, I thought it was made for a designer, but the clothes are so subordinate to the making of the picture that only a very courageous photographer willing to defy the designer's ego would be able to do it. Casati may have liked this, and she may have been a collaborator in it, but it was still a fairly defiant gesture of the artist in control.

MF: I have never read anything that would corroborate what I am about to say, but going along with your idea that this was a fashion shoot, at this time Man Ray had just started to work for Paul Poiret, the prominent Parisian designer. It's conceivable that Man Ray had gone to Casati's apartment to do a fashion shoot and then they started playing around.

WN: That would account for carrying a crystal ball. He knows he's going on a shoot; he needs some props that he can rely on.

FN: He depicted a crystal ball in an airbrush drawing in 1919 that was called *The Eye That Beholds All*. Perhaps it isn't pure coincidence that what comes out of this photo session is a portrait of eyes.

MF: And it is the eye that sees all, the crystal ball, that holds the photographer with the camera, which is indeed the eye that sees all.

DF: The next picture we're going to consider is *La prière* (pl. 27).

WN: This photograph is both erotic and adorational; it's so contrary to the style of all of Man Ray's other nudes. Does anyone know who the model was?

MF: At one time I thought it was Meret Oppenheim, the artist associated with the Surrealists whose most famous piece is the fur-covered teacup. I found an album in Man Ray's studio with lots of different contact sheets of people organized by subject. A contact print of this photograph appears on both of two pages that were devoted exclusively to Oppenheim, so I drew the conclusion that if he included this picture on two pages of portraits of her, it must be her.

WN: The problem is that the print is dated 1930, but he didn't meet Oppenheim until 1932.

MF: Yes, so the identification is inconclusive, but to me it looks like it could be her body. She seemed to be very comfortable with being nude.

WN: This is one of those intriguing technical details. It can't be Kiki, because she left in 1929; it can't be Oppenheim, because she didn't arrive until 1932, unless that date is wrong. The person he was seeing at this point was Lee Miller—could she have been the model? Or did Man Ray hire someone to pose for this? He was using professional models at the time.

MF: I thought this might have been somebody for hire, too, just because it is such an extreme posture. It's a very vulnerable pose to be in while somebody is standing behind you with a camera. It would be hard to find a friend who would do this.

KW: I don't know that this necessarily has to be a professional model. There were a number of women who were part of his group for whom this would have been a Surrealist performance.

DT: It's certainly Surrealist in the sense that it's antireligious, possibly anticlerical.

MF: It's almost as if somebody had read Breton or listened to his most recent tirade at a café and then made this picture as an illustration of it.

DT: I see this as an ideological statement. It's a satiric comment on the whole idea of prayer and the church.

FN: He probably came up with the title after he took the picture. I don't think he was setting up to make a prayer. It's just a beautiful idea of the woman grabbing that far back to cover herself and bending over at the same time—he seized the opportunity. In the end, it is made irreverent, if nothing else, by calling it *Prayer.*

JC: Even on a formal level it's Surrealist, with the big, round shapes that these two hands, which are disembodied, are holding like two melons. And then there are the feet. I think this would appeal to Man Ray's Surrealist affinity.

WN: That's true. One of the Surrealist elements here is the decontextualization, what Jo Ann called disembodiment. We don't know where the rest of her body is or what may be being done to it. That part is left to our imagination.

DT: You can talk about the photograph in a formal way, but does that override everything else that's going on here?

JC: Oh, no. I think it's about sex! About women, and the joy of photographing them.

DT: You do? She's so vulnerable here; it's a very disturbing picture.

JC: It is, but that's a part of the pleasure of it. It's forbidden, but there's good taste in that she's actually covering herself. It's definitely a sexual image, but by covering her he leaves it to your imagination to fill in the part that's covered. It's very vulnerable, but it invites you.

DT: What if you take away the title, what happens to it then?

WN: We know that Man Ray loved titles, but he didn't seem to care whether the title came before, during, or after. He loved titles that somehow were a latch to understanding his work, that created a further enigma.

KW: Not ambiguity exactly, but resonance. You might not figure out exactly what he meant by naming it *Prayer*, but the title sets up an atmosphere of understanding.

DT: Is this supplication, then? Prayer as supplication, if we take it nonironically?

WN: Prayer is a very complicated statement. Every religion has a different kind of prayer. We assume this is Christian prayer, but Muslims pray in a way more like this. They kneel and supplicate. But let's just talk about methods of Christian prayer. When you kneel to pray, you kneel to ask for forgiveness, understanding, or a favor. That's where the word *supplication* comes in, because prayer is usually to subordinate yourself to a higher being, no matter which faith you're talking about. The problem here is the misogynist aspect of the picture. When you first see it, it's an adorational image born out of, "Hey, this is why you're in Paris; this is wine, women, and song," and it's very simple. It gets more complicated once you take the title into account. Once it is seen in the context of Surrealism—the decontextualization and the disembodiment—it starts getting into the uglier phases.

JC: Could this be like Andres Serrano's *Piss Christ*?

MF: Very much. Such a large part of the Surrealist agenda was an anticlerical, anti religion commentary. In this picture there is so much forbidden knowledge, boundaries you are not supposed to cross. This is set up for a very particular agenda.

KW: It's worth mentioning in this context that Man Ray's family was Jewish, but his own religious heritage wasn't an active part of his life.

FN: When this picture was made, Picasso was famous for being able to take a woman apart and reorganize her in different positions. There are paintings by Picasso where the breasts take the place of buttocks; here Man Ray has put a woman in such an unusual position that the image is intentionally ambiguous. Imagine any other time when the back of your hands can be flush with the back of your feet. Hands don't normally hold your own rear end; if anything, they hold your breasts. Maybe the visual metaphor here is similar to what Picasso was doing.

DF: Photographs like *La prière* reflect Man Ray's ties to Surrealism, but that influence is also seen in his fashion photographs, and it was really this work that brought him his greatest public recognition during the 1930s.

KW: This photograph of an Augustabernard gown (pl. 35) appeared in *Harper's Bazaar* in October 1934, although this print is dated 1936.

WN: Nothing could be more opposite to darkroom drudgery than working with these elegant people and fancy materials.

DT: Right. Man Ray found the darkroom work, and I think commercial work ultimately, a drudgery. In the 1940s he decided that he was going to give up photography. He continued to take all sorts of photographs, but he rarely did commercial work in the 1940s. Throughout the mid- to late 1930s he primarily worked for *Harper's Bazaar*; he became one of the first celebrity photographers during that time. In an interview later in life he said that he could talk the language of the fashion editors, that he liked to deal with the fashion models because it was all about sex appeal and getting close to these beautiful women. I have always suspected that this was Man Ray talking tough as usual, trying to act macho, but at the same time it's clear the man really did love women. He worked very hard as a photographer, not simply going through the motions of doing those sessions. His fashion photographs are extraordinary, not only for their technical quality but also for the imagination that went into them. Man Ray was quite different from someone like Salvador Dalí, who would do anything to make a buck.

MF: He didn't just take the picture, he composed it and often made the background. He really changed the way fashion was presented in magazines. In this photograph there is a wonderful anonymous face, and the dress becomes a silhouette. This kind of thing was not done before; a much more elaborate set would have been used.

DT: This is like a takeoff on the distorted nudes André Kertész did.

WN: Do you think that he knew the work of Kertész?

DT: Yes. This is a kind of domestication of that work. It's clearly not Surrealist in the way that Kertész's distortions are, but nevertheless I think that Man Ray was able to take someone else's technique and use it to his own advantage.

MF: He is also totally sympathetic with the designer here. This dress is all about

Man Ray. *Self-Portrait in Hollywood Studio,* 1944.
Gelatin silver print, 24.8 × 19.6 cm. 84.XM.1000.71.

elongation and the line from the long part of the torso to the flare at the bottom. That's what makes this dress extraordinary, and what does he do? He uses a technique that emphasizes it even further.

KW: He's not only being stylized as a photographer but also contributing to the understanding of the designer's vision.

MF: This is less Surrealistic than some of the fashion work he did for *Harper's* during the mid-thirties. What I think Man Ray understood so thoroughly is how much the context in which the image is published or shown matters. Whether it's *La Révolution Surréaliste* or *Harper's Bazaar,* the image doesn't change, but the context changes. The audience changes.

KW: This is one of the starker fashion images Man Ray did. It's so streamlined, and the model's face is so much in shadow. It's not a picture that you look at and think is beautiful immediately, but the more you look at it, the more you appreciate this incredible form.

WN: It's easy to look at for a long time. It's clean and simple and also exaggerated in a strange way, but what can we say about it beyond that? Is this merely a decorative photograph that was made very skillfully with a lot of beauty?

DT: I think there's a lot of content to the fashion work; it's very erotic.

WN: Where do you see it? Is it in the shape of her waistline?

DT: I see it in the curves, in the mysterious shadows on her face.

JC: Sometimes you look at fashion photographs and immediately have a different set of standards because of what they are. What saves this is that her face is in shadow. It's a person, but it's an elongated person; there's an abstraction to it and an enigmatic quality because of her face being hidden.

MF: It's an interesting photograph because you can't figure out how she stands up. She becomes nonhuman, a picture. Where are her feet? How is she pinned to that page? What's fascinating in a lot of Man Ray's fashion pictures is that he removes any visible signs of support. It's something that the next generation of fashion photographers picked up; people like Irving Penn learned volumes from looking at these pictures.

DF: I have a question about the use Man Ray would have made of these fashion photographs, based partly on the discrepancy between the 1936 date on this print and the published date of 1934. When he sent a photograph in for reproduction, did he sign it in the same way that he signed his portraits of artists? Did he have some occasion to present this as an art photograph in 1936, and he signed it then?

KW: It's also inscribed "1936: Credit, *Harper's Bazaar*" on the back, but in an unknown hand.

MF: So it was produced and published in 1934 for *Harper's Bazaar*, and this is a print seemingly made in 1936 for someone and signed. That's fascinating, because 1936 was a big year for Man Ray, the year of the Surrealist exhibition in New York.

DT: He also photographed Dalí for the front cover of *Time* that year, and he was in New York for his own exhibition of drawings.

MF: If it were any other year but 1936, I'd wonder, but that year there were a lot of reasons why he might print it again and sign it.

DF: Despite Man Ray's creative success in the late 1930s, the threatening war made life in France increasingly difficult. In 1940, after he had lived in Paris for twenty years, he was forced to return to the United States.

MF: He left Paris in July of that year, practically kicking and screaming. He went the usual route, by going south and across the border to Spain, where he caught one of the last boats to leave. On board with him were the composer Virgil Thomson, Dalí, and the filmmaker René Clair. Man Ray was very unhappy about coming home because he knew that he would have very little of the cachet as an American in America that he had as an American in Paris. He probably had a good sense that the New York audience was not going to treat him as well as he was treated in Paris. And when he arrived, all of his visions of this came true. My favorite story is that the boat was mobbed by reporters when it arrived. They all rushed by Man Ray to meet Dalí, who called Man Ray over to interpret for him. That must have been a blow.

He stayed in New York for a short period of time and very quickly realized that it was not the place for him. In unpublished notes for his autobiography he said that for a while he considered going to New Orleans, which of course had something of a history of harboring French artists, Degas among them. He continued on to Los Angeles, where there was a very large expatriate community of German, French, Italian, and British filmmakers, musicians, and writers. Most of them were working for the motion picture industry, and it's very clear from conversations that Man Ray had with other people that he too thought he could work for the movies. Everybody talked about how much money could be made. While it's probable that the Hollywood filmmakers thought it very glamorous to have Europeans come over and hang around the movie set, they weren't about to let these people behind the camera to waste time making art films.

DT: Man Ray would also have wanted total control of the filmmaking process, and they weren't going to allow him to do that.

MF: He said once that he gave up filmmaking in the 1920s because it became more of an industry; you had to have all of these people doing it, and you lost control.

DT: And he wasn't going to work by committee.

KW: No. But he did become a part of the Hollywood European artists group.

DF: And within a few days of arriving in Los Angeles, he met Juliet, a woman with whom he would spend the rest of his life.

DT: Juliet Browner was a young woman, thirty years old when she came west, who had been associated with the bohemian artistic circles in New York.

FN: She was a dancer and had been a girlfriend of Willem de Kooning's. She was very proud of that to the end of her life.

MF: She came out to California with a friend. They were trying to get work in the movies; I think they wanted to be actors.

DT: She and Man Ray met on the second or third day that he was in Los Angeles. A friend of hers in the East had told Man Ray, "Hey, would you look up Juliet Browner when you get to L.A.? I'm kind of worried about her." So he did, and they fell in love. He asked her to move in with him, and that was it for the rest of their lives.

MF: At this point, Man Ray thought life was wonderful. His immediate American response was that "I felt I was in the swing of things." He had a new car, a place to live, and a new girl—he was set.

KW: This is like what he did with Kiki, but it seems to have developed even faster.

FN: He was fifty, though, and she was thirty; a twenty-year difference is a lot.

DF: Our next photograph—*Henry Miller and Margaret Neiman* (pl. 42)—shows another expatriate who had migrated to Los Angeles during the war.

DT: Miller came to California a little later than Man Ray did. He met Man Ray and Juliet, who by that time were living together on Vine Street, through Gilbert and Margaret Neiman.

MF: Juliet told me that these pictures were taken at their Vine Street apartment. There was a courtyard area there, and they would have parties on Sunday after-

Man Ray. *Self-Portrait in Graham Hollywood*, 1941.
Gelatin silver print, 6.5 × 11 cm. 97.XM.54.2.

noons. Man Ray had made these masks; the women would put them on and have little performances.

WN: This stucco wall is very typical of California, but the doorjamb was obviously distorted somehow when the print was made.

KW: This picture is a variant of another that we have that is not distorted, so he was clearly playing around with the image.

JC: What I find curious about the picture is that it's a Sunday afternoon picnic and Miller has a seminude woman behind him wearing a mask, and he's wearing a shirt and tie with suspenders.

DT: It's wonderful!

KW: Can we link this Henry Miller picture back to the earlier portrait work in Paris? Here again Man Ray is photographing the cultural elite, but it's a very different kind of portrait.

MF: I think he was trying to reestablish his career and reputation as a painter while he was here. His photographs were, for the most part, casual or in more informal kinds of situations.

FN: He certainly was not doing this to make money.

DT: Henry Miller was as poor or poorer than Man Ray at that time. He didn't have a dime to his name, so this was just done out of friendship.

DF: Didn't Man Ray find commercial viability in Los Angeles the way he had while he was in Paris?

DT: He could have done a lot of commercial work, and he did do some studio photographs. He also made a number of pictures of movie stars.

MF: In California he really tried to keep himself out of the commercial photography market. The job offers he got in New York from the fashion magazines were considerable, but he said, "No, I am not going to do this."

FN: When he came out to Hollywood, some newspaper account identified him as "Man Ray the photographer." That must have hit him hard, and he decided, "Wait a minute; this is going too far. I might be good at photography, I might earn a little money at it, but if you're going to peg me as just that, no matter how lucrative, I'm not going to continue taking photographs."

MF: Right. In America he was constantly being categorized, whereas previously he had not been.

KW: In Paris he was an artist working in photography.

FN: Remember that the fashion photographs he did in Paris were being published in America. In Paris he wasn't being identified as just a fashion photographer. He took pictures of people, but he also had art exhibitions. In Hollywood he must have been disappointed to realize he had been so thoroughly typecast. Every time he was introduced, I'm sure he was described as a famous photographer.

MF: There was grumbling in Paris about his being a fashion photographer and making money in commercial art, but that wasn't over the categories of art, it was over politics. The Surrealists were being split by affiliations with Communist organizations, and those who were moving in that direction saw anything conceived as commercial as suspect.

KW: Do you think there may also have been a sense that he had already mastered portraiture and fashion work, and also that he was dispirited by the war and being in California?

DT: He was really dispirited by the fact that he thought that he had lost over twenty years of his work. He left it behind with friends and with Ady, his most recent lover before he left.

MF: He really didn't have much work to show when he got to Los Angeles. He had a box full of negatives and some photographs, but most of his negatives were left in Paris.

DF: Is it correct to say that Man Ray never really found recognition during his stay in Los Angeles?

DT: That's right. He had a major exhibition in December 1948 at the William Copley Gallery in Los Angeles, but only a couple of works were sold.

MF: I think it is significant that by that time he had been able to make a trip to Paris and bring back some of his major paintings. Those were in the Copley show, but they still didn't fire his reputation. It was too late.

DT: Once the war was over, he was elated to learn that all of his work in Paris had indeed been saved. He went back in 1947 and managed to sell his bungalow in Saint-Germain-en-Laye, but he decided that life in France immediately after the war would be too hard. When rent controls were relaxed, in about 1950, he felt that the situation in Paris was improving and that it was time to go back to Europe. So he held a yard sale at his studio at Vine Street and Fountain.

MF: Literally, with his paintings and drawings and photographs all out there for sale.

WN: Man Ray took the Copley show very seriously, because Copley was a rich young man whom he hoped could launch his career again, but the balloon was punctured when the exhibition happened. Copley bought *The Lovers*, a painting of a pair of lips, as a kind of consolation. It would be interesting to know how much he paid for the picture.

FN: It was $500.

WN: And that picture stayed in Copley's collection until 1979, when it was sold at auction for $750,000.

DF: The final photograph we are going to consider—*Juliet in a Blonde Wig* (pl. 47)—was done after Man Ray and Juliet returned to Paris. She was a constant subject for him.

KW: He made many photographs of Juliet, but this is not all that typical of that body of work. He has been called a proto-Surrealist, but here he's a proto-contemporary photographer.

WN: Here Juliet is looking a little like Cindy Sherman.

MF: But unlike Sherman, Juliet is not in control of the picture.

WN: The young woman in this photograph is trying to be an actress. She is attempting to tell her story, not through painting or photography, but through dance or something else. I see this picture as a performance, a recording of a woman trying to express herself through her body. And Man Ray is more of an instrument, as he was with Duchamp (pl. 15), in the consecration of a performance.

FN: You give her too much credit for being the performer; I don't think she was at all. He dressed her up, he put the wig on her—she had nothing to do with it.

MF: I find this very posed, more than was the case with any of his other models. In fact, I have a feeling that, perhaps because Kiki and Lee Miller and other women had walked out on him, by this point Man Ray did not allow Juliet to participate in the art-making process at all. She didn't know the art world, and he kept her outside of his creative process.

WN: That's true. He gave the women before Juliet the tools to establish their own creative base, but in giving them that freedom, he allowed them to do what they finally did, which was to leave. Could this be considered his revenge?

FN: Well, he did give her something. He gave her himself. Her role was to carry on after his death, and she did. She did exactly what every artist's widow should do— she perpetuated the myth.

KW: I don't find many of the Juliet pictures that interesting, but this one intrigues me because there's a real discomfort to it, much more psychological tension.

DT: I sense a greater presence here, almost in the way that Picasso has a presence in his portrait (pl. 36). We really sense Juliet in this picture more than in others where she is decorative or simply the beautiful subject.

KW: This reminds me of some of the Stieglitz pictures in which Georgia O'Keeffe is clearly fed up with being told how to stand and how to move her arms. I get a sense of Juliet as herself here, although she is participating willingly in this enterprise of being photographed.

JC: This picture is interesting to me because it's a kind of reprise of some of the ideas that we have been finding with Man Ray from the beginning. I think of this in relation to *Violon d'Ingres* (pl. 17), of Kiki dressed up, and to the idea of dressing the model. It's far from the anatomical, classical drawing aspect of that, but it is about the nude in the studio and being the model.

FN: It seems like a very informal picture. The fabric in the back I read as being the bedspread. This picture just happened one afternoon.

MF: Yes, it just happened instead of being set up. I think that they often worked this way. Juliet would talk later about how they would do things with costumes. There are a lot of photographs from Paris that clearly were made before or after costume balls. She'd have on leopard-skin outfits and things like that. But this image with the cheap wig is the polar opposite of the beautifully done and very stylish photographs of Man Ray's earlier career.

WN: Yes, it's diametrically opposite the fashion pictures.

JC: This picture seems to have more heart than a lot of his pictures of her. There's something about the way she looks at the camera. Her body is slim, but it's not idealized. It's very confrontational. This one gets me emotionally.

MF: I think it might have something to do with a rupture that Man Ray was experiencing. Here is a man who is trying not to deny his career, but to get away from his reputation as a fashion photographer.

WN: He's trying to obliterate the fact that he knew how to get rid of that background, that he knew how to make her hair and skin right.

MF: He didn't want it to be a fashion photograph, because he was trying to get rid of that reputation and be a pure artist again.

FN: The position she's in is right out of a Degas painting of a woman emerging from her tub, or even a Toulouse-Lautrec. With the obviously fake hair, Juliet looks more like a prostitute here than the traditional artist's muse.

When I first met Juliet, she showed me a shoebox filled with photographs—there had to be a thousand, all of her naked—taken by Man Ray right up to 1976, when he died. Within months of his death, he was still photographing her naked—on the stairs, on the side of the couch, lying down, everywhere.

JC: That's how he knew he was alive.

FN: But it's interesting that she showed these photographs to me. In 1976 she didn't look that good, but she still was proud of the fact that he was taking pictures of her, that she was still serving the role that won her Man Ray.

DF: To bring our discussion to an end, perhaps each of us can put forth a few concluding thoughts about Man Ray. I'll start by saying that what I find fascinating is what it meant for him to be an expatriate. Paris has always been a strong magnet, and not just for artists. But for Man Ray, it seems that the most important part of his being in Paris wasn't what was happening there, but that being there freed him from all these categories that he was trying to run from. In France he was relieved of the burden of being an American; the milieu of Paris allowed him to be different things—a painter, a photographer, a filmmaker, a sculptor—without categorizing himself as any of them. When he came back to the United States, all of a sudden that burden and those restraining categories were controlling him again. Then when he went back to Paris in the 1950s, he was freed again.

FN: Everyone who hears for the first time that Man Ray shunned photography, or wanted it to be a secondary consideration when he was classified, jumps to the immediate conclusion that he didn't give photography the same kind of credibility that he gave painting. It's easy to say that while painters might be represented in the Louvre, he would never make it into that or any other major museum if he were exclusively labeled a photographer. I don't think Man Ray consciously avoided photography for the purposes of not being classified; he didn't want to be classified for anything. It wasn't just photography; he did it systematically on every level. He didn't want to be just a filmmaker or just a photographer. He didn't want to be put into any given category where certain conclusions could be drawn automatically on the basis of how he was classified.

DT: That's true. If he was the enfant terrible of Paris, it was not because he was immoral or believed in the precepts of the Marquis de Sade or that sort of thing, but because he didn't want to be categorized. What he did was to transgress the boundaries that were set around each art form that let people say, "Oh, you're a painter," or "Oh, you're a photographer." He wanted to be able to move back and forth freely among the various media.

This leads me to say that it's impossible to talk about the photographs alone. I understand the emphasis today to focus on them, and I think we have, but at the same time I think one necessarily talks about the way photography was related to and was an intimate part of his life, especially with the pictures of his lovers and of Juliet. But to talk about his photographs as if they stood alone is somehow misleading. Often they are of objects in other media. Are these documents or are they art photographs unto themselves? This is the kind of question I think we've all wrestled with today.

There are motifs that run back and forth among various images, not only in the photographs but also in the paintings. There are objects that have the same names that paintings have. *La fortune* is a painting and then it becomes an object. It's also seen as part of a photograph of his studio. Are we talking about photographs, objects, paintings, or what? He gets us lost in a labyrinth of media, and I find that absolutely fascinating because it's difficult to understand.

FN: Man Ray said he would use whatever technical means were available that made the end result most expedient. He did use photography to take portraits, but when he created the picture of the Marquis de Sade, for example, he had no idea what Sade looked like, so he painted an imaginary portrait of him.

MF: I have been mulling over a couple of ideas as you've been talking. One is that

Man Ray had a very long and extraordinarily prolific career. I can't think of many other artists who worked as consistently and kept producing images throughout the greater part of the twentieth century. He worked in this labyrinth of media—the phrase Dickran used is quite wonderful—and sometimes the labyrinth worked for him and sometimes it didn't. Sometimes he got lost in it, and sometimes no one came to look for him when he got lost.

So I think that drawing overall conclusions and thinking about his whole career can be a mistake. There are moments when it all works. His first New York period certainly is an initial time that it all came together. I think it came together again in the late 1920s—perhaps it was Lee Miller's influence—when he was making photographs, shooting films, starting to paint again, and doing the fashion work for *Vogue*. This almost didn't happen again; he became more hermetically sealed. But I do think that another moment happened at the very end of his life, when he got back to Paris. Not many people were listening then, but he was working in a lot of different media and playing and reproducing and replicating; there was a last burst of energy.

What's of lasting importance, I think, is the idea that he chose the medium most expedient to the idea. Looking back from the final part of the twentieth century at Man Ray's career, what makes him most relevant to us and to working artists today is that he maintained that concept.

JC: I think Man Ray's inventiveness seems his strongest suit. Sometimes I don't get a great feeling of depth to the pictures—I don't mean that in a pejorative way—but it's the inventiveness that survives. He has different themes—the women, the still lifes, the Surrealist work—but overall I don't get the feeling that it connected to his life. The work itself doesn't let me know him so much; it's more about the effect and what can happen. His greatness, I think, is that he had the freedom to try all these things, and that's where the inventiveness comes from.

KW: I concur with you. I find his inventiveness at these moments that Merry was talking about the most vitalizing thing about his work. For me, 1922 is one of those moments—he was going crazy trying things. I also think his facility with language—his writing and his titles—is something that's as much a part of Man Ray as the visual artist.

WN: I tend to focus on how successfully Man Ray harnessed the elements of accident and chance in his photographs. He was a true master of some of the most important elements of photography, such as controlling what is out of control and doing it in a way that gives the illusion of great simplicity, or to take it even further, to make art out of emptiness. How easy this picture is. It's like a great dancer who moves with such elegance on the stage that it makes you think you could get up there and do it yourself. He also balanced intuition and logic in an amazing way. One of the themes that we talked about here is that he moved through life acting on intuition, but he always applied the brakes of logic when they were needed. He was both a classicist and an expressionist. He was limited on one hand, and unlimited; he was one of those artists who reconciled contradictions as a process of making his art.

JC: Those contradictions are so important to the work, I don't know if they were really reconciled.

WN: He wanted to reconcile the contradictions, but whether he was successful or not is another question. I think he anticipated the present moment in art, which I see as one with a great apprehension about the future of art itself and about the role of the individual as a force in the creative process. Man Ray, like many younger contemporary artists today, thought of himself as powerless in a large structure where there were people and forces bigger than himself, and he expressed this ambivalence by continuously appropriating his own art. He never hesitated to quote himself, to repeat himself. In the past, artists were always admonished to invent something new every time, so this contradictory element of his being an artist who always wanted to invent but didn't hesitate to repeat himself is important.

Finally, I'd like to quote Marcel Duchamp talking about Man Ray. He said, "Man Ray treated the camera as he treated the paintbrush, a mere instrument in the service of the mind." This interplay between the mind as the controlling force and the tools and what they achieve is an important element. Man Ray always said that he would photograph what he couldn't paint and paint or draw what he couldn't photograph, and he lived out these precepts continuously for seventy years.

Man Ray. *Self-Portrait, Paris,* 1921.
Gelatin silver print, 13.2 × 8.3 cm.
97.XM.54.1.

Chronology

1890

Emmanuel Radnitsky born in Philadelphia on August 27, the eldest of four children.

1897

Family moves to Brooklyn.

1908

Graduates from high school, where his studies included mechanical drawing. Offered scholarship to study architecture but decides to become an artist. Works in New York as a draftsman and graphic designer.

1910

Enrolls in life drawing classes at the National Academy of Design, New York. Is exposed to modern art and photography at 291, the Fifth Avenue gallery run by Alfred Stieglitz (1864–1946).

1911

Attends anatomy classes at the Art Students League, New York. His parents change the family surname to Ray.

1912

Studies at the Ferrer Center, New York. Begins to sign work as Man Ray.

1913

Sees Armory Show in New York. Moves to artists' colony in Ridgefield, New Jersey. Meets Belgian writer Adon Lacroix (1886–1980). Paints Cubist portrait of Stieglitz.

1914

Marries Lacroix and publishes *Adonism*, a collection of poems dedicated to her. About this time, acquires first camera to photograph his artworks.

1915

Publishes Lacroix's *Book of Divers Writings* in an edition of twenty and creates the maquette for a single issue of the *Ridgefield Gazook*, a satirical bulletin. Meets the collector Walter Arensberg (1878–1954), who introduces him to Marcel Duchamp (1887–1968). First one-man exhibition at the Daniel Gallery, New York. Moves back to New York.

1916

With Arensberg and Duchamp, founds the Society of Independent Artists. Second one-man exhibition at the Daniel Gallery.

1917

Society of Independent Artists exhibition held in New York. Creates aerographs, pictures made with an airbrush. The American photographer Alvin Langdon Coburn (1882–1966) begins making Vortographs in London.

1919

Third one-man exhibition at the Daniel Gallery features aerographs. Separates from Lacroix.

1920

Joins with Duchamp and Katherine Dreier (1877–1952) to establish the Société Anonyme, the first museum devoted to modern art; shows work in Société exhibitions. Begins freelance work for *Harper's Bazaar*, an association that continues until 1942. First known exhibition of his photographs (*Homme* and *Femme*) at the *Salon Dada: Exposition Internationale* in Paris.

1921

Société Anonyme sponsors "What Is Dadaism?" symposium with Man Ray as participant. With Duchamp, publishes the sole issue of *New York Dada*. Awarded honorable mention for a portrait photograph of Berenice Abbott (1898–1991) entered in the annual photography competition sponsored by Wanamaker's department store in Philadelphia. Duchamp leaves for Paris in June; with the patronage of Ferdinand Howald (1856–1934), Man Ray is able to follow in July. Duchamp introduces him to the Paris Dadaists, whom he photographs. Has one-man show at Librairie Six, which is operated by the wife of the Dadaist Philippe Soupault (1897–1990). Meets and photographs Kiki (Alice Prin; 1901–53), who soon moves in with him.

1922

Decides to support himself by becoming a portrait photographer; begins to receive attention for his pictures of such cultural luminaries as Jean Cocteau (1889–1963), Gertrude Stein (1874–1946), Alice B. Toklas (1877–1967), the Marquise Casati (1881–1957), and James Joyce (1882–1941). Tries his hand at fashion photography for designer Paul Poiret (1879–1944). Makes first Rayographs (cameraless photographs). Rayographs and photographs reproduced in numerous journals, including *Aventure, Der Sturm*, and *Broom*; Cocteau publishes "Lettre ouverte à Man Ray, photographe américain" (An open letter to Man Ray, American photographer) in the spring issue of *Les feuilles libres*. Full-page feature on Rayographs in November issue of *Vanity Fair*. Publication of *Les champs délicieux* (The delicious fields), a limited edition album of twelve Rayographs with a preface by the Dada leader Tristan Tzara (1896–1963).

1923

Abbott becomes his darkroom assistant until 1926. Makes Rayograph film *Le retour à la raison* (The return to reason). Publishes Rayographs in the March issue of *Broom*, for which he designs the cover, and in the Dada journal *Littérature*.

1924

Monograph on Man Ray published in Paris by the Dadaist Georges Ribemont-Dessaignes (1884–1974). André Breton (1896–1966) publishes *Manifesto of Surrealism. Violon d'Ingres* published in *Littérature*. Appears in *Entr'acte* (Intermission), a film directed by Francis Picabia (1879–1953) and René Clair (1898–1981).

1925

Fashion photographs appear in French and American editions of *Vogue*. Photograph of Sinclair Lewis (1885–1951) published in *Vanity Fair*. Participates in the first exhibition of Surrealist art at the Galerie Pierre, Paris.

1926

One-man exhibition at the Galerie Surréaliste. Films *Emak Bakia* (a Basque expression for "give us a rest"), which premieres in Paris. Société Anonyme exhibition at the Brooklyn Museum.

1927

Travels to New York for an exhibition of his work at the Daniel Gallery.

1928

Produces the film *L'étoile de mer* (Starfish).

1929

Publishes *1929*. Produces the film *Les mystère du château de dés* (The mystery of the château of dice). Meets Lee Miller (1907–77), who becomes his assistant and lover until 1932. One-man show at the Chicago Arts Club. The Museum of Modern Art opens in New York.

1930

With Miller, projects hand-colored film onto guests at a ball given by Count and Countess Pecci-Blunt in Paris.

1931

Publication of *Électricité*, a portfolio of ten gravure prints of Rayographs commissioned by the Paris electric company CPDE (Compagnie Parisienne de Distribution d'Électricité).

1932

Work included in the *Surrealist Exhibition* at the Julien Levy Gallery, New York.

1934

Publication of *Photographs by Man Ray 1920 Paris 1934*, with 105 pictures by the artist and a frontispiece portrait by Pablo Picasso (1881–1973). Creates *Échiquier Surréaliste* (Surrealist chessboard), which features portraits of Joan Miró (1893–1983) and other movement members.

1935

One-man exhibition of photographs at the Wadsworth Atheneum in Hartford, Connecticut. Publication of *Facile*, poems by Paul Éluard (1895–1952) with thirteen photographs by Man Ray. Publishes "Sur le réalisme photographique" (On photographic realism) in *Cahiers d'art*.

1936

Buys a small house in Saint-Germain-en-Laye. Begins relationship (until 1940) with Adrienne Fidelin (Ady). Work shown in the *International Surrealist Exhibition* in London. Valentine Gallery, New York, hosts an exhibition of his drawings. Attends opening of *Fantastic Art, Dada, Surrealism* at the Museum of Modern Art, New York, which includes his work in many media, including photography.

1937

Shoots his last film (in color) with Picasso and Éluard near Antibes, where he remains for a time to concentrate on painting. Publishes *La photographie n'est pas l'art* (Photography is not art), with twelve of his photographic images and a preface by Breton. Volume of poems by Éluard, *Les mains libres* (The free hands), published in Paris with drawings by Man Ray.

1938

Participates in *International Exhibition of Surrealism* at the Galerie des Beaux-Arts, Paris. Paints *Portrait imaginaire de D. A. F. de Sade* (Imaginary portrait of D. A. F. de Sade [1740–1814]).

1940

Leaves Europe for New York after the German occupation of Paris. After a short time there, travels to Los Angeles by

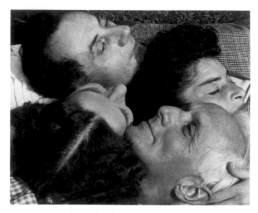

Florence Homolka. *Double Wedding Portrait*, 1946.
Gelatin silver print, 20.6 × 25.4 cm. 95.XM.89.
Clockwise from upper left: Man Ray, Juliet Man Ray,
Max Ernst, and Dorothea Tanning.

car. Meets Juliet Browner (1911–91) after
a few days in Hollywood; the two soon take
up residence together.

1941

Show of works on paper at the M. H. de
Young Memorial Museum in San Francisco.
One-man exhibition at Frank Perls Gallery
in Hollywood. Publishes "Art in Society" in
California Arts and Architecture.

1942

Exhibition of portrait photographs at Frank
Perls Gallery. Photographs the author Henry
Miller (1891–1980).

1943

One-man exhibition of works on paper
at the Santa Barbara Museum of Art.
Publishes "Photography Is Not Art" in *View.*
A selection of five photographs appears
in *Minicam Photography.*

1944

Retrospective exhibition at the Pasadena
Art Institute.

1945

One-man exhibition at the Los Angeles
Museum of History, Science, and Art.
Solo exhibition at the Julien Levy Gallery,
New York. Resumes connection with Société
Anonyme. Work included in Julien Levy
Gallery exhibition *The Imagery of Chess*, a
show of chess sets designed by artists.

1946

Marries Browner in a double ceremony
with Max Ernst (1891–1976) and Dorothea
Tanning (b. 1910).

1947

Publishes *Mr. and Mrs. Woodman*, a limited edition album of thirty-seven photographs and one engraving. Visits France to secure his goods and sell the house in Saint-Germain-en-Laye. Niece Naomi Savage (b. 1927) joins him as a darkroom assistant.

1948

Publishes *Alphabet for Adults*, an album of drawings. Uses photographs of mathematical objects as basis for Shakespearean Equations, a series of paintings. Premiere of *Dreams That Money Can Buy*, a film by Hans Richter (1888–1976) that includes a segment written by Man Ray. One-man show opens at the William Copley Gallery in Beverly Hills. Awarded honorary Master of Fine Arts degree by Fremont University, Los Angeles.

1951

With Juliet, relocates to Paris.

1952–57

Exhibits work in Los Angeles and Paris.

1958

Commissioned by Polaroid to work with their black-and-white film, resulting in the series Unconcerned Photographs. Experiments with color photography.

1959–60

Exhibits work in Los Angeles, Paris, New York, and London.

1961

Awarded a gold medal for photography at the Venice Biennale.

1962

Retrospective exhibition at the Bibliothèque Nationale, Paris.

1963

Publication of autobiography, *Self Portrait*, and *Portraits*, a book of photographs. Exhibition of Rayographs in Stuttgart.

1964–65

Exhibition of *31 Objects of My Affection* in Italy and New York.

1966

Retrospective exhibition at the Los Angeles County Museum of Art. Publishes *Résurrection des mannequins*.

1967

Awards Committee of the Philadelphia Arts Festival recognizes Man Ray for his accomplishments and the honor reflected upon his native city.

1968

Work included in two exhibitions at the Museum of Modern Art, New York: *Dada, Surrealism, and Their Heritage* and *The Machine as Seen at the End of the Mechanical Age*.

1970

Oggetti d'affezione (Objects of my affection) published.

1971

Traveling retrospective exhibition seen in Rotterdam, Paris, and Humlebaek, Denmark.

1974

Eighty-fifth birthday exhibition held at the Cultural Center, New York. *Analphabet* published.

1976

Dies in Paris on November 18.

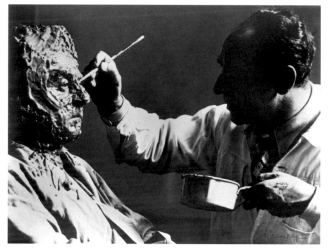

Man Ray. *The Life Mask*, 1932.
Gelatin silver print, 22.7 × 29.8 cm. 84.XM.1000.150.

Editor	Gregory A. Dobie
Designer	Jeffrey Cohen
Production Coordinator	Stacy Miyagawa
Photographers	Charles Passela
	Ellen M. Rosenbery
Printer	Gardner Lithograph
	Buena Park, California
Bindery	Roswell Bookbinding
	Phoenix, Arizona